SPORTS PUBLIC RELATIONS

SAGE has been part of the global academic community since 1965, supporting high quality research and learning that transforms society and our understanding of individuals, groups, and cultures. SAGE is the independent, innovative, natural home for authors, editors and societies who share our commitment and passion for the social sciences.

Find out more at: **www.sagepublications.com**

Jacquie L'Etang

SPORTS PUBLIC RELATIONS

SAGE

Los Angeles | London | New Delhi
Singapore | Washington DC

Los Angeles | London | New Delhi
Singapore | Washington DC

SAGE Publications Ltd
1 Oliver's Yard
55 City Road
London EC1Y 1SP

SAGE Publications Inc.
2455 Teller Road
Thousand Oaks, California 91320

SAGE Publications India Pvt Ltd
B 1/I 1 Mohan Cooperative Industrial Area
Mathura Road
New Delhi 110 044

SAGE Publications Asia-Pacific Pte Ltd
3 Church Street
#10-04 Samsung Hub
Singapore 049483

Editor: Mila Steele
Editorial assistant: James Piper
Production editor: Imogen Roome
Copyeditor: Rose James
Proofreader: Bryan Campbell
Indexer: David Rudeforth
Marketing manager: Michael Ainsley
Cover design: Francis Kenney
Typeset by: C&M Digitals (P) Ltd, Chennai, India
Printed in Great Britain by Henry Ling Limited at
The Dorset Press, Dorchester, DT1 1HD

Library of Congress Control Number: 2013940301

British Library Cataloguing in Publication data

A catalogue record for this book is available from
the British Library

ISBN 978-1-4129-3618-7
ISBN 978-1-4129-3619-4 (pbk)

For Deek

Contents

Acknowledgements

I am indebted to those sports practitioners, commentators, journalists, communicators and marketers who shared their perspectives and experiences of sports business and its practices.

Some material appeared in an earlier form in:

L'Etang J (2013) Critical perspectives in sports public relations. In P Pedersen (Ed.) *Routledge Handbook of Sport Communication.* London/New York: Routledge Taylor Francis.

L'Etang J (2010) Cross-cultural sport and public relations. In M Hopwood, P Kitchin and J Skinner (Eds) *Sport Public Relations and Communication.* London/New York: Butterworth-Heinnemann Elsevier: 153–186.

L'Etang J (2009) The public relations and promotion of adventure sports. In J Ormrod and B Wheaton (Eds) *On the Edge: Leisure, Consumption and the Representation of Adventure Sports* (LSA Publication No 104). Eastbourne: Leisure Studies Association: 43–70.

L'Etang J (2006) Public relations and sport in promotional culture. *Public Relations Review,* 32(4): 386–394.

I am grateful for permissions granted by Routledge, Taylor & Francis, Leisure Studies Association. Effort has been made to trace all copyright holders, but if any have been inadvertently overlooked, the publishers will be pleased to make the necessary arrangement at the first opportunity.

The project would not have got off the ground or been completed without the enthusiasm, commitment and patience of Mila Steele and the expertise of her colleagues Imogen Roome, James Piper and Rose James.

Preface

What is Sports PR?

Sport involves struggle, success and failure. Its intrinsically competitive nature produces drama and evokes emotion. A central feature of human culture for centuries, its playfulness carries deeper meanings in terms of dominance and identification. It is not only intrinsic pleasure to participants and spectators but has complex symbolic significance. Thus sport is a medium and a focus for human communication. Sport reflects societal preferences and concerns and may be a focus for debate about contemporary issues. While there are benefits arising from sport with regards to individual health and well-being, and sport may be used as a tool to improve societal relations or specific communities, it is also the case that sport can be a focus for hostilities, or lag behind social change, for example in relation to gender. The relationship between sport and society is therefore complex, and its multiple meanings contested. The professionalization of sport in the context of **digital networked society** and **converged media** has stimulated the expansion of sport as mass entertainment, which has coincided with sport's rise up the political agenda. Sport's location in business and politics has engendered the development of a complicated series of networks, investments and policies. Sport is one of the world's major businesses but it is also entertainment, celebrity, participation, fandom and a crucial part of our culture and social identification (Boyle and Haynes, 2006). Public Relations (PR) is implicated at all levels whether handling major sponsorship and media rights deals, events, promoting stars or increasing participation. In the UK even the most modest sports club seeks local media coverage and requires effective stakeholder relations to 'improve its profile' and to gain community support and sponsorship, or even chartered status. Sports PR is a specialist area of PR practice that reveals particular insights into the role that PR plays in contemporary society. The role and practice of PR, which includes media relations, promotion, corporate communications, issues and crisis management, advocacy and public affairs and lobbying, is therefore an important aspect of sports business. PR and sport are both facilitators of communication and relationships and sport is a focus of strategic societal interventions by a variety of actors.

   This book endeavours to delineate areas of practice, and to give some idea of the immense range of work that might be described as sports PR but may also be seen under the umbrella terms **sports marketing** or **sports communication**. A deeper understanding of PR concepts and practice highlights the unique contribution they can make to understanding sports business and organizations. The book is intended to reflect the diversity and scale of sports business and the varied and potential roles of PR within it. The book provides an argument for a more strategic approach to PR work in sports business, and highlight aspects of sport and sports organizations that encourage communicators to reflect upon the role of sport in society, and the nature and limits of sports PR. It also reflects upon strategic intentions that lie behind technical communication and provides some critical perspectives.

What is this Book About?

This book aims to explore the relationship between sport and PR and to reflect upon the following basic questions:

- What is, and should be, the role and scope of PR in sport?
- How are the concepts of PR employed in the sports industry?
- What is the relationship between promotional culture, sport and PR?
- How and why is sport used as a tool of PR, and in what international, national, regional and organizational contexts?
- How are PR services and expertise understood and used within the sports business industry?
- What opportunities exist for sports business to avail itself further of PR concepts?

The aim was to try and capture the dynamic processes of the rapidly industrializing sport business, because it seemed that such rapid transformation would inevitably require PR work focused on communications to enhance relationships and reputations, as well as more basic promotion. Therefore, understanding the ideals, values and rhetoric of the sports business and its practitioners' understandings of networks of relationships was important. A central interest was the extent to which PR is understood as a business function within the sports industry – how was such work described, realized, exemplified and valued by sports business people? The project aimed to capture, at a point when the sports industry must surely need PR experts, the extent to which promotional ideas had diffused within sport, not just at the capitalized and lucrative end of the industry, but also in amateur and minority contexts – **sportscape** and **mediascape** are constantly changing and new 'products' (sports) are being capitalized and commercialized all the time. Therefore the book extends beyond the most popular or the richest sports, which dominate the media.

This is not a 'how to' book, though it may be of interest for practitioners reflecting upon their practice and its wider implications. Instead, this book considers some broader societal themes in relation to PR concepts, such as globalization, nationalism, ethics in sport, gender issues, cultural identity, racism, sport as part of health promotion or tourism. The book aims to go beyond a description of communication techniques, although there are many examples and quotes to illustrate sports business approaches and practices in relation to public relations issues.

While the scale and impact of major sports is recognized, an effort is made to include a range of examples, and this coverage is tempered with some discussion of less commercial sports. Consideration has been given to the sports business processes that transform and industrialize some sports rather than others. Sport, like language, is an arbitrary sign system comprising multiple symbolic meanings dependent on context, culture and readership. The aim has been to elucidate the dynamics of the relationship between sport and PR at the societal level, at the interplays between economics, politics, culture, ideology and technology, at the business level, but also at the level of specific actors and agents in those dynamic processes.

This book reflects upon the specialist skills and knowledge required of sports PR practitioners and their business and commercial relationships with other key actors such as sports journalists, sports marketers, sponsors, sports agents, sporting associations and governmental bodies. It raises questions about contemporary PR practice in relation to a number of interrelated occupations to which it may offer some new self-understanding. The book aims to define a specialist field of practice within PR and to give an understanding of the nature of work, and the requirements for knowledge in that field. Quotes from business and sports practitioners offer opportunities for reflection on their discursive practices and what these reveal about their values and ideologies. Finally, the book raises a number of critical issues in relation to sport which are relevant to PR practitioners. Thus it blends the pragmatic and critical, to draw out tensions and problematics in the field that will necessarily impact relationships and communication.

The book partly responds to Neupauer's 'plea for helping an unknown field' (2001: 551) but it aims to elucidate exploratory or interpretive lines of enquiry, and to incorporate a more specifically sociocultural perspective. Implicitly it draws attention to the idea that there is more work to be done to explore links between PR and grand-scale social projects, events, media representation and the lifeworlds and lifestyles of citizens drawing on insights of Zaner and Engelhardt Jr (1973), de Certeau (1988), Habermas (1989 and Debord (1994) (cited in L'Etang, 2006).

Why Take a Cultural Perspective?

It is well documented that sport activities have long been part of human cultural activity. Examples include wrestling depicted on a seal and boxing on a relief carving dated at 3000 BC, and there is evidence of spectatorship at public festivals around 2000 BC and during the Cretan-Minoan period (Zauhar, 2004: 24, cited in L'Etang, 2006). However, sport has not always been available to all and, worldwide, access remains restricted in various ways either by economics, politics, ideology, gender, or religion. Thus sport remains contentious, not only in terms of access but also in terms of economic provisions and sport development, both at elite performance and mass participation levels, indicative of requirements for argument, persuasion, lobbying and change. Media representation appears biased and limited since lucrative male sports are dominant in terms of coverage and economic investment and sponsorship, thus shaping at least to some degree social and cultural agendas, discourse, norms and values. Because sport is a sociocultural praxis, it reflects host community norms in relation to gender, age, class and communities' expectations about sports-appropriate behaviour. For example, in some cultures female body-builders defy conventions about female muscularity (Choi, 2000); and images of active people in their sixties and seventies are rare in broadcast or print media (news, lifestyle and sports magazines), at least in the UK (L'Etang, 2006).

Sport's political heritage is well demonstrated by the long history of sports tourism in which various empires and regimes used sport to articulate or reinforce national identity or provide entertainment for the masses. Examples here include international games in the Egyptian period (Egyptians, Libyans, Syrians and other parts of Africa). and during the Greek Empire 140 cities held athletic events, which stimulated a sports tourism industry (Zauhar, 2004: 32, cited in L'Etang, 2006). Rural communities developed forms of sport that might be played at local festivities, such as at harvest time. Such folk sports are the origins of many contemporary sports. Some remain in ritualistic form, such as the annual Kirkwall Ba' Game which involves kicking a bladder around the capital of the Orkney Islands between the 'uppies' and the 'doonies' (those born on one side of the town versus the other) at Hogmanay. These examples demonstrate dynamics between sport, 'events', tourism and culture.

According to Riordan and Kruger, contemporary modern sport, at least in developed capitalist secular countries, dates its history to the late-nineteenth and early-twentieth centuries when industrial capitalism began to accede to social reformers by legislating for leisure time. In fact 'worker sports' developed as an outgrowth of socialist and **communitarian philosophies** in the late-nineteenth and early-twentieth centuries, imbued with non-competitive values (Riordan and Kruger, 1999: 105, cited in L'Etang, 2006). Originating in Germany in the 1890s they developed into a fully-fledged alternative to bourgeois sport and Worker Olympics were held in 1925 and 1931, and by 1930, 'worker sport united well over 4 million people, making it by far the largest working class cultural movement' (Riordan and Kruger, 1999: 105, cited in L'Etang, 2006). The worker movement ultimately failed because bourgeois sports, funded by capitalist and totalitarian states alike, drove them out of the market both by making better provisions and gaining extensive mainstream publicity (worker sports were marginalized, only gaining coverage in the socialist press) (Riordan and Kruger, 1999: 114, cited in L'Etang, 2006). This example highlights the connections of sports practice to class, the economy and to organizational internal practices. The relationship between sport and employment as a form of communication is discussed in the third chapter.

Sports have been shaped by social, economic, legal, technological and political change, culture and ideology, managerialism and technology, science and the media. Linkage between these broad-scale developments and the evolution of PR has not received particularly close attention. Sport is a microcosm of social life, which reveals underlying values and power relations. Social practices are reflected in sport and sport is an arena in which a variety of conventions, mores, ethical issues and problematics are played out. Since agency and action are facilitated by communicative action, an understanding of the role of PR in sport can contribute a more subtle understanding of the formation and circulation of public discourses about a range of societal issues.

Who is This Book For?

This book was written with several distinct groups of people in mind: those whose main interests are in sports management, sports marketing, sports business, event management and sponsorship, but who would like to understand better how their expertise relates to that of PR; enthusiasts of sport who are curious about the role of PR in sport; and last, but not least, specialists in PR interested in its application to sport. Consequently, a wide range of disciplines and sources have been drawn on, including sports studies, particularly sports sociology; cultural studies, including the sociology of consumption; media studies, especially sports media; sports business and marketing; as well as the relatively limited literature on sport within PR which provided a reason for attempting to write this book in the first place.

For those unfamiliar with PR concepts and literature, a conscious effort has been made to include definitions and explanatory examples. Furthermore, the second and third chapters provide an introductory explanation of the PR field and core concepts accompanied by illustrative sports examples.

What Research Underpins This Book?

At the outset, the approach to the project was influenced by Bourdieu's recommendation:

‘ The researcher should focus on competing interests, the conflict they generate, and the whole logic of a field, which can still only be done by plunging into the particularity of an empirical reality, historically located and dated, but with the objective of constructing it as a special case of what is possible. (Bourdieu and Wacquant, 1992: 107) ’

Empirical research included analysis of the trade journals *SportBusiness International* and *PR Week*;[1] interviews with PR and communications practitioners working for sports organizations, sports PR/marketing organizations and journalists from which a variety of themes and issues emerged. Overall, the aim was to give critical consideration to the role of sports PR in promotional culture and in relation to wider issues. Challenges and issues in sports PR are highlighted, alongside a descriptive overview of work that appears to characterize the fields of sports business. The implicit knowledge, values and assumptions that underpin sports business knowledge are necessary for PR workers to operate successfully in this sector. An interest in sport is obviously helpful, indicated by an emphasis on 'passion' that suffuses the business and is a key discourse (see L'Etang, 2013: 308 for examples), but at least as important is curiosity about the complex fields of sports business. PR practitioners in the field not only have to have excellent media and promotional skills, but to understand the links between PR and marketing,

---

[1] These are presented throughout text and references in their abbreviated forms, *SBI* and *PRW*.

events management, sponsorship, sports agentry and celebrity management and how these functional relationships affect the realization of PR priorities. Political lobbying at both local and national levels is an important dimension in relation to events bids and resource allocation. Financial acumen and legal competencies are also important in relation, for example, to sponsorship, licensing, media rights and intellectual property.

From an analytical perspective **structural-functionalism** shaped the pragmatic approach to seeking an understanding of PR work in the sports business context, and within sports culture and its subcultures. Bourdieu's concept of **distinction** was employed not only to understand dynamics between different sports cultures but also the apparent understandings about, and structuring of, PR work. Since sport is a rapidly expanding world business embedded in cultures as social practice and as a form of communication, it permits exploration of PR's cultural and symbolic role. Taking a cultural approach to PR assists exploration of its role in the commodification of lifestyles, values and relationships.

Cultural studies provided the **circuit of culture**, a communicative framework in which meaning is created, modified and reinvented during processes of symbolization, representation, regulation, consumption and identity formation within particular cultural contexts, which provided a useful insight into the relationship between culture and economic practice in the sporting context. The concept of **cultural intermediaries** was helpful in describing sports PR practice in society.

Such work is consonant with that of Palmer's interest in **cultural brokers**. In her ethnographic work on the Tour de France she explored 'the institutional power exerted by sporting and administrative elites of world sport' (2000: 364) in which,

> 'Like the IOC in the case of the Olympic Games, La Société du Tour de France acts as gatekeeper of cultural traffic, ensuring that only a select range of myths and narratives about the Tour de France are fed into popular consciousness. (2000: 367) '

Palmer's concept of media content and influence might be linked to **propaganda models** of the media (Herman and Chomsky, 1988) but also highlights the importance of PR work as mediation between producers and consumers. Furthermore, the reference to **myths** and **narratives** highlights the role of media sources (PR) in the definition and **framing** of news stories (**primary definition**) and the creation and circulation of news stories and discourses.

Concepts of **professionalism** and **professionalization** were useful in considering the status and expertise of sports PR, while **strategic communication management** highlighted those aspects of practice which do not, at present, appear to be within the **jurisdiction** of many practitioners. **Critical theory**, **rhetoric** and **discourse ethics** were useful background concepts, useful in highlighting **power**, and the discursive work that is carried out on behalf of sports and sports business. Critical questions relate to the existence and reproduction of discursive inequalities within sports and the business that attaches to it, and the role of PR in that process. There are wider power relations within the sports public sphere, and those with economic power may dominate discourses. Culturally and financially important sports, their routines, values and language are central to societal communication.

Some individuals may capitalize on their sporting success to gain real political power. For example, *SBI* commented of former British middle-distance Olympic athlete Lord Coe that 'Coe the athlete morphed into Coe the ultimate sports politician' (*SBI*, 2009e: 26–28). The relationships among and between sports, media and politics highlighted the significance of **source-media relations** and the ability of sport to present itself as a social good raised interesting questions about the ability to raise critical perspectives about sports practice and the influence of sports business in society.

Sport engages with, and contributes to the formation of, elites and their distinction from others, yet it is claimed to be a solution to problems that are at least partially the responsibility of governments and global imbalances. It has become embedded in capitalist economics and involves multiple overlapping networks within governmental, financial and social contexts. Communications are therefore central to a very complex global sports system with numerous subsystems. These perspectives position sport as part of social change and development – and PR is implicitly, if not explicitly, an intrinsic part of such change processes. Change entails the promotion of new agendas, probable resistance in some quarters, advocacy and persuasion, stakeholder communication, and engagement with public opinion. These are all central elements of the work and occupation known as PR, the role of which is defined and discussed in this book. Sport and PR share optimistic ideals about their global roles and contribution to society, and both have been seen as a way of developing **bonding** and **bridging** strategies to develop **social capital** and **communities**.

However, idealistic claims regarding the role of sport in promoting **civil society** may be counterpointed by allegations of child exploitation, lack of accountability, corruption and the use of performance-enhancing drugs, and such dualisms imply a clear role for PR advocacy and reputation management. Idealistic claims regarding the role of PR in promoting democratic practices, consultation and dialogue may be countered by critiques that see strategic communication as a form of propaganda. Throughout this book there will be reminders that opinions about sport and PR are socially constructed, open for debate, and not fixed meanings. The corollary of this is that there are in circulation a number of competing discourses both of sport and of PR, some of which are subjected to scrutiny in this book.

How This Book is Organized

The book is written thematically, so concepts and ideas cross-fertilize and accumulate throughout. Examples are integrated throughout the text in order to illustrate day-to-day realities, to bring issues and contexts to life, and to illuminate concepts. More developed examples are boxed out separately. Some examples are distinguished under headings **Discuss!** and **Think Critically** providing exercises for student readers and tutor directed tasks. Chapters conclude with a list of **Further Reading**.

The book covers three main aspects that are integrated throughout: the cultural and business contexts and issues of sport (the various dynamics between sport, business, media, culture and PR); operational contexts and issues (specialized areas of practice); and occupational contexts and issues (the role and scope of PR activity and key concepts). The early chapters explain key concepts in PR and communications and then proceed to concentrate on delineating the dynamics between sports business, communications and PR practice in global and organizational contexts. Later chapters bring together a range of interdisciplinary perspectives to understand the nature and role of PR practice in a sports context, and to identify problematics in the field.

Chapter 1 draws on a range of disciplines to provide an overview of previous work relevant to a consideration of PR work in sport. It sketches key aspects of the media environment and introduces relevant concepts of celebrity and commodification. Chapters 2 and 3 build understanding of different facets of PR concepts including key terminology, frameworks and examples. Chapter 4 takes a global perspective, looking at issues such as public diplomacy. Chapter 5 positions PR within sports business. Chapter 6 links PR to events, while Chapter 7 looks at sport designed for social impacts. Chapter 8 discusses lifestyle and minority sports. Chapter 9 reflects back on the PR role in the sporting environment and considers wider implications for its occupational role.

Further Reading

Jackson S (2012) Reflections on communication and sport: on advertising and promotional culture. *Communication & Sport*, 1 (1/2): 100–112.

Pedersen P (2012) Reflections on communication and sport: on strategic communication and management. *Communication & Sport*, 1 (1/2): 55–67.

1

Introducing PR and Sport

Introduction

This chapter aims to provide an overview of key discipline sources and to provide contextual background to sports PR in relation to the media environment, celebrity, commodification and representation. It provides an introductory review positioning sport and PR in relation to one another; an overview of sport in its sociocultural context, and introduces issues surrounding sports' media representations. The relationships between PR, sport and politics, and between sport, celebrity and PR are also introduced. This chapter begins with an overview review of some historical literature relevant to a consideration of the role of PR in sport. PR is contextualized within the converged media environment and journalism practices linked to sports business imperatives.

The chapter covers:

- PR and sport: sources and developments
- Convergent media in a digital networked world
- Sport celebrity and PR
- Commodification and representation
- Personal PR

Key Concepts

- Celebrity
- Commodification
- Convergent media
- Discourse technologist
- Legacy media
- Mediascape
- Moral panics
- News subsidy

- Primary definition
- Representation
- Secondary definition
- Source-media relations
- Sportscape

PR and Sport: Sources and Developments

Within PR relatively little attention has been given to sport. Exceptions include Curtin and Gaither who, writing from an international perspective, noted the value of sports business to PR consultancy and pointed out that the topic is 'overlooked in international PR texts, yet sports can unify nations, promote social change and affect the national psyche, making it a powerful cultural agent' (2006: 29–30). Authors from sports management, sports marketing, sports journalism, events management, and sports media sociology all touch upon PR concerns and activities though with little reference to PR concepts or literature. In the US, sports PR is uniquely defined as a separate occupational and academic specialism, that of 'sports direction' (Johnson, 1996; Helitzer, 1999; Neupauer, 2001; Irwin et al., 2002). Nichols et al. (2002) focused on sports media relations (L'Etang, 2006: 386). Anderson (2006) explored the use of PR to seek support for a business merger between two pro football leagues in the US. Sports marketers (Shank, 2002; Chadwick and Beech, 2006) took some interest in the field but it was Hopwood (2006) introduced public relations perspectives to sports marketing and the role of PR in sports marketing in her study of PR practice in English county cricket (Hopwood, 2005). Sports management and event management texts (for example Bowden et al. 2003) have not generally given PR the attention it deserves. However, Rojek's (2013) text on events written from a sociocultural perspective presents a useful engagement with PR activities. Finally and most recently, Pedersen's (2013) edited collection *Routledge Handbook of Sport Communication* marks a major step forward in the development of the field.

From a PR perspective Hopwood et al.'s (2010) edited text made a specific specialist contribution in presenting an explicitly functional account of the field. They framed the role of PR as response to crisis – all of the examples they give in their opening pages are critical incidents and scandals, although topics covered by contributors range more widely across corporate social responsibility (CSR), marketing, relationship management, fan relations, PR for individuals and international and cross-cultural communications. Critical work including an interpretive analysis of the purchase of a baseball team focused on source-media relations, media content and subsequent impact on media framing (Trujillo, 1992); and a textual analysis of a sports organization's community relationship programme that drew out competing rhetorical positioning (Boyd and Stahley, 2008). A Special Issue of *Public Relations Review* largely focused on reputational issues such as those surrounding player transgressions (Wilson et al., 2008); crises (Bruce and Tini, 2008; Dimitrov, 2008; Pfahl and Bates, 2008); reputation and image repair (Fortunato, 2008; Brazeal, 2008); publicity and marketing techniques (Anderson, 2008; Mitrook et al., 2008) including online (Woo et al., 2008). Several contributions explored rhetorical strategies and discourses including techniques of apology and diversion (Brazeal, 2008;

Pfahl and Bates, 2008; Jerome, 2008) or based on Benoit's **image repair** framework (Benoit, 1995, 1999; Benoit and Hanzicor, 1994). The subject matter in some cases was uncompromising, dealing with violence, sexual attack, activism, professional jealousies and emotions – all unusual topics for PR journals. Benoit's framework is used as the basis for a **Think Critically** box in Chapter 3, p. 57).

Sport studies include a range of sociological themes including gender, class, race, politics, economics, national identity and globalization (Riordan and Kruger, 1999; Gratton and Henry, 2001; Hargreaves, 1994; Allison, 2005; Maguire, 2006; Jarvie, 2006). But there has been a growing interchange between sports and media studies reflected in special issues in *Media, Culture & Society* and the *International Review for the Sociology of Sport; Sports Media*. More journals are now available such as the *International Journal of Sport Communication,* and *Communication & Sport*. Within sports studies, it has taken time for PR to be given attention. A typical approach was taken by Whannel (2000) who focused on media sport failing to take account of PR's contribution to the business development of the sport industry. *The Handbook of Sports Studies* (Coakley and Dunning, 2000) defined the field of sports studies, its histories, paradigms and concerns, and included a contribution focused on production, content and audience, but made only passing reference to the potential for information to be 'controlled by press and PR departments' (2000: 292).

Media studies sociologists have focused on professional sports, news media – especially TV (Whannel, 2000: 291) – TV rights, media economics (Haynes, 2005), sports fans and fanzines (Haynes, 1995; Crawford, 2004), national identity (Boyle, 1992; Blain et al., 1993), concentrating on mainstream team sports covered regularly on sports pages and occasionally on news pages of newspapers (Boyle and Haynes, 2000, cited in L'Etang, 2006). As Campbell (2004: 203–4) pointed out, entertainment, sport and lifestyle media have tended to be 'dismissed or ignored rather than analysed' as mainstream media academics have focused on political public affairs and news media practice and this narrow focus was illustrated in the *Sage Handbook of Media Studies* (Downing et al., 2004) which did not index either sport or PR (L'Etang, 2006).

The media sociological concept of **source-media relations** is relevant to interrogating PR's influence (Hall, 1969, 1978; Ferguson, 1990; Schlesinger, 1990; McNair, 1996; D. Miller, 1998), or PR's role in **primary definition** whereby media sources generate initial and particular interpretations of events, issues and other actors in an attempt to protect reputation or promote particular **frames of reference** or ideologies, thus reducing the media to **secondary definers**. It has been noted that sports journalism has had lower status than other forms of journalism, and sports journalists often find it hard to gain professional autonomy because they may be former sports stars themselves (or fans) and therefore find it challenging to maintain critical distance (Boyle, 2006). Sports journalism encompasses a range of media including magazines that appear to attract different personalities, as one former journalist commented,

' I wanted to work in a magazine because I preferred the environment, newspapers are more pressurized, political and stressful … everything was just about contacts and finding a story, not about the writing. I found magazines much more satisfying and the fact that it is participatory journalism in that I get to do the things we write about, it's service journalism.   ❯

Media sociologists (Boyle and Haynes, 2000; Haynes, 2005; Boyle, 2006; Wanta, 2013) have also produced useful insights into relationships between media, sources, sponsors and sport, but tended to focus on traditional media relations rather than the broader aspects of PR work. The **converged media** context has impacted the sports environment and operation and this is discussed below. Historical studies that focused on the relationships between news sources (including PR practitioners) and the media 'on the beat' – were explored from the perspective of the sports journalist, employing concepts such as **gatekeeper** (people that sift incoming news items and determine which items are retained as possible news stories), **agenda setting** (people and institutions that set the news agenda), disinformation and focusing on the ambivalent interdependence between sports promoter and journalist (Bourgeois, 1995; Lowes, 1987).

Bourgeois considered the **bonding** processes that take place in the sociocultural context of sports journalism and the precariousness of maintaining professional distance from PR sources. Bourgeois suggested that the strategy adopted by sports journalists could be defined in processual terms, within which journalists,

❮ Must transform interactions between sports teams and between athletes into an entertaining sports spectacle … through a process of spectacularization, which is founded on the ethics of entertainment, on the use of the lexicons of fantasy, combat, and passion, and on dramatization … because the outcome is unpredictable. (1995: 199)   ❯

Bourgeois's analysis suggested that stories may begin with co-operative tendencies between PR practitioners and journalists, proceed to an identification of flaws that become socio-dramatic anchors or foci for a variety of narratives and speculative scenarios and solutions (L'Etang, 2006). In short, an initially collaborative relationship might unravel, through inconsistencies or alternative stories and rumours, subsequently developing into a reputational crisis for an individual, a team or a whole sport, as has happened with drug-use allegations in various sporting contexts. These processes accelerated with digitization and social media.

The tensions between media and sources are not always unhelpful to sources, however. In September 2011, the International Cycling Union (UCI) hosted the World Road Cycling Championship in Copenhagen. In the weeks leading up to the race, the media was filled with negative headlines predicting traffic chaos and road closures. However, according to Lars Lundov, Sport Event Denmark, the negative media coverage helped organizers to solve problems and communicate alternative modes of transport, claiming that, 'It went in our favour … we didn't have any problems' (Evans, 2012a: 26).

Collaborative tendencies may also be mitigated by competitive pressures and the temptation for **sting journalism** that may involve tempting sportspeople into compromising situations.

What Happens on Tour, Stays on Tour?

In the UK *The Sunday Times* highlighted alleged corrupt practices by two members of FIFA's Executive Committee. These were pursued and the two members were disciplined. However, the Head of the Federation's Ethics Committee criticised the media exposé. Commenting on this incident Kevin Roberts, Editor of *SBI* noted the changing relationship between media and sport, and urged closer co-operation,

> In an ideal world [media and sport] would feed off each other, making the other stronger and richer. But today the relationship is driven by distrust and fear rather than the mutual respect which was once the case ... early Test Match cricket ... was a six-week journey by sea. Players and the gentlemen of the press travelled on the same ships, often with the journalists in first-class and the cricketers ... in standard. Inevitably, men who spent time together travelling formed bonds and friendships, which overlapped and supported their professional relationships. One of the results was the 'what happens on tour stays on tour' mentality, which recognised that humans – whether or not they are sportsmen – are likely to do dumb things from time to time. Today everything has changed. Intense competition, in the print, online and broadcast media sectors creates unprecedented pressure for journalists to go way beyond match reports. Journalists and professional sports people might as well live on different planets and deep personal relationships between the two sides have become extremely rare. (Roberts, 2010b: 7).

Discuss!

How close should journalists be to their subjects or their PR representatives in the pursuit of a story and why? What are the societal implications of close or hostile relationships? How close should the relationship between sports businesss and the media be? How does social media influence these relationships? Finally, what does the quote reveal about historic gender assumptions that prevailed upon the cultures and practices of sport and sports journalism, and to what extent may these affect sports in society today and social attitudes more generally?

Convergent Media in a Digital Networked World

Following Meikle and Young (2012), the term **convergent media** is used in this book to capture the range and linkages between contemporary media. **Networked digital**

media (Meikle and Young, 2012) suffuse private and public spheres offering multiple opportunities to consume, remediate and participate in online discussion. It is self-evident that this communicative potential has been taken up by sports business and the PR industry and is a matter for much debate and experimentation. **Social media** offers multiple spaces for communicative interactions and experiences. Globally there are cultural preferences, for example Facebook is ubiquitous in the UK but elsewhere there is Friendster (Asia), Orkut (Brazil and India), Cyworld (Korea), Mixi (Japan), QQ (China) and Vronktahte (Russia) (Meikle and Young, 2012: 63). Social media organizations themselves use PR services, for example Twitter employed M&C Saatchi to challenge the view that Twitter 'is mainly used as a resource for journalists and as a promotional service for celebrities ... the brief [was] to present the social network as a people-focused brand' (*PRW* 2012a: 1).

Within PR the shift in communication dynamics is fundamental, because a major part of PR work has traditionally been around media relations, publicity and promotion based on models of **mass communication** and **media effects** and two-step dissemination of messages to key **opinion formers**, relying on the media to reach wider audiences. The provision by **sources** (Nike, national associations, government departments responsible for sport, sponsors) of issue-relevant, newsworthy, appropriately written and presented material performed the function of a **news subsidy** (Gandy, 1982) and facilitated the chances that those messages were reproduced or represented as closely as possible in key media (relevant sections of the most important titles written by influential journalists). One-to-one, face-to-face relationships with journalists also facilitated close understanding between journalists and PR practitioners, despite underlying tensions over who was really making the news and journalists' resentment of their dependency on PR sources (particularly since many former journalists 'crossed over' to PR, eliciting criticism of 'poacher turned gamekeeper'). It was not unusual to be asked at an interview for a PR job which journalists you knew and had in your **contacts book**. However, now it is the case that although,

> ' Media relations was (and is) important in terms of editorial status (often referred to as third-party endorsement) and in terms of its power to circulate organizational discourses and ideologies ... it is now one of many information sources and is not the societal filter it once was. The historical model of filter then publish has been reversed. (Shirky, 2008: 81–108) '

PR is often evaluated in terms of media coverage, for example counting the number of times key terms/phrases (**content analysis**) were used in editorial or looking at the extent to which source material was used. However, analysing media coverage on its own does not provide any insight into reader perspectives. It is still the case that some PR campaigns are flawed in their design in that they state objectives of attitudinal or behavioural change among particular stakeholders or demographics but then proceed only to evaluate media content, which provides some insight into the media but does not give any information about the targeted readership. The fact that much PR evaluation is limited to media evaluation implies an underlying assumption that readers believe what they read in the media. However, there has been a long tradition in media and mass communication studies that has argued that readers are not passive but active, using media to their own ends, constructing their own interpretations and judgements – and it is precisely this process that has moved to some extent from the private to the public sphere. The Internet provides the potential to view processes of opinion formation within particular networks. A multiplicity of media forms are now integrated with one another and easily consumed through a single device, but are also diverse in form, style and reach offering consumers the ability to make interventions and edits. The opportunity to **reconfigure** or **recombine** enhances participation, interactivity and communicative action (Lievrouw, 2011).

These opportunities have changed the way in which reputation and relationships are formed and the methods employed by PR practitioners. Nevertheless, communicators need to retain their prime focus as Matt Farrell, Chief Marketing Officer of USA Swimming pointed out,

> Connectivity should not depend on technology, but should rather *build relationships*. Content creates connection, not the device. … Connectivity is a *mission*, not a device. Accomplishing connectivity takes *trust*. We *work hard* to earn the *respect* of members and communicate USA Swimming to them and explain how our sponsors represent their values. We seize opportunities to tell stories about our sport and how our organization is trying to lead it. This is a real opportunity to make a *deeper connection* beyond venue signage. And it works – 74 per cent of our members are likely to purchase our sponsor's products: 91 per cent of members feel sponsors are promoting their brand positively; and we are on track for a 100 per cent renewal rate of our top partners. When I think about connectivity, I focus less on technology and more on *trust, loyalty, authenticity, leadership* and *inspiration*. Then I tweet it. (*SBI*, 2013d: 114) (Author italics)

Continuous development in converged media impacts the structures and practices of PR. For example, Aloft Hotels invited PR consultancies to pitch for a business proposal via Twitter, and to participate in an ongoing discussion over a period of four weeks after which the client would draw up a shortlist for a formal pitch and meetings (Stein, 2012: 9). PR campaigns are now expected to integrate all forms of available media as Kindred MD Laura Oliphant pointed out,

> Our clients want to see digital and social media as part of their campaigns at a time when the lines between these disciplines are becoming increasingly blurred. (Hay, 2009: 13)

Discuss!

What does the quote above reveal about the nature of public relations work? How might the qualities 'respect', 'trust' and 'loyalty' be gained?

This has been an important development because for a period specialists in social media were recruited, and although this is still the case, the trend is now for integration, as the social media manager Kerry Bridge at Dell pointed out,

' We are moving from a central social media team towards it being embedded into people's roles across the board. We've trained more than 1,000 employees globally and we will continue to roll that out. (Wicks, 2010 10) '

Converged media profoundly affects the way in which PR activity is conceived and enacted because it is now only one of many sources of discursive influence. And it is particularly challenging for those accustomed to a communication outputs and publicity approach that did not go beyond basic content analysis of print media or the comparison between media releases and media coverage. The effects of PR generally are rather under-researched, although groundbreaking work was carried out by Cardiff University's School of Journalism that showed how dependent the non-tabloid newspapers were on PR-generated news releases for their content (Lewis and Franklin, 2008). The problem with the dominant media-centred approach in PR is that it stops short of evaluating actual impact beyond the media (even though the campaign objectives may specify attitudinal or behavioural change of a particular group). If PR is defined as being purely about influencing media content then it is not surprising that the sobriquet 'spin doctor' is applied to the occupation. PR practitioners have been described as **discourse techno-logists** (Leitch and Motion, 1996) but they are not alone in this activity. This historical approach to media relations was typically predicated on one-way communications in which publicists tried to write in a sufficiently newsworthy style to pass media **gatekeepers**. The **one-way** model was criticised for its similarity with propaganda models' persuasion (Herman and Chomsky, 1988), and early PR theorists endeavoured to deal with this critique by formulating a model of PR which was dialogic and met equal exchange conditions of **two-way symmetrical communication**. The difficulty with this model has largely been that it has failed to engage with notions of power or to indicate criteria in which the process of communication might be judged to have been truly dialogic. Thus it has been posited as a largely idealistic model that appeared not to bear a great deal of relation to a practice largely concerned with dissemination to the media, publicity, persuasion and lobbying. Networked digital media has clearly changed the context in a way that facilitates user-authorship and editorship and has a different sort of communication potential: the question is whether communicators adapt to the paradigm or retain standardized approaches; established models may be too rigid.

On the other hand, if PR is seen as being around **stakeholder relations**, then that is going to demand a more sophisticated approach to evaluating PR work (advocacy/persuasion, reputation, relationships). Networked digital media offer a lot of communication options but they are not just 'one more medium' or 'another technique', they require a different approach, namely investment in thought and time to develop communication strategies that will engage key opinion leaders and develop and enhance interactive relationships. However, practitioners who overly focus on how to evaluate this or that digital medium miss the point that the sum is worth more than the whole of the parts. It is the way in which users relate to, use, and recreate media as part of multiple networks that matters. Media convergence forces PR practitioners to think holistically and consider usage rather than in terms of particular tools or techniques and outputs of corporate messages.

In other words, what still matters is understanding meaning-making processes and their wider implications within a community (much more accessible with digital networked media), and being canny about approaches that appear to offer clear metrics, for example, Facebook pages offer a 'like' option, but not 'bored', and methodologically such counts give no indication of the motivation or significance that lies behind the click.

'The International Association for the Measurement and Evaluation of Communication (AMEC) meets annually to discuss and review the progress of evaluation practices in the industry, including those that relate specifically to social media. AMEC's Social Media Task Force recommended that 'Social media measurement needed to focus on outcomes, not outputs, so basic quantitative measures like number of followers was useful but not particularly valuable, and that the PR industry needed greater transparency from vendors of measurement'. (Magee, 2012b: 25) '

In other words the same problems that were encountered with print media evaluation also exist in converged media, the fundamental challenges are that PR has not been perceived as a research-based discipline, which has contributed to the unwillingness of clients and employees to pay for research into impacts as opposed to outputs; some of its practitioners lack the social science expertise either to do the job themselves or commission someone else to do it on their behalf; evaluation is frequently not measured against behavioural or attitudinal objectives. Current models on social media evaluation are often adapted versions of an historic model referred to as AIDA – Awareness, Interest, Desire, Action. These models are predicated on persuasion and change that is supposed to follow the dissemination of messages via blog post, videos, blogger events and briefings, and evaluated by calculating visitors, fans, followers and likes. There are technical products on the market that will collect quantitative data on traditional media (media evaluation packages), but those designed for social media appear, at least in part, to be based on a pre-digital media paradigm. The challenge is not only to capture visits and usage but also the meaningfulness of any engagement in relations to other variables (competing discourses and relationships) and the dynamic of shifting relationships within key networks. Converged media offer a great deal of feedback potential, but evaluation needs to take account of multiple perspectives and the interplay between them in relation to a topic and connected relationships.

Thought also needs to be given in PR to the changed balance between remote and face-to-face communication and its implications. In the same way that in mid- and late-twentieth century London journalists used to network in pubs around Fleet Street to exchange gossip and leads, so PR practitioners shared collateral in wine bars and clubs. Now that so much can be achieved instantaneously but remotely, it is interesting to reflect on what is or is not lost in a range of professional relationships, and how central an issue that is for communication professionals and the advice they give their clients. In short, while the quantity of communication opportunities for interaction continues to increase, practitioners also need to be able to contribute to and assess the quality of relationships, their sincerity, intensity, reliability and uniqueness. This is important because PR practitioners are (presumably) recruited for their overall understanding of human communication, of which digital networked media are a major part, but not the whole.

Within PR literature some maintain a distinction between 'old' (print) and 'new' media (which now it is not), occasionally referring to 'old' media as **legacy media** (for example see Holladay and Coombs, 2013). However, this is an artificial divide that obscures the way in which developments have extended and reincorporated a media mix that is built on assumptions of interactivity and remediation. This also has implications for the way in which PR works with other specialists such as marketing and branding. Corporate and consumer communications need co-ordination across digital platforms that still reflect their distinctive purpose, as do media relations for announcing news, for example sports celebrities often use Twitter and news journalists frequently source and cite Twitter. The London 2012 Olympics were billed as the first 'social Olympics': 9.7 million tweets were sent during the opening ceremony on 27 July 2012, 125 times more than on the equivalent day in Beijing when the platform was still in its infancy (Shearman, 2012: 15).

From an analytical perspective, it is important to understand strategic intent, policy, communication context and the fact that opacity, distortion and manipulation are still features of communication spaces. Responding to allegations, rumour and gossip demands immediacy, and it should not be forgotten that converged media offer opportunities for creative reinterpretations of stories and organizations that subvert the original meaning, known as **culture jamming** (Lievrouw, 2011: 22–3), interventions that can be subversive and defined as **activism,** indeed the proliferation of low-cost communication options has facilitated the growth in the numbers of new social movements. This has implications for sports business because:

> ' All businesses are media businesses, because whatever else they do, all businesses rely on managing information for two audiences – employees and the world. The increase in the power of both individuals and groups, outside traditional organizational structures, is unprecedented. (Shirky, 2008: 107) '

Access to digital networked media creates an expanded public sphere for debate and its openness encourages multiple commentators. These compete with established paid journalists and PR practitioners raising interesting issues over expertise, legitimacy and professionalism and professional status. There is now, according to Shirky, an age of **mass amateurism**, which is really the corollary of democratization and dissemination of publication and interactivity tools – 'the linking of symmetrical participation and amateur participation' (Shirky, 2008: 98, 107).

In sports business, converged media open up many opportunities in terms of new products and services, such as gaming. Owners and managers of major sports face communication opportunities and challenges, for example in being sufficiently responsive to their fans, who have been empowered and given a 'voice' that can endlessly resonate through re-mediation, re-Tweets and hashtags, repeated (if deemed significant) by news media in the dynamic spiral that is contemporary communication space.

However, in **sportscape**, converged network media have also raised expectations regarding the availability of the sports person and the extent to which they will communicate via Twitter and Facebook. Sponsors expect that professional sports stars will make themselves available, and will regularly comment on issues other than sport. Their 'private' spaces are also to be consumed as a crucial part of their individual commodification. Professional sport is one job, promoting sponsors is another, subjecting oneself to the voyeuristic gaze a necessary condition of celebrity. Predators, prey and parasites are virtually present in the self-promotional space, but which is which is not always obvious. Converged media has often been claimed by PR specialists as a new dawn of interactivity (which it is) but that in itself does not guarantee ethical communication (whatever we might mean by that) or authentic trustworthy relationships; people may not always think what they Tweet.

Sport 'Celebrity' and PR

The phenomenon of sports celebrity is not new. The English cricketer W. G. Grace had 'a special place in the lives of people in Victorian England' and professional football players in the 1890s were feted in their neighbourhoods (Smart, 2005: 2) as were professional runners in the same era (Askwith, 2004: 60). Some sports have benefited from their association with stars from other cultural domains. For example, tennis became popular among Hollywood silent film stars such as Tony Moreno and Enid Storey in the 1910s and 1920s, and talkie stars such as Joan Crawford, Groucho Marx, Barbara Stanwyck, Carole Lombard, Marlene Dietrich, many of whom were taught by Eleanor 'Teach' Tennant at the Beverley Hills Hotel (Spain, 1953). From a modest background herself, Teach's social circle included William Randolph Hearst and Marion Davies, and she attracted stars to the hotel and brought it considerable publicity, so that soon Teach 'found herself very busy with the unpaid job of PR Officer' (Spain, 1953: 26). Ranked third in the US as an amateur, Teach later coached world-beaters Alice Marble, Bobby Riggs (who many years later, in 1973, lost 'the battle of the sexes' to Billy Jean King) and 'Little Mo' Maureen Connolly, who won the Ladies Championship at Wimbledon three times before the age of 20. This historical example illustrates the synergy between celebrity circles that generate glamour and mystique around particular trends or fashions. The notion of 'stars' and 'stardom' could easily cross from entertainment to sport, something taken for granted by sports business practitioners today who regard sport as an entertainment business.

Celebrity can be defined as being well-known for being well-known (Boorstin in Andrews and Jackson, 2001: 2) and while sporting heroes have always existed, the development of 'mega-celebrity' has been facilitated by converged media and processes of globalization. According to Rojek (2001) democratization, the commodification of daily life and the decline of organized religion have been the key developments leading to the cult worship of mass-media celebrities (Smart, 2005: 9). Sports celebrities are commodified and become part of the currency of sports business and, more widely, in promotional culture. Andrews and Jackson identified key aspects of promotional culture, which helped manufacture celebrity:

> The representation industry; the endorsement industry; the publicity industry; the communication industry; the entertainment industry; the coaching industry; the legal industry; and the appearance industry. (2001: 4)

These multifaceted aspects of postmodern Western-style cultures make a convincing case for analysing PR within broader cultural and less technically focused vocational frameworks. PR students often note popular culture's assumptions regarding synergies between PR and celebrity, yet anecdotal evidence suggests that academics are often keen to deny or belittle the connection, regarding it as trivial. This academic evasion is as puzzling as it is interesting, suggestive of the desire to 'scientize' and 'neutralize' PR into a technocratic organizational practice. Sport celebrity is intrinsic to the commercialization of sport because sporting heroes are required to inject media interest and sponsors' cash and that consequently,

> Sporting heroes therefore offer themselves as products of the 'culture industry', to be fashioned into sports stars ... The modern sport star ... is ... both cultural product (as a brand to be sold) and process (part of the chain of advertising and brand or product endorsement that underpins the regime of capital accumulation. (Gilchrist, 2005: 126)

Achievement is not necessary for fame in an era of branding, and an environment in which 'the celebrity as role model is both made and undone by press and television coverage' (Smart, 2005: 8). The news agenda has long included an interest in sleaze, noted by Boorstin as 'our morbid interest in private lives, in personal gossip, and in the sexual indiscretions of public figures' (1962: 255 cited in McNair, 2000: 52). Converged media exacerbates and stimulates the 'rumour mill'. Sporting victims include Tiger Woods (allegedly treated for 'sex addiction'), John Terry the Chelsea and English footballer (allegedly involved with a team-mate's partner), Ryan Giggs (who not only allegedly had an affair with a women but had apparently requested, and obtained, a super-injunction to prevent media coverage). Such examples are not simply moments of individual tragedy or public scandal, but have wider ramifications for consumer brands (and their values), sponsors, brand consumers, event and hospitality managers. We simply cannot understand sport unless we engage with the phenomenon of contemporary celebrity and associated paparazzi, celebrity magazines such as *Hello, OK, Heat*, and their online versions as well as news values and media and social **moral panics**.

Boorstin implied that such events have authority because they are not pre-planned, are not **pseudo-events** and therefore have an **authenticity**, but much has changed in media content, particularly entertainment media. Publicists, producers, media and participants (or are they actors?) in 'reality' TV tease viewers with performances that can dupe. A good example of this is the sport of wrestling and how it is performed on TV as entertainment. Serrels explored the various conventions and rituals regarding the 'masculine melodrama', the 'search for a moral order', and its own ethical system (Serrels, 2006): the wrestling industry presents performances staged as real but actually fake – outcomes are normally established prior to the contesters entering the ring. Afficianados and experienced fans will not be taken in, except in rare moments of reality (known in a wrestling argot supposedly based on pig Latin as 'The Shoot'). As Boorstin noted in his discussions of authenticity and pseudo-events (the creation of which have often been denigrated and blamed on PR by the media),

' Many sports become pseudo-events; and some (professional wrestling, for example) have actually flourished by exploiting their reputation for being synthetic. (Boorstin, 1992: 254) '

Such fake performances also affect other sports, for example in 2012 there were suggestions that 'diving' in English football (giving the impression that the footballer has been fouled by the opposition) had increased due, it was interestingly and xenophobically suggested, to foreign influences.

Yet part of sports business is concerned with the creation and subsequent promotion of new styles and forms of sport, and the generation of new structures such as 'world series' are often central to re-branding or reinventing a sport that is not realizing its desirable commercial value.

Commodification and Representation

The injection of capital means that sports and sports people become **commodified**, in that they acquire economic status through celebrity, a concept that in itself is no longer entirely dependent on sporting prowess. Promotion is an essential part of the process that translates physical expertise not only into events to which tickets may be purchased, but makes the image of the athlete(s) in question so desirable in terms of the values and ideals it conveys that it can be sold many times over through multiple media. PR expertise includes understanding of media values and their implications in terms of the way in which athletes are presented; the way in which reputation can be built through wisely chosen associations and activities to build a particular image. However, athletes can and do take an active role in their own digital media promotional activities, and in less popular (and therefore less government or corporately funded) sports, gaining even small amounts of local sponsorship can make a difference in terms of being able to be a full-time athlete. Therefore athletes often participate in the process of **self-commodification** early in their careers when seeking sponsorship, consequently attractive women emphasize their looks alongside their sporting talents to potential sponsors, and sponsors seek out attractive sportswomen, for example,

> ❛ Sharapova ... [an] ... intoxicating blend of commercial appeal of a huge, public person-
> ality ... movie star good looks ... Ivanovic ... smouldering looks surely guarantee her
> a fortune off the court [topped the UK tennis magazine *Ace*'s poll to find the world's
> sexiest player] ... IMG are rubbing their hands together in anticipation when it comes
> to young Nicole Vaidisova. The attractive Vaidisova has already adorned a number of
> high profile magazine covers and fronted Reebok ads. (Britcher, 2006: 36–7) ❜

Likewise, an *SBI* feature exploring the most powerful sports personalities for endorsements listed a top ten of which two were women (Maria Sharapova and Michelle Kwan),
both of whom were defined by their 'great looks' and 'elegance, beauty, grace', whereas
no mention was made of the physical appearance or attractiveness of the men, all of
whom were described in terms of their sporting prowess (*SBI*, 2007b).

Thus the sports business trade magazine reinforces expectations about the demands
laid upon elite female athletes: it is not enough to perform at an outstanding level at their
chosen sport, they must have 'the look' and perform heteronormative gender roles in
order to meet the expectations of sponsors. The process is viewed critically by those who
see this as a form of patriarchal exploitation. As Vincent and Crossman point out,

> ❛ Many of the narratives of sport journalists on female athletes conform to a White,
> hyperfeminine, heterosexual ideal ... Narratives about female athletes are frequently
> imbued with socially constructed sex-role stereotypes and are replete with refer-
> ences to their heterosexual familial roles as wives, mothers, girlfriends, and daugh-
> ters. This mediated discourse of female athletes' heterosexual familial roles serves to
> reproduce the pattern of male dominance. Many of the mediated narratives about
> female athletes are predicated on how they conform to socially constructed gender
> stereotypes or how they 'do gender' rather than their athleticism. This process of
> devaluing and trivializing female athletes serves and reifies patriarchal ideology.
> (Vincent and Crossman, 2007: 80; see also Brookes, 2002; Giese, 2000) ❜

Processes of **commodification** dictate that good-looking men and women will generate
more income. Sports business practitioners try to talent-spot attractive performers who
will be able to generate brand income regardless of their sporting talents. This is particularly the case for female sports stars who are closely assessed on looks and personality,
for example, US gymnast Nastia Liukin was dubbed 'Queen of Olympics Gymnastics'
after winning the Beijing title. *SBI* commented,

> ❛ Liukin has a bright future ... has become the darling of many sponsors and advertisers ...
> presented with a slew of non-sports opportunities, appearing on a variety of TV shows
> and magazine covers, including a shot with Maria Sharapova in New York ...What Liukin
> has done is place herself in the realm of Mary Lou Retton, the 1984 US gymnastics gold
> medallist ... Liukin seems to possess those same traits [bubbly personality and the gist
> of veracity] plus the kind of looks that Sharapova has used to attract more sponsors and
> endorsers than almost any other woman on the planet. (*SBI*, 2008b: 17) ❜

Commodification is linked to media representation; media texts and images are often gendered and heteronormative, and any image may be digitally enhanced to produce the most favourable aesthetic impression. Numerous studies have shown that coverage of women is limited, for example Lopiano (2000) found that 90 per cent of sports newspaper content was devoted to male sport, 5 per cent to women and 3 per cent to horses and dogs (women only overtook horses and dogs in 1992) (cited in Wanta, 2013: 80). Sports journalists are more likely to be men than women; sports business is also dominated by men as discussed later.

News-formation processes were put under the microscope by Knoppers and Elling (2004) in relation to the gendered processes of news selection by journalists, which, they argue, leads to the consistent under-representation of women's sport. Sports journalism is still a man's world (Knoppers and Elling, 2004: 58; Boyle, 2006) and Knoppers and Elling focused on how, within the structural constraints that shape journalism practice, journalists legitimize their choices. They found that giving more attention to women's sports was defined negatively as **promotional journalism,** clashing with a particular notion of (gendered) 'objectivity'.

Journalism values are made apparent in the quantity and quality of gender and race representation across a variety of genres including news media and specialist magazines. Inequality is evident across the board. Some magazines exclude women entirely, or, on the other hand, select the most photogenic examples. Despite an aging population, leisure sports magazines rarely, if ever, portray older men or women on their inside pages, and certainly not on covers. Likewise, covers do not reflect the ethnic make-up of the UK population. In some cases (see below) magazines overtly sexualize content.

Such predispositions within the media inevitably affect the way some sportswomen present themselves, for example one female golfer said 'I am careful to be well-presented and I am fortunate to be pretty'. PR is necessarily implicated in these processes in its impression management of individuals who are produced groomed and presented as brand representatives for products and services to be consumed.

Gendered and Sexualized Representation in Golf Magazines

Golf World

In one issue there were 188 images of men in 210 pages (including three on the front cover). The only images of women portrayed (except for one tiny unnamed image on page 210) were ghettoized in a single article about the Royal & Ancient's decision to permit women to compete in the Open. Passport-size photographs appeared of Isabelle Beisiegel, Mhairi McKay, Trish Johnson, Nina Reis, Laura Davies, Sophie Gustafson, Heather Daly-Donofrio, Laurette

(Continued)

(Continued)

Martiz and Sandra Carlborg. Stephenie Louden appeared in a studio shot holding a golf club laterally behind her shoulders so that her breasts, encased in a purple cashmere twinset, were emphasized. Michelle Wie was the only female golfer shown in action in the whole of the magazine. Annika Sorenstam was depicted at a press conference. Sophie Sandolo – the only woman to merit a full-page shot – appeared sitting slightly backwards on a space-age sofa that on close inspection was comprised of giant golf clubs. Wearing a strapless virginal-white mini-dress, slit at the side and bondage-type knee-high boots that consisted only of a large tongue of silver leather clasped onto her legs with four straps, Sandolo pouted down at the camera, her expression ambiguous since her eyes were sunk in pools of dark eyeshadow. Her hands were clenched, appearing to be virtually manacled together.

Golfpunk

The magazine leaned towards the *Playboy* end of the magazine market, possibly unsurprising since its editorial team had backgrounds in *Loaded* and *GQ*. In one issue was a section on 'Bunkerbabes' where 'we fly the Golfpunk lovelies to Las Vegas for a night on the fruities. Nudge, Nudge' and pictures of a bikini-clad woman accompanied by the by-line 'You little tees' ('Contents' *Golfpunk*: 1). Scantily clad women posed provocatively with gold clubs, tees poking out of tiny shorts. A similar approach was taken on the magazine subscription form, where a model wearing black velvety underwear and a lace garter, peeks out from under a black hat while holding a golf club in her right hand behind her head (and thus emphasizing her right breast) and with her hand on the head of a (dead) stuffed cheetah. 'The Golf Nurse' gave basic golfing tips in a double page spread that included seven pictures of the nurse wearing hot pants, sleeveless top, stripy long socks and a mohair cap. Golf clothing was modelled on fully dressed men accompanied by bikini-clad blondes in killer stilettos. There was not a single image of a professional female golfer.

Sport reflects but also shapes societal patterns and flows, and there are some fundamental issues in the sports industry with which PR becomes implicated through the reproduction of discourses. These are strongly gendered and shaped by heteronormative assumptions and discourses. Gender inequality structures sports business. The most highly paid professional sports stars are inevitably men, an imbalance that the sports media complex connives in, and justifies on the grounds that male sports are more popular and therefore attract more sponsorship.

Inequity in Cricket

In January 2012 BBC News interviewed the England Women's Cricket team about the possibility of winning the World Cup for the fourth time in a row. In passing it was mentioned that they had travelled on the same plane as the men, but the men had flown in the comfort of business class while the women travelled tourist class. The (female) interviewer asked the team if they were bitter. The answer was along the lines of, 'Not at all, we do it for the love of the game, not the money'. While this comment could be interpreted as graciousness or perhaps as a sideways dig at their much less successful but much more generously funded male counterparts, it also suggested submission, or at least accommodation to the inevitability of the status quo.

Sport business itself is a largely male occupation as is sports media and journalism, apparently reflecting and reinforcing societal stereotypes about feminine and masculine appropriate behaviour. Evidence of awareness of this issue was acknowledged by *SBI* in an article that reported major gender imbalances (Gillis, 2013: 36–40). The article quoted Sally Hancock, former director of Olympic marketing and group sponsorship at Lloyds TSB Bank and a high profile figure who won sponsorship personality of the year at the Hollis Sponsorship Awards,

> It's depressing to say the least. The industry can often feel like an exclusive boys' club and does nothing to inspire confidence in women looking to move up the ladder in industry. I started out in sponsorship in 1988, and at the time there were significant numbers of women at agency account managerial level with very few in senior roles within sports administration. Twenty-five years later I am not sure that much has changed. (cited in Gillis, 2013: 37)

While inequality and prejudice in sports practice is challenged by lobby groups such as the Women's Sport and Fitness Foundation (WSFF), in the UK progress is slow. WSFF have highlighted issues of lower participation in sport among women from the teenage years and have argued that strong role models and media coverage are the way to correct the gender imbalance as well improving women's health and fitness.

Discuss!

How does this issue affect the reputation of sports business and how should the industry respond?

It has been documented that lesbian, gay, bisexual and transgender (LGBT) sports people are less well rewarded for their abilities in terms of sponsorship and brand opportunities. It is still the case that in some sports, such as rugby, it may be hard for sports stars to acknowledge LGBT and publicly fluid identities. Some LGBT sports stars elect to announce their sexuality in a formal press conference, for example, on the verge of his WBO world title fight Puerto Rican featherweight Orlando Cruz who competed at the 2000 Olympics announced 'I have been and always will be a proud Puerto Rican. I have always been and always will be a proud gay man' (BBC teletext, 6 October 2012).

Sport reflects society in relation to prejudicial attitudes, something of which some sporting associations are aware. For example, Anna Rawson was asked by a reporter what ladies' golf could do to become more popular like ladies' tennis. As *SBI* reported,

> Rawson was familiar with the line of questioning. When she's not playing golf she makes a good living as a fashion model so her views on 'sexing up' golf have an added frisson. She threw out a few suggestions but said that, on the whole, she felt things were improving. But she didn't just say that. She said that the game was shedding its 'dyke' image. Mistake. The interview was quickly relayed to LPGA headquarters in the States where, a few weeks later, the then tour commissioner Caroline Bivens welcomed Rawson to the LPGA by making her stand up and apologize for using 'the D word'. (Gillis: 16–17, cited in L'Etang, 2013: 507)

Discuss!

How can sports PR practitioners avoid stereotyping and practise authenticity? Are sports cultures and business heteronormative and if so, why? What implications does this have for PR practitioners?

Think Critically

Choose a sample of sports and fitness magazines from a variety of sports. Analyse the covers in terms of representation of gender, race and age. Choose individual magazines and carry out more detailed qualitative and quantitative analysis of the editorial and articles, noting any links between sponsors, advertisements and editorial. What does the exercise reveal about apparent journalism values? Finally, analyse news stories in the magazine and consider how those stories were sourced and what PR activity may have lain behind the stories.

Personal PR

Individual sports stars need a PR specialist in personal PR. Personal PR is all-inclusive in terms of its approach and is not limited to the star's sporting activities but includes their personality, private life and networks, including the inevitable scandals. In some sporting contexts there may be overlap between the roles of press agent, agent and PR.

Personal PR also helps the sport with which that person is associated. As Barry Hearn, Chairman of Matchroom pointed out,

> 'Having characters in sport is important. I've always had a concept that sport is a soap opera played out by characters. People talk about those characters and that helps the sports PR machine'. (*SBI*, 2013a: 56)

Nurturing of sports talent to celebrity status for long-term economic gain is central to sports business and marketing, but controversy can tarnish satellite brands and even squeaky-clean stars can be subjected to critique. Tom Daley is a British swimmer who found fame when he competed at the Beijing Olympics aged 14 and then again at London where he won a bronze medal. Clearly he was a marketing and public relations dream especially since he was articulate and relaxed in front of the camera. Professional Sports Group represented Daley and explained his brand potential,

> Today's stars have to be more than winners; they must have something extra to offer their sponsors and that means developing personal brands and media platforms that complement their athletic achievements … Tom is a very unique mix. He's a perfectionist who wants to be the best he can be. The 2016 Olympics is his focus. He is really bright – an 'A-star' student – and a fantastic communicator who understands and enjoys modern media. He is not bad-looking either and he has an incredible story. (Cunningham, 2013: 70)

However, somewhat ironically, in the run-up to 2012 Daley was criticised for spending too much time on promotional and marketing activities and was also the subject of offensive tweets that triggered further media debate.

One aspect of personal PR is to maximize the value of the sports star by extending their career beyond sport. Fame delivers economic rewards but has the potential to lead to success in other areas as boundaries between sport and entertainment have become porous and sports stars may be reinvented in new roles. This reinvention or 'cross-over' process is part of the personal PR remit as shown in the following examples:

> Facilitated by the professional marketing and public-relations services offered by global sport agencies such as IMG, Octagon, and SFX, many sport celebrities have transcended sport and crossed over into popular entertainment (Rowe, 1995).

> Serena Williams, whose celebrity image is carefully managed by IMG, has acted in a television sitcom and appeared in numerous television commercials. (Vincent and Crossman, 2007: 91)

Sports stars have generally relatively short careers in their prime area of expertise (less true in some areas that are not so physically demanding such as snooker or darts), and from their perspective they need to make the most of the financial opportunities that arise and capitalize on their achievements and fame to develop a post-competitive career. Obvious routes are coaching, sports management or sports development, but in the era of media sports, the media itself is also a clear option. In the UK examples include Sue Barker (tennis), Gary Lineker (football) Clare Balding (amateur flat jockey) all of who commentate on a variety of sports. Balding also commentates on other countryside matters and animal-based events such as Crufts.

The ultimate transformation is from that of sports star to general and life-lasting celebrity. A sports start will be 'tried out' in various media chat shows to see if they can 'cross-over', for example Michael Phelps did many talk shows and hosted *Saturday Night*

Live on NBC (the network for the Olympics in the US), presented the VideoMusic Awards and became the face of a trading card (Wilner, 2008). Phelps also attracted a wide range of non-sports business sponsorship including Visa, Hilton Hotels, Omega Watches, AT&T, and Rosetta Stone language-learning software.

While sports business increasingly relies on sports stars to market themselves, display 'personality' and share personal details and opinions, the demands and availability of digital information may backfire, particularly where opinions are problematic or not directly related to sport. For example, in spring 2013 a new manager was appointed at the English football club Sunderland AFC – Paolo di Canio from Italy. On his appointment, the Vice-Chairman and Director of the Club, politician David Miliband, former Foreign Secretary, resigned from the Board in protest because di Canio had allegedly previously professed a belief in fascism (and had made a fascist salute when he played for Lazio in 2005, an act for which he received a ban). On 2 April 2013 di Canio arrived at his new club, but following intense media debate over the Easter weekend refused to answer questions about his political beliefs, stating that his beliefs were personal and that he would not talk about them. Many fans expressed criticism and the local miners' association threatened to remove their official flag from the ground out of respect for the role that former miners had played in the fight against fascism in the Second World War. Subsequently, a statement was issued from di Canio on 4 April 2013 in which he declared

> ' I am not political, I do not affiliate myself to any organization. I am not a racist. I do not support the ideology of fascism. I respect everyone. I am a football man. This and my family are my focus. Now I will speak only of football. (BBC Sport, 4 April 2013) '

The case draws out some interesting points: apart from likely reputational damage to Sunderland, it suggests that not only sports stars but those in prominent leadership positions also need personal PR. Media coverage quickly extended. Sunderland's executive had been seeking to rejuvenate the club's finances and in autumn 2012 signed a shirt sponsorship deal with Invest in Africa for £20 million a season. Invest in Africa is an organization founded to dispel misconceptions about African commerce, to promote and encourage new investors; and to showcase companies already operating successfully on the continent (Harman, 2012: 16). Evidently Invest in Africa approached Sunderland because Sunderland's Foundation of Light supports 120 employees working with 44,000 children each year, paralleling similar programmes in Africa associated with Invest in Africa. The connection also offers business and football opportunities in Africa. The crisis that was catalysed by David Miliband seemed likely to throw all of Sunderland's activities, and more crucially, its values under the media spotlight for some time to come.

Think Critically

Choose a local sports person aged between 15 to 20, possibly someone at your college or university. Consider how you would go about gaining relevant sponsorship that would allow them to train or attend events. What would the sponsor gain? Why should they choose this person above another person? And why this sport rather than another sport? How does the sport and the person align with the potential sponsor's values or extend them in a way that could be beneficial in terms of marketing or media coverage? How would you make the sponsor–beneficiary relationship a genuine relationship? Can you avoid stereotyping your sports person?

Discuss!

Consider the relative celebrity status of the following athletes relative to their achievements. Why do some have a higher profile than others? How is that profile achieved? Is that profile justified, and if so, why and how? Who handles personal PR for these stars?

- David Beckham
- Juan Manuel Fangio
- Florence Kiplagat
- Nichol David
- Li Xueni
- Usain Bolt

- Rafael Nadal
- Chrissie Wellington
- Victoria Pendleton
- Ma Long
- Alexandra do Nascimento
- Luis Scola

Summary

Modern sport is deeply embedded in image-making, celebrity, promotion, elite and intra-elite relationships. Sports events have cultural significance relating to individual processes of identification and punctuate societal flows. PR practitioners and journalists are meaning-makers and storytellers, combining corporate and populist concerns with human interest stories. PR is embedded in sports business, its promotion, sponsorship, events and hospitality, its risks and crises, and, most fundamentally of all, its policies and relationships. This chapter has summarized some key sources in PR, sports and media studies to provide background concepts relevant to contemporary sports PR practice. It has highlighted tensions and co-operation amongst media, sports business and PR and elaborated issues around sports PR and celebrity.

Further Reading

Andrews DL (2013) Reflections on communication and sport: on celebrity and race. *Communication & Sport*, 1 (1/2): 151–63.

Boyle R (2013) Reflections on communication and sport: on journalism and digital culture. *Communication & Sport*, 1 (1/2): 88–99.

Carlson B and Donavan DT (2013) Human brands in sport: athlete brand personality and identification. *Journal of Sport Management*, 27 (3): 193–206.

Claringbould I and Knoppers A (2012) Paradoxical practices of gender in sport-related organizations. *Journal of Sport Management*, 26 (5): 404–416.

Eagleman AN (2011) Stereotypes of race and nationality: a qualitative analysis of sport magazine coverage of MLB players. *Journal of Sport Management*, 25 (2): 156–168.

Hambrick M and Mahoney T (2011) 'It's incredible – trust me': exploring the role of celebrity athletes as marketers in online social networks. *Journal of Sport Management and Marketing*, 10 (3/4): 151–179

Kane MJ and Maxwell HD (2011) Expanding the boundaries of sport media research: using critical theory to explore consumer responses to representations of women's sports. *Journal of Sport Management*, 25 (3): 202–216.

Moore AJ (2012) The masculine image of presidents as sporting figures: a public relations perspective. *Sage Open* 2. Available at sgo.sagepub.com/content/2/2/ 21582440 12457078

Schultz B and Sheffer ML (2010) An exploratory study of how Twitter is affecting sports journalism. *International Journal of Sport Communication*, 3 (2): 226–239.

Sheffer ML and Schultz B (2010) Paradigm shift or passing fad? Twitter and sports journalism. *International Journal of Sport Communication*, 3 (4): 472–484.

Smith E and Hattery A (2011). Race relations theories: implications for sport management. *Journal of Sport Management*, 25 (2): 107–117.

Waters RD, Burke K, Jackson Z and Buning J (2011) Using stewardship to cultivate fandom online: comparing how National Football League teams use their web sites and Facebook to engage their fans. *International Journal of Sport Communication*, 4 (2): 163–177.

Wanta W (2013) Reflections on communication and sport: on reporting and journalists. *Communication & Sport*, 1 (1/2): 76–87.

Whiteside E and Hardin M (2012) On being a 'good sport' in the workplace: women, the glass ceiling and negotiated resignation in sports information. *International Journal of Sport Communication*, 5 (1): 51–68.

2

Theories and Critiques of Sports PR

Introduction

This chapter defines the role and scope of sports PR, its specialized areas, explains the diverse nature of sports PR work and the importance of PR to sports organizations. The chapter also introduces the academic discipline of PR, some of its terminology and themes, and explains its managerial, organizational and societal scope, giving emphasis to the strategic relational purposes behind PR, rather than specific techniques. Throughout this book functional and critical approaches are employed. Functional approaches are largely focused on the needs of the sports client (for example, sports organization, sports sponsor or sports star) and the organizational practical aspects of PR such as its role and scope, processes and techniques, and its effectiveness (measurement and evaluation) from the point of view of that client. Critical perspectives take a broader view and look at the societal impacts of sports PR, including negative impacts such as unfair influence in the corridors of power and connections to propaganda.

The chapter covers the following:

- Defining PR
- Terminology
- The role and scope of strategic PR
- Reputation
- Reputational threats
- Sponsorship ethics
- PR, marketing and advertising
- Approaches to theorizing PR – an historical synopsis

Key Concepts

- Communitarian
- Co-orientation
- Civil society
- Critical theory
- Dialogue
- Excellence
- Framing
- Functional
- Persuasion
- Propaganda
- Public affairs

- Public opinion
- Public sphere
- Publics
- Reputation
- Rhetoric
- Situational theory
- Social capital
- Systems theory
- Symmetrical/asymmetrical communication

Defining PR

PR can be defined in a limited way as an organizational function designed to improve the effectiveness of a (sports) organization's relationships and reputation where effectiveness is defined as furthering organizational and client interests. Within those parameters there are a number of strategic and tactical aspects to PR work. The issues-led nature of PR is highlighted as being particularly important to sports business. PR practice may also include advocacy and persuasion, for example, to convince the IOC to choose one city over another as the host for the next Olympics; or to include synchronized skating, sport climbing, wushu, rollersports or squash as an Olympic sport in 2020. PR is therefore interest-led in practice, which is why it is important for citizens to be able to 'read' PR activity behind the scenes and understand how PR produces discourses that circulate in contemporary society. PR represents particular interests, and is responsible for rhetorical utterances in public communication that seek to influence and achieve a particular effect. PR is purposeful strategic intention. Reputation is a central focus for PR work that requires ongoing monitoring in terms of issues (or, less euphemistically, 'problems') on the public agenda: problems that are ignored or mishandled may develop into crises (relating to confidence, trust, hostility).

PR appears multifaceted because it employs a wide variety of communication tools and techniques in order to facilitate relationships with a range of different but sometimes overlapping stakeholders – employees (including sports administrators, ground staff and caterers; spectators and fans); sponsors and financiers; manufacturers of sports equipment and clothing; volunteers; local communities; funding bodies; local, national and international governmental agents; sports governing bodies; corporations; health boards; international organizations (such as the International Olympic Committee [IOC] or Fédération Internationale de Football Association [FIFA]); lobbying groups such as the Independence Governance Committee (IGC) in football; print, digital and social media.

PR is present at all political, economic, sociocultural and technological change in contemporary, post-industrial cultures in a globalized world. PR notably takes place at points of organizational or societal change. In other words, changes in the global landscape, political, social, environmental, technological, or economic changes require complementary organizational responses and may trigger activism. Consequently, PR activity (whether or not it is conducted by paid PR specialists) clusters around:

1. public policy formation;
2. organizational change and development;
3. public issues such as health, the environment, transport, financial stability;
4. media coverage including digital and social media;
5. major global shifts (L'Etang, 2011).

PR may be understood as **flow** (Edwards, 2012) or as connected to power and dominance through creative focused energies (drawing on Bourdieu for this latter point).

Terminology

Defining PR can be tackled at different levels of analysis (technique, specialism, orientation, purpose, impacts/effects). If that were not enough, it is the case that because PR does not have a particularly good reputation itself (a painful irony for the professional bodies and the occupation more widely): consequently, a variety of alternative terms are used, such as **communication management**, **strategic communication**, **corporate communications**, **reputation manager**, **relationship manager** as well as the specialized term for **media relations**, **public affairs**. These terms themselves do not have consistent definitions, but may be employed rhetorically to imply a sophisticated organizational function or specialized area of practice. The degree of overlap between these more recent terms ('PR' emerged as a term in the early twentieth century) and PR can be readily identified, for example, Joep Cornelissen describes communication management as 'any type of communication activity undertaken by an organization to inform, persuade, or otherwise relate to individuals and groups in its outside environment' (J Cornelissen, 2008: 1), a definition that could equally be applied to PR. Corporate communication may be employed variously: to refer to PR on behalf of corporations; to refer to employee communications (the corporate body of the organization); to refer to non-consumer organizations; to refer to communications specifically related to the organization's identity, For example, corporate culture, corporate identity and images. Some aspects of PR work are technical and administrative (writing media releases and promotional/publicity material, managing websites and social media sites, organizing events) and others more strategic (policy level briefings, **corporate culture** and identity, change management, **corporate social responsibility** (CSR).

PR can be defined as the organizational function responsible for the management of an organization's stakeholder relationships, and for monitoring organizational reputation and public opinion, for example, sponsors, fans, athletes, employees (of sports organizations and sponsors), volunteers, geographical and online communities, govern-ment (local, regional, and central as well as international sports bodies that regulate sports). At a strategic level it will also endeavour to establish risks to reputation. PR may be seen as risk communication, although for some this is a separate function that supports 'the science of risk assessment and the process of risk management' relating to the communication of environmental, safety and health risks (Lundgren and McMakin, 2009: 1). However, many different types of organization will undertake risk assessments as part of their crisis planning functions, and will interpret risk specifically as being about 'risk to reputation'.

The function of PR is to establish and monitor internal and external relationships with stakeholders; to monitor the public agenda including converged media for rising issues and social concerns, and to protect the reputation of the organization. PR is not just promotion or media relations, although these aspects are the most visible parts of the work and dis-course work is central to its **framing** activities, shaping messages and stories in the public sphere. PR practitioners monitor stakeholders, publics and opinion leaders, the blogosphere and locate the organization into relevant 'public conversations'. PR gives an organization voice and identity. It is also responsible for ensuring that the organization thinks through the likely impact of organizational practices and policy on organizational reputation. In the course of their work, PR practitioners engage with fluctuating cultural beliefs and practices, communicative action, discourse ethics, organizational cultures and climates, formation of public agendas and debates and interest group activism.

Functional approaches to PR concentrate on the importance of the role to organizational effectiveness and the achievement of managerial aims. One school of thought in PR suggests that the PR practitioner acts as a **boundary spanner** between the organization and its wider environment (composed of political, eco-nomic, sociocultural and technological **systems**) (Grunig and Hunt, 1984; Grunig, 1992; Toth, 2006). According to this approach organizational systems have to adjust to their environments (issues and publics) and the PR function can help them to do this. Since organizations and environments are constantly in flux, PR needs to sup-ply early-warning systems (scenario and crisis planning); but also helps to provide stability and international integration (employee communication, corporate culture); as well as co-creating and communicating organizational mission and vision (cor-porate identity, corporate communications).

PR practitioners take feedback from **stakeholders**, **publics**, public opinion polls and the media on behalf of the organization in order to help the organization to adapt, and take advantage of, external change. This adaptive model of PR informed the basis of much thinking and research in the second half of the twentieth cen-tury (Cutlip and Center, 1950; Grunig and Hunt, 1984; Dozier et al., 1995; Grunig, 1992; Toth, 2006). This approach to PR played down the role of persuasion and the distorting effects of power, and instead emphasized the importance of **dialogue** and **co-operation**. Recent work on **dialogue** (Kent and Taylor, 2002; Theunissen and Wan Noordin, 2012) has traced its links to **deliberative democracy** and **public engagement** (Pieczka, 2011; Pieczka and Escobar, 2013).

Public Opinion and Issues Management

Public opinion is an important concept, for example, public opinion about Tibet challenged the IOC prior to the 2008 Beijing Olympics because public sentiment fuelled public protests. A fundamental democratic value requires that policy is supported by public opinion and both governments and organizations need to show that they take account of public opinion to avoid charges of dictatorship, corruption or corporate bullying. PR is sometimes described as representing an organization's interests 'in the court of public opinion', which suggests that the PR function is akin to that of a legal advocate, though operating much less formally or rigidly. PR practitioners need to use all forms of communication – interpersonal, group, network, mass-mediated, Internet – selectively and appropriately with a range of stakeholders and publics.

Public opinion is a challenging concept and many political philosophers have struggled to construct a satisfactory definition. There are two main approaches that have emerged to thinking about the concept: public opinion as an expression of the general will, or a broad consensus; or public opinion as simply the majority opinion (Price, 1992; Pieczka, 1996). Issues emerge from the intersections between public policy, public opinion, PR and the converged media and may gather momentum, moving up the public agenda. They may have short, medium or long-term life cycles moving up and down the media agenda as in the case of corporate responsibility and governance, bankers' salaries, and environmentalism. The specialist area of issue management may refer to topics on the converged media agenda including social media, or to a very particular issue that is facing an organization, such as a merger.

The Role and Scope of Strategic PR

PR strategy is concerned with the reputational positioning of an organization, stakeholder reputation and the representation of the organization in the public sphere (rhetorical positioning). Strategic PR takes place when the PR function is integrated with organizational/corporate policy-making, indicated in large organizations by membership of the Board and close access to top management – Chairperson, CEO, Managing Director. Such status remains an aspiration rather than a reality for many workers in PR, who are often restricted to the production of communication outputs (media releases, web page management, blog management). At a technical level PR entails a range of communication techniques including media relations, networking, interpersonal communication and face-to-face meetings, Internet communication (social media, web pages, blogs and forums), lobbying, event management and hospitality and exhibitions.

For those in sports management and sports marketing, PR is likely to be best known either for media relations or for publicity events to support the marketing of a sports event, service or product, but PR is most effective when these are linked to an overall

PR strategy as part of the organization's objectives. PR supports the management of an organization; the achievement of organizational objectives, and helps to articulate organizational policy and ambitions. The PR function should therefore be properly involved in processes of policy formation, where decisions that might affect reputation or stakeholder relations can be explored from multiple perspectives. A PR analysis of public issues and reputational threats may lead to a programme of CSR for example.

Public affairs describes work that seeks to influence policy formation (politics) and legislation (civil service) and includes communication with government, not just politicians, at all levels: local, regional, and international bodies. Public affairs entails opinion monitoring, issue management and lobbying and may be conducted at local, national or international levels. It may entail collaboration with interest groups, and respond to their advocacy or that of activists. The PR function of public affairs deals with the implications of public policy for an organization and is both strategic in its research function and tactical in its lobbying. Common public affairs issues are: regulation, governance, ethics and organizational responsibility. One example would be the amount of government regulation regarding the amount of sport taught in schools, the provision of sports facilities, and the amount of extra time teachers are required to spend in extra-curricular activities supporting sports activities. In the UK a running issue has the been the sale of school sports grounds to property developers at the expense of children's sports facilities. Another example would be convincing governments and the IOC that women should be allowed to compete in certain sports, such as the marathon, or, more recently, boxing.

Public affairs also includes lobbying political interests on behalf of sport, and moving in elite circles. Sport also provides a milieu for lobbying, for example Hartmut Zasttrow, CEO of the marketing and sponsorship company Sport + Markt commented,

> ' Government ministers and other decision-makers often attend [sports] events in their countries' capitals or centre of power. For investors, these kinds of clubs can be more attractive as they present an opportunity to lobby and influence. (Miller, 2011: 12) '

This highlights the role of sport and sports PR in power relations and behind-the-scenes influence.

Reputation

Reputation is fluid and dynamic. PR is frequently presented as the organizational function designated responsible for the organization's reputation (Eisenegger, 2005: 1; Fombrun and van Riel, 2003: 225–30). According to John Mahoney, Reputation Inc's founder,

> ' An effective reputation strategy has to be in line with the business's DNA … [and focus] on objective study of stakeholder sentiment and behaviour, the formulation of business-critical reputation objectives and ensuring corporate affairs functions and CEOs have the right skills to drive reputation. (Mattinson, 2013: 19) '

However, PR in itself cannot control reputation. Organizational members have the power to influence reputation, both in their working lives, but more importantly, in what they say about the organization privately to friends, family or in their local community and social media. Second, reputation is the consequence of multiple experiences and judgements made by stakeholders and the wider public, influenced by on- and offline interactions. Thus reputation is variable, multi-perspectival and largely formed outside the organization in response to organizational acts (behaviour) and rhetorical positioning. Reputations are the consequences of processes of interpretation, meaning-making and re-construction. PR cannot construct 'an image' of an organization and then control its consumption, but it can engage organizational communities in the co-creation of identity through ongoing discussion and debate.

Reputational Threats

Athletes and Sponsors Behaving Badly

There are multiple examples of athletes getting the wrong sorts of headlines of the sex, drugs and rock'n roll variety and, as indicated in Chapter 1, this has been a clear focus of attention in the sports communication and PR literature. Falls from grace and fatal flaws make classic stories. Scandal and stories of high athletic performance followed by human frailty play into **media news values** and **media frames** that **socially construct** social phenomena, leading agendas through **schema of interpretation** and sometimes the use of **stereotypes**.

After years of rumours it was announced on 11 October 2012 that there was allegedly convincing evidence that Lance Armstrong, seven-times winner of the Tour de France, had been a key figure in allegedly bullying team mates to take performance-enhancing drugs. What this case particularly highlighted, according to British cycling journalist Richard Moore, was the dependence that sports federations may have on their major stars. In a BBC interview (11 October 2012) Moore argued that it was difficult for federations and journalists to gain access to the necessary evidence because deceptive drug practices could be carried out within a small inner circle. Moore said that it was very difficult to get 'intelligence'. It was only when there were whistleblowers from within that group that retrospective allegations emerged.

On the other hand *SBI* suggested that outstanding sports stars may accrue at least some immunity, citing Wayne Rooney as an example:

' Come the World Cup he was a shadow of his former self and soon followed tabloid tales of late-night partying and more visits to hookers. His poor form continued and his lifestyle led a number of personal sponsors to drop him or scale down his involvement, and one assumes, his fees. But through all this, the fans – that's the people whose adoration earned him the endorsement deals in the first place – remained remarkably tolerant and supportive ... form is temporary, class is permanent and Rooney has football class in abundance. The fact is that Rooney could have gone six months

Discuss!

How true do you think this assessment is? How could the impact of
controversial behaviour on reputation be assessed?

without a goal and enjoyed regular threesomes with Mother Theresa and Myra Hindley without earning public criticism. (Roberts, 2010a: 7) 〉

Reputation failure has long-term consequences in terms of the type of sponsorship that may be subsequently attracted, for example,

‘ NFL player Michael Vick served 18 months in prison on dog-fighting charges and lost $138 million contract with Atlanta Falcons and high value endorsements. However, he then marketed himself as a re-made man and was taken back by Nike … Vick is known as an 'electrifying' competitor and will continue to attract sponsorship from energy drinks and supplements – but he will be taboo for family products and foods. (Wilner, 2011a: 16) 〉

Digital and social media opportunities, and the potential for moments of indiscretion to be publicized immediately, increases transparency with regard to sports stars and organizations and heightens the risk of public knowledge and possible condemnation. The focus on individual indiscretion or wrongdoing is necessarily part of personal PR practice, as this advertisement for gcigroup.com made powerfully clear:

‘ Did your athlete score last night? In the age of citizen journalism, social media and an ever-expanding blogosphere, the athletes representing your brand are always a click away from internet infamy. (*SBI*, 2008d: 47) 〉

In the contemporary communications climate, more attention has to be given to **impression management,** balancing the needs of the individual to live a private as well as a public life against judgements that **voluntary disclosure** or **apologia** may be a more prudent as well as more honest approach. More will be said about this shortly in the section on **crisis communication**.

Authenticity and a sport's credibility are essential for maintaining fans and income streams, as *SBI* Editor Kevin Roberts pointed out,

‘ Four of Italy's leading football clubs guilty of match fixing … the Tour de France embroiled in its annual doping allegations festival and Britain's leading jockey was banned from the sport on allegations of race fixing … for sport to mean anything at all the audience has to believe … that the content they are witnessing is for real … If there is any suggestion that the outcome has been fixed or influenced it ceases to have any meaning whatsoever and without meaning it has no commercial value. (Roberts, 2006a: 5) 〉

From the sports business perspective it is the financial impact, rather than ethics or the human cost of an incident, that has priority as shown in the case of fallout from alleged drug use in Major League Baseball,

❝ Bank of America's huge five-year deal with Major League Baseball has put the financial institution up front at many of the sport's biggest moments. But with the ugliness surrounding Barry Bond's alleged steroid use, Bank of America had to back off a heavy involvement … As the baseball season was beginning in April, Bank of America and Home Depot both withdrew corporate support of Bond's chase of … the … home run record … Bond was dubbed 'defective product' by some market analysts and Bank of America certainly seemed to support that view. (Wilner, 2006: 16–17) ❞

There is a distinct ripple effect from an individual to their particular sport and all its stakeholders. Once a sport has been associated with drug use, as for example happened in the case of professional cycling, it can be difficult to change its culture and the wider reputation.

Nevertheless, despite the risk of reputational failures such as the scandal surrounding a BBC Panorama programme concerning football players and agents, Clifford Bloxham, Vice-President of Octagon's Athletes and Personalities division commented that

❝ There is still a positive side to player management and athlete marketing … athletes are a great vehicle for bringing products and programmes to life and for connecting with the right target audience. … it is hard to better Tesco's sport for schools and clubs programme. Tesco have successfully utilized Frank Lampard, Paula Radcliffe and Jason Robinson in virtually every marketing communications medium, including television, radio and print advertising, point of sale (POS) materials, direct mind, interactive and internet activity, PR and internal communications. (Bloxham, 2006: 25) ❞

Sponsorship Ethics

Sponsorship can backfire on a corporate sponsor's reputation when athletes misbehave, and it is not only sports stars whose behaviour has to be above reproach:

❝ The arrest in America of David Carruthers, Chief Executive of Alternative Investment Market … has sent shock waves through the on-line gambling market. Indicted on 22 charges, including racketeering and tax evasions, his arrest is the first such action to be taken against an executive from a listed on-line betting company … shares were suspended, the news knocked £900 off gaming stocks in just two days. (*SBI*, 2006a: 51) ❞

These examples highlight the role for PR to monitor sports cultures and raise awareness of reputational currency and the shared responsibility for its maintenance. Sponsorships may not be straightforward, and there has been a shift in what is culturally acceptable. 'Pressure is being applied to sponsors in the alcohol, gaming and food sectors' (Singer, 2008: 18). An EU Directive prohibiting tobacco advertising and sponsorship took effect in 2005 (which particularly impacted F1) and in 2007 the EU did call for an outright ban on alcohol sponsorship throughout Europe on health grounds; and although sponsored events are cross-cultural, alcohol sponsorship legislation is not (Singer, 2008: 18). The gaming industry's close association with football shirts has raised ethical questions over branding on children's shirts, and existing advertising restrictions on high fat, salt and sugar products to those under 16 also apply to TV programme sponsorship (Singer, 2008: 18). These developments all have implications for future sources of funding. The French Tennis Federation (FTF) sought to ban three online betting companies from taking bets on the French Open to avoid the possibility of a betting scandal that could 'stain' the reputation of the event (Glendinning, 2008a: 12–13). FTF also suggested that the online companies were effectively parasites upon events and event organizers because they do not invest in the event from which they generate profit (Glendinning, 2008a: 12–13).

In the UK in 2013 there was media reaction to the announcement that Newcastle football team was to be sponsored by Wonga.com – a pay-day moneylender with a very high rate of interest. This was deemed inappropriate in a club based in an area of low employment and high insolvency exacerbated by the financial crisis. Clearly this example is at least insensitive, but also poor PR in terms of community relations and CSR.

Athlete Relations, Issues and Activism

The relationships between coaches and young athletes may raise ethical issues that affect a sport's reputation. For example journalist Joan Ryan exposed physical and emotional abuse in gymnastics and ice-skating on the basis of more than 100 interviews in her book *Little girls in pretty boxes: the making and breaking of elite gymnasts and figure skaters* (1995) when she described how young girls were subjected to emotional and physical abuse, coerced into harder and harder training regimes and restricted diets (Grand and Goldberg, 2011: 87). Girls identified as weak, rebellious or unappealing in some way were weeded out and the rest enslaved in a subservient regime (Grand and Goldberg, 2011: 87). More recently, in 2008 Jennifer Sey, the US gymnastic champion in 1986, published a book about her personal experiences during her gymnastics training entitled *Inside elite gymnastics' merciless coaching, overzealous parents, eating disorders and elusive Olympic dreams* (cited in Grand and Goldberg, 2011: 87). Coaches have also been implicated for enforcing illegal drug regimes on their protégés. Emotional and physical abuse, which leads to burn-out and long-term psychological problems, is a constant issue in the sports world and certainly one of the key areas for national associations to be monitoring in relation to their practices. Issues are not necessarily new topics on the public agenda, but may well be ongoing possibilities and a serious threat to reputation. Sports communicators need constantly to be aware of such issues and how they relate to practice within the sport(s) with which they are involved, as do those from non-sports brands that may sponsor sports.

Incidents that threaten reputation are quite likely to require communicators to work in partnership with legal specialists. Partner and rights specialist Dominic Farnsworth from Silkin LLP explained,

> ❝ The public has now been in the grip of the cult of celebrity personality for years and their fascination shows no sign of abatement … while celebrities are used to boost brands' images, care needs to be taken to ensure this strategy does not backfire. A few unguarded comments by a celebrity, a skeleton falling out of the closet, or some inappropriate behaviour could leave a campaign in tatters. … Tiger Woods, sponsored by Nike, switched back to an old favourite Titleist club when he experienced a drop in performance … Cricketer Ian Botham, who was appearing in advertising for Dansk low alcohol beer, famously described the product as 'gnat's piss' … The FIFA World Cup 2002 threw up a number of instances where advertisers may have given cause to reflect over their choice of brand ambassadors, particularly since many would have been selected for intensive advertising exposure surrounding the event … The Irish captain Roy Keane, reportedly paid £50K by 7Up, quit the tournament before kicking the ball, leading to public outcry and 7Up posters being disfigured. (Farnsworth, 2006: 50) ❞

There may be tensions between brand protection and athlete freedom and lack of clarity over what constitutes 'bringing his/herself into disrepute' (Farnsworth, 2006: 50). Furthermore, the wish to protect reputation is not limited to the corporation, but is also an issue for the athlete,

> ❝ In this age of corporate social responsibility … certain sportswear manufacturers … have been subject to allegations of exploitative production methods … a player might wish to have the right to terminate an association with the brand … (Farnsworth, 2006: 50) ❞

Indeed, Bob Skinstad from esportif (Saatchi and Saatchi's sponsorship consultancy) reported that

> ❝ We are now seeing commercial negotiation where athletes are contractually requiring sponsors to recognize their own brand values and promise not to act in a way which could compromise those values … [this could include] general behaviour by the company (such as environmental and PR … Players [may] refuse to wear logos, participate in certain sponsored events, play in sponsored stadia … Consider … sportspersons who take a public stance on being teetotal, vegetarian, non-smoking or anti-junk food or refuse to fly for environmental reasons and it becomes clear that many of the global sports sponsors could be in for interesting times. (Farnsworth, 2006: 50) ❞

Other iconic examples of an apparent shift in power balance were evidenced by the Malian footballer Fredi Kanouté (ex-Spurs/West Ham) who signed for Sevilla, a club which gets sponsorship from an online gambling company 888.com. As a devout Muslim, Kanouté refused to play in a shirt that promoted gambling and the name had to be obscured with tape; likewise South African Hashim Amla, whose national team was sponsored by South African Breweries, ensured that his shirt did not feature the beer brand 'Castle' (Farnsworth, 2006: 50). In this case, personal PR trumped corporate PR.

This certainly suggests an interesting shift in the balance of power between elite athletes and sponsors and the ability of a socially motivated athlete to act as an activist and catalyst for change. Normally the specialist function of **athlete–sponsor relations** is concerned with sponsors encouraging athletes to participate in hospitality events, to 'press the flesh', and in many cases this is a distraction or extra work for athletes, so 'athletes … have proved notoriously reluctant to engage with sponsors, beyond the specific stipulations of their contracts' (Roberts, 2006d: 32) and indeed, on the men's ATP tennis tour CEO Etienne de Viliers worked hard to make players more accessible, commenting:

> Players live and work in a fairly sheltered environment, often surrounded by their entourage and it is not always easy to get them to be comfortable stepping out-side that. We are working to train and educate them in new marketing roles and there are now financial incentives in the form of revenue share to encourage them. (Roberts, 2008c: 48)

Likewise, one PR practitioner working for a football club commented that one of his key challenges was

> Getting the players to realise the level of commitment they should all have to the media and the community around the ground; making them understand just how much people admire and idolise them and consequently, how a little bit of their time outside football can mean so much to people.

Discuss!

How can sponsors encourage athletes to participate in hospitality events? What are the pros and cons for athletes in participating in hospitality events?

Issues as Reputational Hazards and Potential Crises: London Olympics 2012 and the G4S Challenge

The Olympics and Paralympics passed off safely, but not without reputational incidents. The first of these related to the amount of available person-power available to support security measures. The company G4S had been contracted to supply security guards, but only days before the start of the Olympics it was revealed that they had not recruited sufficient staff and there was confusion among those they had recruited as to where or when they were supposed to be reporting for duty. The media had a field day.

There was extensive coverage partly because the story conformed twice over to a key aspect of media news values. First the story was yet another example of an Olympic host being not quite ready, so the 'news' was in fact 'olds' (Galtung and Ruge, 1965). Second, the company G4S had been bedevilled by other failures, notably the escape of so many prisoners supposedly under its care 'that references to it got written into the script of sitcoms' according to one commentator, and this history **framed** the Olympic crisis and shaped media interpretations.

The PR industry's publication *PR Week* raised questions over the management of the communication function and the organizational politics that might have influenced the handling of the crisis,

> G4S is handling its current Olympics reputational crisis in-house, despite bringing in Bell Pottinger for a corporate brief that included crisis work last year ... It is understood that support is also being provided by a discrete UK comms team led by longstanding corporate affairs director Paddy Toyne-Sewell. However, one source with close links to the G4S team suggested that a key issue impairing its handling of the Olympic issue is that the G4S global comms operation is conditioned to deal with defensive crisis management or 'damage control', rather than strategic reputation enhancement. UK Head of PR Nicky Savage told *PRWeek* last Friday that the firm was concentrating on sorting out the operational issues before it focused on comms. This decision, the source suggested, was indicative of the lack of importance that the firm's management placed on comms and proactive reputation management. He added that the comms team was 'pretty hierarchical' and that most decisions were made between CEO Nick Buckles and the senior members without involvement from the wider team or agencies. (Cartmell, 2012: 3)

In this case it appears that the company poured its resources into resolving logistical and administrative issues (though in any case they had to be baled out by British security forces) and saw communication as of secondary importance.

Failing to communicate adequately or to update the media caused worse problems. A fundamental issue here relates to the role of PR. If PR is restricted to the production of communication outputs essentially at the bottom of the food chain, then PR practitioners will be unable to raise issues that may lead to reputational challenges and negative discourses in converged media. PR practitioners need to be recognized for their strategic communications expertise, and not just for their technical skills. Specifically, PR practitioners need to be empowered so that they can freely raise sometimes difficult questions, for example about ethical or operational issues, at the highest level within the organizations that employ them. Only if they are given this level of seniority and responsibility can PR practitioners execute their role fairly and with the greatest effect.

Unpredictable events can become crises or ongoing issues that form the focus of media and public debate, highlighting the significance of relations between source (sports organization) and converged media. Fact, rumour and gossip intermingle to develop pressures that may not only apply directly to the organization, but to policy-makers and stakeholders (including sponsors).

Online Reputation Management

Reputation management requires constant monitoring, internal as well as external scrutiny and a willingness for ongoing engagement and discussion as Mike Robb, Head of Corporate Communication at Cicero Consulting explained,

> In a world of 24/7 news with more than 200 social media platforms, reputation management is harder than ever … Keeping your head down and being unwilling to partake in the debate is no longer an option. If you are not out there talking about and defending your brand, you can bet your bottom dollar that someone else is … [But] it is important to acknowledge there is only so much that reputation management can do in communicating the positive stories an organization has to tell. If those stories leave a sour taste in the mouth, it is the job of communicators to ask the tough, probing questions of senior management … With so much scrutiny now placed on high profile organizations, underlying stories are harder than ever to 'spin' in a way that might have been possible even five or ten years ago … Twitter has more than 340 million tweets on a daily basis … Never before has the corporate communications environment been changed so much in such a short space of time, and by a single platform. This is why a long-term conversation is now the only option – one that needs to be based on strong business values that pass the test of public scrutiny … no amount of positive messages will change a corporate reputation if the underlying business values are out of kilter. (Robb, 2012: 13)

Reputation attacks in social media are leading to further collaboration between PR practitioners and media lawyers according to Gideon Benaim, a partner at media lawyers Michael Simkins specializing in reputation protection,

> 'We are seeing more PROs (PR Officers) taking action around social media sites and then pursuing legal recourse … the law [is] becoming more accommodating to this' (Owens, 2012a: 3).

This development brings together two advocacy occupations in collaboration in a particular context of reputation defence, although public relations practitioners and lawyers might often have conflicting views about appropriate communication in times of crisis.

PR, Marketing and Advertising

PR is distinct from marketing in that it is simultaneously concerned with all organizational relationships and with public opinion more widely. In contrast, marketing's priority is focused on the consumer and the supply chain, described as 'The management process responsible for identifying, anticipating and satisfying customer requirements profitably' (J Cornelissen, 2008: 260). From a marketing perspective, however,

PR is a tactical part of 'marketing communications' which includes advertising, personal selling, direct mail, sales promotion, trade fairs and exhibitions, sponsorship, and packaging. Promotion includes celebrity endorsement, special events, and hospitality. PR and marketing overlap but each has a distinct focus. Increasingly, PR and marketing functions coalesce in the sports business because much of the work focuses on branding and media relations in a competitive environment in which 'sponsors fight for media interest' (PRW, 2012b: 3). This may affect organizational structures: for example Claire Furlong, Head of Communications and Marketing at UK Athletics, has 'overhauled the comms function by integrating it with marketing and improving its reputation internally' (Magee, 2012a: 26).

PR can be more easily distinguished from advertising. Advertising is paid-for, controlled space. One of the specialist subfunctions of PR is media relations, the purpose of which is to respond to media enquiries, but also to supply media with newsworthy stories and background information that is useful to the journalist looking for, or researching, a story. PR cannot control the media, neither can it ever guarantee a client media coverage, but it is a major source of news stories and coverage in print and broadcast media. PR provides source materials or **information subsidies** for journalists in the form of on or off the record oral and written briefings and backgrounders, and also in press or media releases written in a factual journalistic style. Press releases may be used by journalists as the basis for a story on which they conduct their own Internet or interview-based research, but under pressure, journalists may 'cut and paste' the press release so that PR-produced material appears almost verbatim. There is also a hybrid form of media coverage that is prepared by media relations practitioners, paid for as in advertising, but written in a style to mimic the editorial style of the magazine or newspaper – this is known as an **advertorial** and is usually labelled as such by the publication in a heading at the top of each page.

Approaches to Theorizing PR: an Historical Synopsis

There are various theoretical approaches to the definitions, research and analysis of PR and many new ideas are emerging all the time, making PR one of the most exciting disciplines in which to be working. PR is a relatively new academic discipline and therefore takes its ideas from a wide range of sources, including management, media and cultural studies, social theory and philosophy of social science, and they are invaluable in understanding PR as sense-making and identity-construction. In this section the main approaches are presented in a broadly historical way, with the earliest theorizations being presented first.

The **systems approach** was drawn from the **General Systems Theory** by early US scholars (Cutlip and Center, 1950; Grunig and Hunt, 1984) who sought to explain the role and value of the PR function to organizations. **Systems theory** explained that organizations are comprised of numerous interconnected specialized subsystems, usually functional areas (accounting, research and development, human resources) or hierarchical (managerial); organizations were connected to external environmental systems and subsystems through the input and output processes (intake of resources developed into new outputs) (Grunig and Hunt, 1984; Grunig, 1992). Systems theory is a metaphor that sees the world as living interacting organisms that require a balanced and stable environment and the capacity to adapt and interprets the world as a series of interlinked and interdependent systems through holistic connections (Pieczka, 1996). Systems are dynamic and evolve and adapt, developing specialisms and differentiations. Organizational systems exhibit different qualities of openness or closedness, for eample the comparison between a military base and a coffee-house chain. The role of PR was explained as the organizational function responsible for boundary spanning and conducting both external and internal intelligence to identify issues that could cause reputational problems. PR was identified as the organizational function that could help the organization adapt to environmental changes. Thayer's (1968) theory of **diachronic** and **synchronic** organizational communication was renamed symmetrical and asymmetrical communication and it was argued by PR systems theorists that collaborative and mutual communications processes produced the best outcomes for organizations. Systems theory provided a framework that justified a strategic-level role for PR. Strengths of the model are its ability to express the fluid and dynamic nature of organizations in their environment and delineate a clear role for PR. But systems theory is a functional theory based on an ecological metaphor of adaptation, and does not deal with questions about the power and influence of organizations, morality, intention, agency, or effects. It also tends to assume that organizations are ideologically neutral and of benefit to society. On the other hand, one of the strengths of the metaphor is its interconnectedness, which fits well with networked societies. **Situational theory** was a diagnostic tool developed from the process of subdividing publics into smaller groups based upon their relationship to a particular issue, and their degree of activity or passivity (Grunig and Hunt, 1984). It was argued that practitioners should base their PR programmes on research into the activity or passivity of publics and also explore degrees of **co-orientation** between publics and the organization, finding out, for example, the degree to which different publics shared or opposed or were indifferent to issues that affected an organization; the extent to which they could accurately predict the organization's view of a particular issue; and what they thought an organization believed the public's views would be on an issue. This research-based approach offered practitioners the opportunity to refine their efforts more subtly.

The '**Excellence**' approach adopted and adapted the managerial literature on 'excellence' made famous by Tom Peters and Robert Waterman's 1982 bestselling book *In search of excellence*. These authors deduced eight attributes characteristic of excellent companies based on research into 62 companies (Linstead et al., 2009: 223). The excellence approach was a 'one best way' philosophy and, similarly, assumptions that there is one best way to do PR framed the empirical research funded by the US professional body, the International Association for Business Communicators (IABC). Excellence incorporated the systems framework and focused on a number of key themes and propositions, including organizational effectiveness (goal attainment); interdependence and adaptiveness; measurability; functionalism; and two-way symmetrical communication as an ideal from functionalism; which, taken together contributed to a prevailing idea that excellence and systems could, would and should lead to a general theory of PR. The prescriptive and somewhat didactic promotion of this perspective over a number of years meant that it took time for other points of view and different research questions to emerge. The theory was so dominant that it became a worldview within the discipline,

> What started as a literature review has ended in … a general theory of PR – a theory that integrates most of the available body of knowledge in PR and expands it to an even more powerful body of knowledge … the general theory provides a theoretical explanation for the best current practice of PR – which our theory says is excellent – that organisations and society do not understand or appreciate. (Grunig, 1992: xiv)

The approach is still used, for example in a case study of Aston Villa Football Club to explore the implications of the takeover of an American owner (Sarver Coombs and Osborne, 2012). Although, Excellence theory is limited in focusing on managerial and organization needs, and critical scholars raised challenges emphasizing the importance of sociocultural perspectives, community, ethics, politics and power (L'Etang and Pieczka, 1996). Within PR literature a number of varied approaches have now emerged which highlight a range of alternative perspectives on PR, briefly summarized below.

Relational approaches focused on the ongoing evaluation organizational–stakeholder relations employing largely quantitative methodologies focused on variables such as intimacy, trust, control, perceptions, communication behaviours and relational outcomes (Broom et al. 1997, 2000). Subsequent studies drew on interpersonal literature to highlight the importance of professional, personal and community relationships (Bruning and Ledingham, 1999). Although the relational approach appears collaborative in its approach, in reality it is focused on organizational interest, minimizing 'the risk of protests from activist groups' (Hung, 2007: 446) and statistical measurement that operationalizes concepts.

The **communitarian** approach highlighted a loss of community in US society and proposed that PR was 'best defined and practiced as the active attempt to restore and maintain a sense of community that had been lost because of the development of modern means of communication/transportation' (Kruckeberg and Starck, 1988: 118–19). Kruckeberg and Starck thought that PR should build a sense of community and combat anomie or alienation through **social bonding**. The loss of community has been highlighted by other US scholars, notably the philosopher Etzioni and the social theorist Putnam, both of whom were publishing their ideas in the 1990s. Kuckeberg and Starck developed their communitarian approach as an argument for social responsibility and corporate citizenship to benefit the public interest. Drawing on Putnam's work, Luoma-aho (2009) argued that the aim of PR should be to create and maintain organizational **social capital**, a term that 'owes its origin to such concepts as social connectedness … formal memberships as well as informal social networks, and generalized reciprocity, social trust and tolerance' (Luoma-aho, 2009:

234). It is trust and collaboration that facilitates collective problem-solving in society through organizations engaging in communication and civic engagement. A conceptually similar approach was developed and promoted by the US academic Maureen Taylor, who argued that 'PR role in society is to create (and re-create) the conditions that enact civil society' (Taylor, 2010: 7), arguing that PR made civil society possible. Taylor also drew on the rhetorical approach to **civil society** when she argued that 'the heart of civil society is discourse' (Taylor, 2010: 9). These ideas have purchase in the sports context, for example, in understanding ideological and rhetorical positioning of sports organizations that may have innate tensions between community values and corporate rhetoric, as Boyd and Stahley argued in their analysis of the US National Collegiate Athletic Association's community relations programme (2008: 251–70). They are also relevant in understanding volunteering, grass roots and community sport, and to ideas about sport as a major contributor to community.

Critical perspectives and research draws on **critical theory** to highlight the role and impact of PR in society and its links to power and initially emerged from Scotland and New Zealand in the mid-1990s (L'Etang and Pieczka, 1996, 2006; Motion and Leitch, 1996). This now includes **cultural studies** (the role of PR in the political and cultural economy), **postcolonial** and **subaltern** approaches (the perspectives of alternative voices and disempowered groups – see Pal and Dutta, 2008) as well as rhetorical work, which explores PR practitioners as **discourse workers** (Pieczka, 2000). These ideas deepen understanding of globalization and its potentially exploitative and commodifying effects, relevant to sports business and PR practitioners in terms of socio-economic effects, but also in terms of the symbolic and language-choices of PR practitioners in their impression management strategies. **Rhetoric** has been a major theme in the literature since the late 1980s exploring processes and ethics of communication (Heath, 1980, 1991; L'Etang, 1996; Ihlen, 2002). Consequently, it can be seen that there is no single way of understanding PR practice, and that there are a range of theoretical approaches and perspectives that can be brought to bear upon particular organizations or cases to generate a breadth of meanings and understandings. Throughout this book a range of ideas will be used to highlight multiple interpretations of sports PR, as well as providing the functional detail necessary to understanding the operational context.

Gender and **LGBT** perspectives facilitated critical questions about the ways in which sport and sports people operate and are represented, and this approach could be extended to the analysis of those who work as sports intermediaries. The discourse approach explores how PR practitioners use language for strategic gain. This work connects PR to the classical Greek Sophists who acted as argument and persuasion consultants. **Postmodernism** has become a focus for alternative perspectives that generate non-managerial meanings within and about organizations (Holtzhausen, 2000, 2002; McKie and Munshi, 2007). Significant contributions have sought to understand the role of PR within the **cultural and creative economy**, as a **cultural intermediary** between production and consumption that produces social meanings within the economy (Curtin and Gaither, 2007; Edwards, 2011, 2012; Hodges, 2011; Edwards and Hodges, 2011; Valentine, 2004). On this account, sports and sports business (including sports PR) are part of intertwining processes between culture and power.

Critical theorists seek to explore the relationship between PR and power, and argue that PR theory should go beyond the interests of management and organizations to take account of the societal impacts. On this account an exploration of sports PR practice should not only be about the effectiveness of practice on behalf of sports organizations but also consider wider issues such as power, exploitation, and ethics, for example issues relating to child rights, environmentalism and sustainability, relationships between the developed and developing worlds, postcolonial diasporas, cultural imperialism, the promotion and representation of certain body shapes, ageism, gender issues, racism and the impact of commercialization of sport.

Critical perspectives on the role of PR in society have argued that PR is a negative force in democracy because it supports dominant elites and corporate interests, especially via lobbying; that 'deep pockets' can purchase more PR services and therefore dominate and shape the news agenda and the **public sphere**; and that PR engages in dirty tricks and subterfuge (Miller and Dinan, 2008; Dinan and Miller, 2007).

The **public sphere** was a concept developed by the German sociologist Jurgen Habermas to describe a theoretical space in which public as opposed to private issues could be debated by all citizens. Critics suggest that the conditions and price of access to the public sphere have been raised by the genesis and growth of the PR occupation. PR expertise includes that of instigating and contributing to public debate on behalf of organizational clients. The cost of PR expertise may price some out of the information market. However, technological developments facilitate the proliferation of cheaply available forums for debate among diverse communities. Questions remain over the extent to which such developments weaken PR influence, or simply facilitate another opportunity for persuasive discourse; the crucial difference now is the capability for feedback and argument from relevant communities and the purchase such informal communication may have.

Persuasion and Propaganda

Persuasion and PR are conceptually and historically linked to propaganda. Common definitions of the three terms tend to overlap, much to the concern of PR practitioners. Some, especially academics from cultural and media studies, use the terms interchangeably. Crucial to distinctions between these concepts are the notions of information-distortion, filtering, transparency, authenticity, exploitation and coercion.

Propaganda is more strategic and all-encompassing than simple distortion of information given to the media, although that may be part of it. Propaganda suggests control of information and interpretation operating at the level of state or organization. Propaganda is more than 'lies', though lies may be a component. However, in communicating complex information it is possibly not helpful to think in such dichotomous categories as 'truth' and 'lies' – there may well be room for competing interpretations of available evidence. The term propaganda is problematic because of its historic association with totalitarian regimes. It is often the case that 'one person's propaganda is another person's PR', and it is a term open to relativistic interpretation depending on an individual's ideological viewpoint. Propaganda is relevant to discussion of sports PR because sport has been and continues to be utilized as political communication by many nations, especially in relation to nation-branding and enhancing prestige externally, and fostering national pride internally.

Psychologists have argued that persuasion in itself is not unethical. Indeed, some have suggested that persuasion is an intrinsic component of all communication, and that persuasion is part of human beings' nature and intellectual make-up, allowing them to enjoy a good argument and debate. The PR discipline has therefore absorbed significant elements of social psychology and theories of persuasion and incorporated them into functional frameworks, similar to those in sister disciplines, such as health promotion and social marketing.

Think Critically

Choose any sports organization and identify: (1) the key external and internal issues and changes that face the organization; (2) risks and threats; (3) relevant changes and trends in the economic, political and sociocultural environment nationally and internationally; (4) impacts that the organization has on its environment; (5) organizational stakeholders/publics. How may PR practitioners make use of this information to determine their priorities? How may we understand the role of sports PR practitioners in society more widely?

Discuss!

Consider the following functional questions and ways in which you would endeavour to carry out research to answer them:

- When and why are the efforts of communication practitioners effective?
- How do organizations benefit from effective PR? Why do organizations practise PR in different ways?
- How does PR help the sports industry to achieve its objectives?

These functional questions are important, but they are not the only questions that might be asked in relation to sports PR. Consider the following critical questions and reflect upon the theoretical frameworks you might use, alongside empirical research to answer them. Also, why are these questions of importance to sports PR practitioners?

- How does sport benefit society?
- Who benefits most from the sports industry?
- Does the sports industry gain privileged access to the corridors of power and what benefits does it gain from this?
- Are there any negative features of the sports industry? Are these made evident and transparent in a way that citizens can contribute to debate and influence the funding of sport?
- Is there such a thing as sports ideology? How does PR contribute to this?
- Are there equal opportunities in sport and in sports business (including the PR specialism) regardless of ethnicity, gender, sexual orientation, class?

Summary

This chapter started with a descriptive overview of PR practice and some of the important terminology and concepts that are important to its operation. It proceeded to introduce a more diverse and critical array of ideas that can be used to generate alternative perspectives of PR, including sports PR. Key points for reflection and debate may be focused around discussion of the following statements (drawn from L'Etang, 2011):

- PR aims to contribute to the effectiveness of organizations by improving organizational relationships and facilitating public conversations and debate.
- PR has a remit for corporate social responsibility through its issues-management function and responsibility for reputation, for example, organizational change to meet new agendas of sustainability.
- In understanding PR practitioners as being, in some aspects, discourse workers it becomes easier to see that the functional role has the potential to contribute to the ideal of a more enlightened and better-informed society.
- PR takes place at points of change and moments of transformation in complex contemporary societies. Typically, PR activity clusters around (i) public policy formation; (ii) organizational change and development; (iii) public issues such as the environment; (iv) major global shifts such as conflict, unstable international environments, globalization, natural disasters or human disasters such as war or global financial collapse.
- PR is embedded in the contemporary issues of the day in a very wide range of environments (political, economic, technological, sociocultural, regulatory/legal) and contexts (sports, health, religion, tourism, development, regeneration).
- Much PR work itself is fundamentally educational in helping organizations and publics to understand each other's points of view and those of the wider society.
- PR is embedded in networks of influence and is part of the articulation of power through discursive, rhetorical and relational activities.

Further Reading

Babiak K, Mills B, Tainsky S and Juravich M (2012) An investigation into professional athlete philanthropy: why charity is part of the game. *Journal of Sport Management*, 26 (2): 159–76.

Boyd J and Stahley M (2008) Communitas/corporatas tensions in organizational rhetoric: finding a balance in sports public relations. *Journal of Public Relations Research*, 20: 251–270.

Carter M (2013) The hermeneutics of frames and framing: an examination of the media's construction of reality. *SageOpen*, April–June: 1–12.

Clayton Stoldt G, Milner LK and Vermillion M (2009) Public relations evaluation in sport: views from the field. *International Journal of Sport Communication*, 2(2).

Cortsen K (2013) Annika Sorenstam – a hybrid personal sports brand. *Sport, Business and Management: an International Journal*, 3 (1): 37–62.

Edwards L (2012) Defining the 'object' of public relations research: a new starting point. *Public Relations Inquiry*, 1 (1): 7–30.

Farrelly F (2010) Not playing the game: why sport sponsorship relationships break down. *Journal of Sport Management*, 24 (3): 319–37.

Galloway CJ (2013) Deliver us from definitions: a fresh way of looking at public relations. *Public Relations Inquiry*, 2 (2): 147–59.

Kristiansen E and Hanstad DV (2012) Journalists and Olympic athletes: a Norwegian case study of an ambivalent relationship. *International Journal of Sport Communication*, 5 (2): 231–45.

Meng J and Pan P-L (2013) Revisiting image-restoration strategies: an integrated case study of three athlete sex scandals in sports news. *International Journal of Sport Communication*, 6: 87–100.

Pratt A (2013) Integrated impression management in athletics: a qualitative study of how NCAA Division I athletics directors understand public relations. *International Journal of Sport Communication*, 6 (1): 42–65.

Sarver Coombs D (2012) A case study of Aston Villa Football Club. *Journal of Public Relations Research*, 24: 201–221.

Wehmeier S and Winkler P (2013) Expanding the bridge, minimizing the gaps: public relations, organizational communication, and the idea that communication constitutes organization. *Management Communication Quarterly*, 27 (2): 280–90.

3

Corporate Communication in Organizational Contexts

Introduction

This chapter aims to explain linkages between strategic analysis, corporate policy, issues management and CSR and to discuss the role that sport can have as a tool of communication in an organizational context. This corporate focus highlights the organization as a site of sport communication. The chapter draws on examples from the sports business operational context that highlight the role for PR. While the strategic practice of issue management was introduced in Chapter 2, this chapter presents more detailed examples in relation to the concept of **risk management, crisis communication** and **corporate social responsibility (CSR)**.

The chapter covers:

- Issues management
- Risk management and communication
- Security and terrorism
- Governance
- Crisis management and communications
- CSR
- Sustainability
- Employee communications
- Sport as business communication: networking and hospitality

Key Concepts

- Activism
- Apologia
- Communication audit
- Corporate communications
- Corporate culture
- Corporate hospitality
- Corporate identity
- Corporate social responsibility (CSR)
- Corporate sport

- Crisis communications
- Cultural capital
- Employee sports communication
- Issues management
- Reputation
- Risk management
- Sustainability
- Volunteering

Corporate PR in Organizations

The terms 'corporate PR' and 'corporate communication' may be used inter-changeably with PR but are employed in this chapter because they draw attention to the organizational context and agenda and also highlights the important connection between the policy-making level of the organization and PR's issues management and public affairs functions that derive from the need to respond to external pressures and regulation. The process of monitoring the environment allows the organization to think through its position on emerging issues and to respond promptly. Some of these issues may not be directly related to the organization, but implicitly linked, for example health and fitness. In cases of general societal issues, a sports organization may decide to step forward and engage with stakeholders through a long-term **corporate social responsibility programme (CSR)**, for example provision of sports equipment, facilities, or training. In short, scanning leads to the detection not only of organizationally focused issues but of public issues, some of which may be societal in scale and to which the organization may decide **voluntarily** to respond via a CSR programme. The intention behind such decisions may be beneficience, but is usually strategic, a calculated choice to bolster or improve reputation. This has moral implications and more will be said about this later.

As the specialist communications function PR should engage management in discussion about the internal organizational communities and the culture of the organization – the social practices, rituals and relationships. **Organizational culture** has been described very simply as 'the way we do things round here' but can be thought of as the daily life, language, interactions, dress codes, and behavioural conventions. Within the organization, the PR role should lead intra-organizational reflection to construct the corporate identity, which consists of the public presentation of the organization's personality, history, values, vision, mission and relationships. **Corporate identity** is the consequence of an organization's history, culture, values, people, ideologies, political affiliations, and positioning in relation to other organizations. The outward expression of identity can be understood as organizational personality. **Visual identity** is a term used to describe the design elements used to express and communicate the organization, such as logos, letterheads, websites, office design and architecture, uniforms etc. **Aural identity** is the term used to describe sounds associated with the organization such as telephone answering systems and organizational music. These aspects of **projected identity** are open to multiple interpretations by those external to the organization (and indeed within the organization, since the final design will be the outcome of much deliberation and even dispute resolved by internal politics and power). The PR practitioner needs to carry out in-depth qualitative and quantitative research structured into an organization-wide **communication audit**, a mixed-method approach that explores internal perceptions, emotions, networks and internal informal power structures and opinion leaders to provide a 'warts and all' picture of the organization.

Issues Management

The concept of issues management emerged from corporate America in the mid-1970s and is generally understood as a public concern or controversy over which there is debate regarding public interest and societal impacts. Issues move on and off the agenda in cyclical patterns and this has been the focus of many forecasting and modelling studies (Jaques, 2009). Since issues emerge and rise and fall on the public agenda all the time, it is advisable for organizations to conduct regular research in order to compare and contrast the way that different issues are moving around in the public sphere. Such research-based reports provide invaluable and rigorous data and guidance for organizational leaders and management. The organization may conduct its own opinion research (for example surveys and focus groups) in order to evaluate the quantitative scale of an issue or specific problem and to carry out some **futurology** in terms of possible lines of issue development. The fictional stories can then be developed further into **scenario planning** – sketching out possible responses to each particular storyline. This in turn can feed into an organization's crisis planning strategy. Much of this process has been adapted from the military, hence some of the language is couched in a somewhat adversarial way. Clearly confrontation may be avoided through discussion and the chance to co-construct the issue and find acceptable compromise or resolution. One of the challenges to such good intentions is that media typically present issues as competitive storylines between two or more interested parties, highlighting their positions with rhetorically driven dramatic headlines. Sports PR practitioners therefore need research and analytic skills in addition to planning and logistical capabilities in order to carry out issues management practice on behalf of their organizations or clients. If issues management fails a full-blown crisis may develop.

The Grand National: Responding to Activism

The Grand National is a major event in the horse racing calendar but regular fatalities have been heavily criticised by Animal Aid, an organization that logs these on an ongoing basis on Racehorse Deathwatch (www.horsedeathwatch.com/) and has commissioned public opinion polls to ensure that the issue is not forgotten; and written to the media to ensure that horse fatalities at races are properly covered and not censored. The Royal Society for the Prevention of Cruelty to Animals (RSPCA) has also increased the pressure on the racing industry. According to *The Guardian* 1 May 2012,

> The RSPCA has set itself in direct opposition to racing's ruling body by calling for a radical overhaul of The Grand National, despite a preliminary report from the British Horseracing Authority saying that the deaths of two horses in last month's race could not have been foreseen or prevented. The charity responded with its own report, calling for 'seven key actions', including the removal of Beecher's Brook, which it described as a 'killer fence'.

> 'Despite safety improvements, the Grand National is still too risky for the horses,' said Gavin Grant, the chief executive of the RSPCA. 'It's the unacceptable face of racing. We must not see horses dying year after year.'

Grant said he had written to the BHA and to Aintree racecourse 'raising major concerns' and calling for an 'urgent meeting to discuss making the race safer'. He said the race should be restricted to fewer than the present 40 runners, the fences should be 'more forgiving' and drop landings should be eliminated ... The RSPCA's reaction was of most concern to the BHA, because it has worked with the charity on welfare issues in the past and has pointed to that association as evidence of how seriously it takes the subject. A BHA spokesman declined to respond to Grant's statement, pending completion of the Authority's full report. (Cook, 2012).

PR commentator Emma Newell, Head of Sport and Entertainment, Lexis PR commented,

> As one of the crown jewels in the sporting calendar, the Grand National was always going to prompt debate. The BHA was in a tricky position but struck the right balance in its statement: sympathy, a focus on the facts and highlighting a commitment to safety. Rather than responding to immediate calls for change from media and animal rights groups, it bought itself time to talk to those involved, confirming a review would take place before it reacted. Owners, trainers, jockeys and sponsors have all been asked to comment on safety this week, and I expect discussions between the BHA and stakeholders will focus on how changes can be designed to reduce the risk further without jeopardizing the appeal of this world-class event. (PRW, 2012d: 2).

A substantial review followed. BHA Chief Executive John Bittar defended the race's heritage and cultural status and financial importance while signalling co-operation with those who expressed concern,

> The Grand National is a unique race and it represents a unique challenge for the sport and for its regulation. It is a thrilling spectacle, but there is a higher degree of risk involved in the Grand National than other races and for this reason everyone in the sport needs to be conscious of how the race is presented to the public, the general consumer perception and their views of how the race is run. This is an event that generates huge public interest and has a global audience of more than half a billion people. We've seen record crowds of over 150,000 in attendance at Aintree this week, following on from record numbers through the gates to British Racecourses in 2011. All of this suggests that British racing is doing many things right in the eyes of the consumer. It is critically important to us that the good work being done in racing is not overshadowed by yesterday's events, and that racing continues to work collectively to develop and maintain this progress. In this context, we will be working with Aintree and its owners The Jockey Club, along with other groups in the sport to find the right balance which enables us to maintain the highest standards of safety for our horses and participants and to promote the sport to the widest possible audience. (British Horseracing Authority, 2012).

However, in November 2012 it was announced that the sponsor for nine years, John Smith Brewery, would not continue to sponsor the event. *The Daily Telegraph* commented

> Heineken, the multi-national drinks company which owns the John Smith's brand, clearly feels uncomfortable about being associated with a sporting event that, rightly or wrongly, has become a target for critical media attention … Lord Daresbury, the Aintree chairman, insisted on Sunday that John Smith's had taken a commercial decision in pulling out, quoting evidence from sources in the brewing trade that the company was making cutbacks … But he acknowledged that the bad publicity the race had attracted with another two equine deaths this year, and the fact that a change of broadcaster will almost certainly mean a smaller television audience, were also probably factors in the decision. (McGrath, 2012)

In the days leading up to the 2013 race it was declared to be 'the safest ever' (following course changes and plastic replacing wood in the interior of the jumps) but TV advertising was bold, carrying the by-line 'The original extreme sport', thus seeming to risk glamorizing a sport over which there is potential for further polarization. BHA has clearly been involved in discussions with key stakeholders but a severe threat would arise should the RSPCA be insufficiently reassured about safety measures. Public opinion and discursive activities within converged media, including all animal rights groups, need to be closely monitored, for example the racing industry has been involved in ongoing discussions with RSPCA and Animal Aid. Scenario planning might include

(Continued)

(Continued)

developing race options should the race ever become as unacceptable to political majority opinion as blood sports. Public affairs and any lobbying activity should also be carefully monitored. It appears that the sponsor has considered the same range of issues and possible influence or impact on their own stakeholders and consumers.

The Grand National 2013 passed off without major incident but the focus of media attention took debate to a new level in the UK. The industry is self-regulated and some claim it lacks transparency and that there is insufficient information about race horses, their lives and their post-race retirement options. Animal welfare critics argue that racing is unnatural, that horses would never race or jump fences in the wild unless in flight (or in the case of a stallion that wanted to reach a mare) and that the only reason that they continue to race even after a rider has fallen is due to herd instinct. Cross-cultural comparisons have also been made particularly the example of Australian provinces banning jumps races, described by one correspondent as 'a sport in its death throes' (McGrath, 2009). There are a wide range of interests in the horse racing industry including the betting industry that faces its own moral challenges particularly at a time of financial downturn, unemployment and loan sharks. Regulation in the horse racing industry is now a fear, which means that the specialist function of public affairs (that includes the practice of lobbying) comes into play.

Think Critically

You have been asked to advise BHA as to how they should continue to manage this issue. What further research would you carry out and why? What advice would you give and why? Which stakeholders would you prioritize and why?

Managing issues frequently requires organizations to deal with the fact that individuals and stakeholder groups may hold different perceptions and views of **risk**, or have varied beliefs about ethical behaviour and responsibility. Consequently, issues management may entail a variety of communication initiatives that involve concerned stakeholders to exchange ideas and to work through problem areas in participatory workshops, focus groups or advisory committees. Face-to-face interpersonal communication in itself communicates a message of the importance of an issue and, equally important, the store an organization puts on stakeholder relationships. The challenge that faces organizations is to ensure that any such events are genuine consultations and not cynical manipulations. A public meeting held to allow people to let off steam at a point when the organization has already made up its mind is not consultation in any meaningful sense, and those present will be aware of this and consequently be even more frustrated and hostile. While digital and social media also have an important role to play, organizations need to allocate sufficient resources so that websites, social media and blogs are regularly updated, interactive and responsive.

Risk Management and Communication

Risk communication appears to be self-explanatory – communication about risk – but is seen by some as a subset of technical communication, defined as the communication of scientific or technical information either to motivate, to inform or to build consensus about how risk should be managed (Lundgren and McMakin, 2009: 2). These various forms of communication can be distinguished from crisis communications specifically related to an immediate and sudden danger. All forms of organized communication are intended to influence reputation.

Risk communication is tied into other processes such as **risk-assessment analysis**, which endeavours to quantify negative effects using probabilities (Lundgren and McMakin, 2009: 5). This in turn is connected to crisis planning and scenario planning or 'storyboarding' (Lundgren and McMakin, 2009: 138), where simulations and gaming are used to give organizations experience in handling risk. It is also possible to see risk management and associated communications planning as part of intelligence-gathering and environmental scanning. However, these approaches tend to be considered from the strategic management and organizational perspective in terms of how to communicate effectively, where effectiveness is judged in terms of the organization's desired outcomes. The difficulty with this is that stakeholders and the wider society may be unable to make their views sufficiently heard or taken into account although the advent of digital and social media has certainly widened possibilities for communication and action.

The emergence of risk management as a distinct discipline has raised industry standards in terms of orientation and management processes. The existence of a risk-management team and procedures in itself communicates something about a sports organization's culture and values, as Lennox Batten, sports specialist at Marsh pointed out,

> ' A major priority for sports events, up there alongside the need to maximise revenue streams to the full, is the imposition of thorough, comprehensive and robust risk management systems (whereby risks are recognised, analysed, controlled or minimised and thereafter actively retained or transferred). (Glendinning 2006b: 46–7) '

This points to the investment in monitoring systems that intersect communications and public relations information systems.

Security and Terrorism

One of the most major and challenging issues facing major sports events is that of terrorist threat. Sports events may be seen as a 'soft target' and easier to infiltrate than buildings which house the centres of power, making sport an example of the concept of 'target substitution' (Glendinning, 2006b: 46–7). This has considerable resource as well as communications implications,

' It is not only the stadia which hold events, or facilities for athletes, which are under threat. Desperate groups could identify other targets, including power stations or even water supplies … as the security threat has developed it has broadened and become more difficult to manage … greater demands on the budgets of organising committees and host cities. The process of identifying threat, sharing intelligence and developing and implementing security programmes around sports events is becoming better understood thanks to knowledge sharing, while security manufacturers are constantly developing and refining technology designed to help make sports events safer … more could be done to facilitate central purchasing and shared ownership of the most expensive equipment. (Roberts, 2006k: 5) '

The sports industry has responded to this issue and,

' Sports event security is now a highly specialised discipline which draws on the expertise of professionals drawn from the armed forces, police and intelligence services as well as event and faculty management and operations professionals. (*SBI*, 2006f: 8) '

However, such developments raise critical questions about the connections and power of the sports industry as it mingles in the higher echelons with those responsible for surveillance, control and the application of force in society. The fact that much of such work is necessarily secret and not in the public domain subtly changes the character of sports business in terms of status and politics. Johnny Cooper, Associate Director, Control Risks, acknowledged the implicit tension in this shift, though inevitably taking a functional view,

' Sport is underpinned by creativity, freedom of expression, openness and shared values. Security … is about armed protection, CCTV and body searches … [there needs to be] extensive planning, design and training … to mitigate the risks for major sporting events … all stakeholders must be involved in developing and implementing world-class confidence-building security risk programmes for each event. The core principles are integration and communication. (Cooper, 2009: 9) '

The threat of terrorism changes the nature of other business practices and issues such as insurance, and now, according to James Hopper, Partner with Jardine Lloyd Thompson's Global Sports and Entertainment practice, 'Terrorism coverage is relatively widely available' (Glendinning, 2006b: 46–7).

Thus far the sports insurance business has not been able to globalize off the back of sports business, as values towards insurance are culturally specific. More to the point the issue of security and terrorism poses some interesting challenges for communication practitioners and for international federations making choices about the location of major sport events and satellite international media (that are central to the revenue generation for the events), especially for mass events where access is easy. For example, the bombing of the Boston Marathon on Monday 15 April 2013 sent reverberations among sports event organizers at all levels. Even quite small events can be the target for activism, for example Etape Caledonia (www.etapecaledonia.co.uk), organized by IMG, encountered activism in 2009 when local residents protested about the race by scattering nails on the road, causing multiple punctures during what was at the time Scotland's only closed-road cycle event.

Governance as Reputational Risk

Governance encompasses organizational political, cultural and ethical values and processes and is an issue for all organizations, including sports organizations. Governance draws attention to organizational power, the way it is acquired (politics), and distributed (between board level and management) how organizational decisions are made and responsibilities distributed, financial rewards, management of staff, and checks and balances in relation to stakeholders and the wider society. Issues of **governance** may be a risk factor for organizations whether it relates to managerial and organizational decision processes, financial practices and transparency, or the need to demonstrate that they are working towards best practice in areas such as diversity. One PR practitioner working at a football club explained 'We're working towards our Preliminary Racial Equality Standard (P-RES) at the moment ... I am very involved, helping the club achieve this is very important to us'.

At a much broader level an inquiry was conducted into English football exploring the ways in which the four aspects of the regulatory system (FA, UEFA, FIFA) related to UK laws regarding companies, consumers, labour, competition; corporate governance code; shareholder activism and stakeholder participation (Hoye et al., 2006: 173) following concerns about financial mismanagement and the way in which this might affect the sustainability of the game (Culture, Media and Sport Committee, 2011).

This inquiry demonstrated how governance is linked to reputation and how poor practice can lead to political intervention and potentially legislation, and it illustrates how sports PR may entail public affairs and lobbying.

Another ongoing problem that has raised issues of **governance** has been that of illegal or irregular betting, where the proliferation of online in-play betting systems in high-level sport plus illegal betting markets apparently partially driven by organized crime syndicates in Asia has now led to the formation of

'A concerted programme across all sporting bodies – Sports Integrity Unit at Sport Accord (the umbrella body for Olympic and non-Olympic international sports federations set up in June 2010). SportAccord's intentions ... are to bring all stakeholders in sports governance together to form a unified effort to tackle the problem head-on ... setting the ball in motion for the creation of a Code of Conduct ...

investigating the feasibility of establishing a sports betting intelligence and investigation systems, a monitoring system. (Cutler, 2011: 12–13)   )

The manager of the Sports Integrity Unit, Ingrid Beutler (former pro-cyclist and international lawyer who led UNO on Sport for Development), was quoted as saying,

(It's been well appreciated there is a problem. But what we have come across
with some of our members is a denial that match-fixing is currently affecting their sport, or even that it could do. It's just like any hard issue for sport
to tackle – doping was exactly the same … There's always denial in the first
instance when it comes to hard issues … with anything negative, the sports
movement is often reluctant to resist. If you look at problems such as hoo-
liganism, violence and human rights abuses – problems sport has been and is
continually confronted with – the reaction time to tackle these issues is often
delayed. (Cutler, 2011 : 12–13)   )

Defensive advocacy may be seen as an attempt to minimize an issue or even to deny a
problem. Those asking questions may scent the fear and journalists may hunt in a pack
in a face-to-face media briefing/media conference. Blandness or denials may prompt
investigative journalism to elicit incontrovertible evidence. Cover-ups are at least as damaging as the initial problem.

Crisis Communications

Crisis communications describes the role of corporate personnel following a profound
event that may or may not be the responsibility of the corporate body. Crises are events
arising from natural or man-made disasters, accidents, scandals, corporate negligence or
wrongdoing, and rumour. In some cases they are simply the consequence of a simmering issue that has either been avoided, or not handled well. In the context of converged
media it is not possible to close down discussion (and it would be damaging to try)
but crisis communicators still have to manage communications so that the organization
provides accurate up to date information to journalists and also online. The function
of crisis management involves risk management, emergency planning (usually in liaison
with the emergency services), scenario planning, crisis simulation exercises and staff
training in preparation for the unexpected. Any organization can be faced with an unexpected natural or man-made disaster or accident, and on such occasions an organization
needs clear plans to cope with media (possibly international media) requirements and to
have thought through the short-, medium- and long-term logistics of staffing, representation, procedures. However, communicators cannot, and should not be expected, to
make the media go away when a dramatic event has occurred, particularly in cases where
an organization has been negligent or immoral and is therefore culpable and liable for
the situation that has arisen.

Oxford and Cambridge Boat Race 2012

On 7 April 2012 the boat crews of Oxford and Cambridge Universities lined up for the 150th annual boat race. The race was predicted to be close, but Oxford, the lighter boat, had the faster start and were marginally ahead when, at around the halfway stage, Cambridge stopped rowing having spotted a man swimming between the two boats. The race was halted and, after some considerable time, re-started, with Oxford again pulling away. The race referee warned that the Oxford crew were getting too close to the Cambridge boat and almost instantaneously an Oxford oar snapped. As Oxford had already been warned, the race continued and Cambridge ran out an easy winner. In attempting to continue to compete (Oxford could have withdrawn from the race) one of the Oxford rowers collapsed at the finish line and had to be hospitalized.

Media commentators and rowing experts appeared taken aback that a swimmer could have got so close to the boats and appeared almost unprepared for that eventuality. The swimmer was an **activist** protesting against elitism, and it seemed that the possibility of **direct action** performed in this way had never been considered by race organizers. The media immediately raised questions about likely incidents at the then forthcoming London Olympics, citing the Marathon and boat races as particularly vulnerable events.

The communications issue here related to the extent and preparation in relation to **crisis planning** and **scenario planning** for the event and preparation for actions to be taken and statements to be made if an incident took place.

Traditionally, crisis management has fallen to PR practitioners to mitigate potential reputational damage following a major dramatic incident and ongoing media attention, and practitioners are responsible for crisis management planning and implementation at a time of high ambiguity (Seegar et al., 2001: 160). Practitioner approaches concentrate on recommendations for response and action, such as accurate fast communication and openness and consistency, while scholarship in the field analyses a range of different rhetorical strategies and schemes exploring a range of argumentative positions and strategies employed in crisis.

The concept of **apologia** has received a great deal of attention within the PR literature, following Hearit (2001) as a way of resolving social legitimacy crises, and is relevant to a number of sports' reputational crises. Jerome's (2008) study adapted from the political communication arena 'the rhetoric of atonement, a prescriptive typology of apologia designed to guide rhetors facing the need to atone for sins that cannot be denied, justified, or transcended' (2008: 124). **Atonement**, according to Jerome, differs from apologia in that it includes within it purgative and redemptive elements that partially constructs a changed identity that arises from the process (2008: 124). **Mortification, reflection** and **the creation of new identities** is seen in sports where athletes have acknowledged that they have taken drugs and, following a ban, returned to the sport as a changed person espousing repentance quite regularly, for example the British cyclist David Millar. It is also the case that members of the specific sports community may respond both with condemnation (of an individual found responsible for drug use) and defence of their sport in comparison with others. For example, it was very common to read in the British magazine *Cycling Weekly* both acknowledgement of drug problem in the sport but also veiled accusations about other sports such as football and tennis with regard to performance-enhancing drugs, in the context of discussions about the Operation Puerto affair. The reputation of cycling was bolstered by besmirching other sports and suggestions that media framing and agendas led to an unfair over-focus on cycling when, it was implied, other sports were less exposed. As Glantz demonstrated, the American Floyd Landis's image repair efforts demonstrated that while some combinations of defence strategies work well together, others do not (Glantz, 2009). Landis's use of denial, differentiation and evading responsibility was particularly convoluted and contradictory. This case demonstrates how denial strategies can leave rhetors with little else to say in their defence, and can place audiences in an either/or bind that forces them to judge accused parties as absolutely innocent or absolutely guilty. Second, there are considerable limitations to third party bolstering. Although several people spoke on Landis's behalf, their efforts, like his own, ultimately failed to clear his name. Finally, attacking one's accuser also has its limitations, particularly when one's accuser has empirical evidence of the accused party's guilt. (Glantz, 2009: 158)

Bruce and Tini (2008) focused on the tactic of **diversion** as a damage limitation strategy in their study of Australian rugby league, but also highlighted weaknesses in the sports industry,

> ' Although professional sports operate in a context where it would seem logical to have well-developed crisis communication plans, it appears that many sports organizations, including those with professional full-time staff, continue to operate in a reactive or ineffective fashion rather than planning and preparing for the kinds of crises that can be predicted (Helitzer, 1999; Marra, 1998) … in both Australia and New Zealand, PR remains an under-skilled and relatively low status arena which is often subsumed under marketing. Fears remain that much PR work is based on gut feelings rather than research or theory. (Bruce and Tini, 2008: 109) '

Walsh and McAllister-Spooner (2011) analysed the **image repair strategies** of the swimmer Michael Phelps and evaluated the 'rhetorical effectiveness of the discourse of Michael Phelps and other stakeholders after a picture of the 23-year-old swimmer allegedly smoking from a marijuana pipe (bong) appeared in the *News of the World* tabloid in London'. They pointed out that Phelps' misdemeanour was less seriously regarded because the drug in question was not performance-enhancing, and that his previous very positive image meant that he had 'reputational capital' in the bank. Nevertheless the incident reminded readers of an earlier reputational challenge when, months after the Beijing Olympics at which he had won eight Gold medals, Phelps was caught driving under the influence of alcohol. Phelps used mortification strategies, apologized and accepted responsibility for his actions while his sponsors employed bolstering and minimization strategies (Walsh and McAllister-Spooner, 2011: 159).

These examples illustrate the complexity of the image-repair process that begins at the same time that the initial crisis becomes public and a focus of media interest, and highlights how particular discourse use and rhetorical strategies interrelate to re-frame and persuade a number of critical or worried stakeholders and the media. It is clear that a crisis need not be terminal but that there is no one set way of tackling an incident, apart from in the rather basic processual approach recommended by practitioners. A major implication of the scholarship in this field is that sports PR practitioners need an understanding of rhetorical strategies, stylistics, ethics and a sensitivity to language choice – in short they need to be **discourse technologists** (Motion and Leitch, 1996).

Image Repair Framework (drawn from Benoit, 1999)

- Denial
- Shifting the blame
- Evasion of responsibility
- Reducing offensiveness
- Attacking accuser
- Compensation
- Corrective action
- Apologia

Think Critically

Analyse Oprah Winfrey's interview (www.oprah.com/own_tv/onc/lance-armstrong-one.html) with the cyclist Lance Armstrong and identify those image repair strategies that were employed by Armstrong, and those that were not, using Benoit's framework[1]. What impact do you think that his rhetorical choices made on his overall reputation?

Lance Armstrong has stated that he would like to participate in a triathlon Ironman. How should the US and international triathlon associations and the Ironman brand handle this issue and why?

Discuss!

On 4 April 2013 UK media reported that Lance Armstrong would compete in his first competitive event – a Masters swimming event at the University of Texas that, according to the Director of US Masters Swimming, is not covered by the anti-doping laws of

(Continued)

(Continued)

US Anti-Doping Agency. The organization is focused on encouraging adults to swim. However, according to the *Daily Mail* the Masters website does give the impression that it falls under the rules of the international swimming agency. The race is evidently not drug-tested. How should US Masters have handled the situation and why? How should the international swimming organization Fédération Internationale de Natation (FINA) handle this and why? How should Lance Armstrong's personal PR representative, Mark Higgins, have handled the situation and why?

Source: Daily Mail (2013).

Corporate Social Responsibility

Corporate social responsibility (CSR) may be understood as corporate activity that goes above and beyond its formal remit and functional organizational goals. It may include corporate philanthropy, best defined as a one-off donation or gift-giving given out of charitable intent. Where CSR differs is in its claim to be making a fundamentally different type of contribution to society, specifically companies will claim to be acting as a **good corporate citizen**. As the communication Director of Coca Cola Joel Morris said in a typical statement,

' CSR is more than just the right thing to do, it's good business sense. (Mattinson, 2012: 18) '

This is a phrase which demands some interrogation and at least a little cynicism. The idea that companies should give more of their profits back to the community sounds very attractive, but it is seldom a 'no strings attached arrangement', because often the motivation that lies behind it is simply to acquire good media coverage and a more positive reputation. For example, if a company sponsorship is claimed as being part of its CSR, is it evaluated in terms of return on investment (ROI), or media hits, or in terms of its brand reputation alone? If these are the sole measures then they are clearly concerned with the company's self-interest. If, however, evaluation is conducted that also explores the beneficiaries of the sponsorship in their own terms, so that they are involved in helping to devise the evaluation methods, then that is clearly more of a partnership and a different type of relationship. In other words, the motivation is self-interested. This has implications for the way in which we judge the moral worth of such acts because, if we follow the philosophy of Immanuel Kant we would discount such acts (with a consequential effect on the way we judge reputation) because they have not been done out of a sense of duty or obligation but out of a sense of **prudential self-interest** (L'Etang, 1994). For example,

> ' CSR investment, particularly through education, community infrastructure and provision of human resources can help mitigate risk, increase audience reach and enhance brand loyalty. This can have a positive effect on sales and importantly can be offered to sponsors as an additional opportunity, thus bringing in additional revenues. (Angus McGougan, Business Director, Fast Track. 'The sports business debate' *SBI*, 2012j: 65) '

It is sometimes argued that CSR is done on utilitarian grounds to benefit all. If this claim is made then it is important to look carefully at the way in which programmes are set up and evaluated and how they are designed. If there are long-term engagement programmes, which clearly take account of the ideas of the recipient group or groups, and these are able to feed back their ideas throughout the process and to report their own evaluations in the public sphere (either via the Internet or the professional media), and if the company has clearly addressed an issue which is directly relevant to their operation and not just a random topic that happens to be high up the agenda and therefore likely to attract media coverage and public attention, then the programme may be taken to be driven by serious concerns and moral commitments. If these conditions do not exist, then there are questions to be asked about motivation and the morality of the action (L'Etang, 1994).

Sport in itself is often positioned idealistically as an intrinsic social good, for example,

> ' Sport has built-in CSR ... kids and their dreams plus health and education' (Jamie Cunningham, CEO Professional Sport Corporation. The sports business debate. *SBI*, 2012j: 65). '

In the UK football has increasingly become involved in CSR and community-building activities and a number of clubs have their own programmes.

> ' FIFA executives say that they are entering a new phase in which the organization is moving from making the game of football itself better to making the world a better place ... Putting to one side sport's role in combating problems of obesity and related diseases which are plaguing many parts of the developed and developing world, there is a broader social role. A simple football match can create a sense of belonging, achievement and identity which generations of politicians would struggle to achieve. (Roberts, 2005/06: 5) '

The notion of CSR produces other challenges and tensions. For some, it is a chance for a company to make a genuine contribution to achieve societal benefits that would otherwise not be funded. In some cases it may directly contribute to notions of **social justice** by improving fairness, transparency, equity, and opportunity. Corporate societal interventions may provide much-needed injections of cash on social projects, but corporate policy-makers are not answerable to voters in the same way that local, regional and national politicians are, so CSR practice is not necessarily accountable. CSR is a complex practice, not least because it does claim moral benefits as well as reputational benefits for the company in question.

Humanitarian hummel

Danish sportswear company hummel's slogan is 'Change the world through sport' and sponsored athletes have to sign up to an individual 'Karma Project' of ethical value. The company's CSR includes 'long-term relief and aid to women and children' in Afghanistan and Sierra Leone (Chauhan, 2013: 18).
   See: www.hummel.net/en-AA/

Demonstrable long-term commitment to projects is important, as pointed out by Matthew Roberts of Eurosport,

' Investment in grass roots has become a common box to tick the CSR objectives of forward thinking companies, but it is not a cheap option and can be hard to measure and account for … Eurosport interviewed 1600 upmarket consumers whose response created a sports marketing code of conduct … the need to invest for the longer term to maximise results … [as] consumers [believe short term deals] show a lack of commitment [and assume] the brand is using sport for financial gain … grass roots investment … although expensive …. is valued by consumers … [and] company employees, 72 per cent of whom claim grass roots sporting investment makes them feel their company is giving something back into the community and two thirds of them claiming sporting investment makes them feel proud of their company and unites employees. (M. Roberts, 2009: 14) '

Since sponsorship has changed radically in the converged media context, so has the implementation of CSR programmes associated with sponsorship as one of the industry's leading figures, Karen Earl, explained,

' I just can't see anyone activating a sponsorship successfully whether that's in sport, the arts or social responsibility … today the pressure on brands to be good corporate citizens is far greater. Everybody needs to be seen to be doing the right things … Social media has made it easier for corporates to achieve their social objectives although there is still some fear out there about how you control messaging and conversations. (*SBI*, 2012d: 32) '

Converged media opens many debate opportunities and the choice of sponsors for London 2012 Olympics was not without controversy. Dow Chemical inherited the Union Carbide Bhopal disaster (despite efforts to distance itself and despite Union Carbide's efforts when the disaster happened to portray the incident as an Indian, not a company responsibility) and BP's Deepwater Horizon oil spill was fresh in memories. Key opposition groups included Greenwash Gold (www.greenwashgold.org), AgitArtWorks and a group that organized Brand Piracy Day (whose website was shut down, see www.agitartworks.com) and The International Campaign for Justice in Bhopal (bhopal.net/).

> **Think Critically**
>
> Analyse communicative strategies and discourses of various parties in the debates over London 2012 sponsors. What approaches were taken by the London Organising Committee of the Olympic and Paralympic Games (LOCOG) and to what extent did they engage with the criticisms of opposing groups? Which groups were able to establish legitimacy in the debate and why?

Sustainability

Sustainability is rising on the sports business agenda.

'The activities encompassed by the global sports industry are so diverse that it is difficult to talk in general terms about its performance on the issue of environmental sustainability. Sports is certainly not a heavy polluter or consumer of natural resources compared to many other industries. It also enjoys a generally positive public perception as being beneficial for society. The sports industry has thus avoided heavy scrutiny of its performance in making its activities sustainable ... Yet there is no doubt that ... activities ... could be performed in a more sustainable way ... in such a wide, fragmented and varied industry, there is often a lack of leadership.' (McCullagh, 2009b: 39)

Globalization of sport produces environmental problems above and beyond the massive amount of air travel involved. For example, golf might be green in Scotland's climate, but it certainly is not green in China where environmental protestors and some governmental officials have pointed out how the expansion of golf course development threatens the country's agricultural base and threatens the livelihood of many low-income workers (*SBI*, 2008e: 65). Golf has grown exponentially in China and its development has been supported by government as a way of generating income through business tourism. Land values have boomed consequently in areas of development, and golf courses are often built as part of large and lavish hotel complexes. Although the Chinese government has concerns about issues such as food security and environmental pollution (and has been subject to criticism for river and industrial pollution) it has waived regulations in the environmentally sensitive area of Hainan, where in an area of rainforest a large golf complex has been built threatening biodiversity. (Watts, 2010)

The terms 'sustainability' and CSR are sometimes used interchangeably although strictly speaking the first term is specifically more focused on the environmental agenda while CSR is (or should be) more focused on business obligations to society and social justice. One example of this blurring was to be found in *SBI* May 2013 where, under a heading 'How significant is social responsibility to your operations?' environmental examples were cited. In the case of rowing, the environment has become a major part of the sport's identity as recounted by the international federation, in which some activities that would be carried out anyway were pitched as moral actions,

'Our sport [rowing] is dependent on clean water and FISA [Fédération Internationale de Sociétés d'Aviron] has long been a leader along international federations in environmental issues. Rowing takes place outside and many of our events – such as those in Lucerne, Aiguebelette and Bled – are staged in beautiful, natural settings. This close connection with nature means many of our athletes and officials are active environmentalists, working hard to put in place green policies and educating others. In 2011, our mutual interest in clean water led FISA and the WWF (World Wide Fund for Nature) to enter into a strategic alliance, with activations at all our major televised events, is now the flagship of our environmental activity and one immediate additional benefit has been the strong interest from both our current and potential sponsorship partners. We are the only international federation with an environment and sustainability officer, on staff, monitoring all activities in this area. We also have leading-edge policies and guidelines for sustainable management of our events and are proud of the fact that we have now included the requirements to meet environmental standards as part of the bid conditions for our major events. In addition, we are working with our national federations and their member clubs worldwide to implement environmentally-friendly working practices during both training and competition. (*SBI*, 2013c: 54) '

Employee Communication and Volunteering

Crucial to any sports event, product or service are those that deliver the event, product or service. Employee communication is a somewhat unglamorous and rather neglected area of corporate communication, yet it is an area which is vital in terms of images that are projected. Managers may publicly acknowledge employees with the cliché 'our employees are our greatest asset', but in many organizations employees do not feel that they are given face-to-face opportunities to express their views. However, companies involved in sport may be in a strong position to motivate staff through association with big events, as Paul Deighton, CEO of LOCOG argued,

'If the [company you work for] is put on the Olympic team it is like having a gold medal hung around your neck. [Such companies] use it to get people skipping to work and everything they do in terms of training and leadership is related to how they theme it and use Olympic values. (Roberts, 2006c: 46–7) '

Julia Mack, Head of Global Sponsorship for Sony Ericsson, acknowledged the challenges but also implied that organizations directly involved in sport had advantages in motivating employees,

'Internally, the employee audience (in some companies) is generally neglected. We produce a quarterly newsletter to spread good news and collect ideas. You have to take the audience with you. We use the tickets we have to involve employees and their families as a way of engaging and involving them. (Roberts, 2006d: 32) '

As in the voluntary and charity sector, the sports sector is often dependent on volunteers such as parents and local communities, or in the case of a large event, thousands recruited more widely, sometimes across a nation. Clearly there is room for exploitation here, as volunteers may not be paid or simply be offered drinks and snacks. If the event in question is generating substantial income for sponsors, media rights and event organizers, then that is a problem in terms of ethics, specifically fairness and the distribution of benefits and burdens.

Volunteers are sometimes seen as a subset of employees but they are a distinct group with particular needs, indeed, an important consideration is the relationship between the two groups since some volunteers might resent employees who are paid for some of the same tasks that they do for free. Volunteering necessarily raises the spectre of advantage being taken and hard work is needed to ensure that volunteers have a meaningful experience.

Volunteering spans a huge range of events and experiences, and while much was made of London 2012's 'Games Makers' (the unpaid workers at London 2012 who functioned as 'meet and greet' guides and helpers to ticket holders) it is important not to forget the many amateur sports that are completely dependent on volunteers, for example marshalling on cold lonely country roads and in the hills at cycling, hill-racing orienteering events, counting laps in swimming events (and woe betide the volunteer whose concentration lapses so that a swimmer has to complete another two laps due to their error), preparing food and drinks, time-keeping, erecting and preparing courses for a vast range of outdoor sports from field sports to sheepdog trialling – these are the everyday realities for most volunteers. Even at this level, efforts need to be made to thank volunteers for their time and support: it might be a t-shirt, or a competitor's 'goody-bag'.

Think Critically

As a communicator how would you support human resources to recruit, engage, motivate and thank volunteers for a local sports event?

What challenges might arise in employing sport as a major part of employee communication? How could such programmes be evaluated? What moral issues arise?

Is employee turnover and absences the best way to evaluate the effectiveness of an employee programme built around the Olympics? If so, why? If not, why not?

Sport may be used by corporations and other organizations whose businesses are not related to sport as a way of building internal organizational relationships. For example, the British Civil Service offers extensive sports facilities and competitive opportunities for its employees that are also open to Royal Mail and BT, with a scheduled plan to open up more widely to the public sector. The Bank of England owns 32 acres in Richmond, London that includes tennis courts and a swimming pool. This form of corporate sport has historical antecedents for example 'worker games' in early-twentieth century Germany set up by paternalistic factory owners keen to distract their employees from trade union activities and to ensure their fitness for work. In such cases 'It assured the identification of workers with *their* company. So the Krupp workers called themselves "Kruppianer", the workers of the Henschel tank factory referred to themselves as "Henschelianer" to demonstrate unity with their company' (Kruger, 1999: 73).

Sport as Business Communication: Networking and Hospitality

Sports events are a major focus for business networking. According to Tim Harcourt, Chief Economist for the Australian Trade Commission, Australians attend international sporting events not as

> A jolly or a junket, but a real opportunity to network, forge relationships and pickup contacts ... At Sydney 2000, many international business visitors came to Australia for the first time. Accordingly, the Australian Government set up Business Club Australia (BCA) to leverage the business opportunities available ... it is estimated that ... (BCA) facilitated over $1.7 billion in export and investment deals from the Olympics, Rugby World Cup (2003) and Commonwealth Games (2006). (Harcourt, 2009: 51)

The fact that social bonds are formed around sport has been well recognized by business, hence the expansion of sponsorship and of corporate hospitality and the use of sport to forge business relationships. Golf is a good example of this, as illustrated by the comments of Gus Morgan, Head of Sponsorship at HSBC:

> The World Matchplay Championship gave us the opportunity to create money-can't-buy experiences for some of our clients. The players work with us and were tremendous, enabling us to deliver what is the coolest ticket in town for our relationship-managed clients ... Golf is more or less universal among the people we need to be talking to ... football works in most parts of the world but not in North American or India, while cricket works in India, but not in markets like Brazil. Golf cuts through everywhere. Golf also provides wonderful opportunities because it gives people time together and the chance to play on some of the world's great courses. (Roberts, 2006e: 19)

Corporate sport, however, also takes place at a totally different level in which business networks are reinforced more formally by opportunities to 'play' together. One example of this is the Golf Corporate Games, publicized and supported by the magazine *Golf World* and the sports promotion agency ProSportsPromotions where one participant explained,

> Golf makes it easier to shake hands afterwards ... because you are more relaxed and know each other better, it makes things easier.

Golf as bonding and business relations is especially apparent at the economically elite level. Golf operates internationally as **cultural capital** (a capitalist competence that exemplifies economic power and reproduces a distinctive class) and the benefits to business are apparent, as an interview with the top CEO golfer Curt Culver demonstrated,

' It's been very important in business for me. I have had numerous occasions where relationships that developed on the golf course have led to more business for our company … for my career it was very, very helpful. (*Corporate Golf World*, 2005a: 8–9) '

Likewise the Chief Executive of Phones International claimed 'Golf has been a constant feature of my business life … As you move around the course you can relax, and as you relax you become more yourself, and as a result true friendships are born' (*Corporate Golf World*, 2005b: 11–12).

Golf is a competence that is often practised in spaces requiring economic power and where capitalism is practised. Events such as the Corporate Masters, designated as 'the UK's leading networking golf event', communicate an elite identity and the international business class is enacted at exclusive clubs, where the opulence and personal service creates a superior and largely male preserve, pretty much a sanctuary, equivalent to the female-dominated health spa. Yet in Scotland, the home of golf, the game still straddles the classes because public courses still exist alongside the exclusive Archerfields and the Loch Lomond Golf Club, the latter of which claims, somewhat pretentiously, that it aims

' To foster international communication, sportsmanship and friendship in a setting without peer … a sanctuary not just for golf aficionados but for world thinkers … those who receive the privilege of Membership will become among a select group. (Loch Lomond Golf Club, n.d.) '

Professional golfer Robert Karlsson emphasized the connection between the competitive worlds of golf and business, appearing to brand himself as a future sports business executive once his playing days are over,

' In particular, I believe business leaders and high-performing golfers can learn from one another. We both have to deal with pressure in our own different ways. Business leaders could tap in a lot more to the similarities and encourage golfers to share their experiences … I think US golfers can contribute an interesting and welcome addition to corporate events as speakers. Being a professional golfer is about so much more than playing golf and I have to think of myself not only as a brand but as a business leader as well – as CEO of Robert Karlsson Inc. … managing pressure and making strong tough decisions in challenging situations is probably what really brings together the leading pro golfer and the CEO the most. I have learned a lot about making decisions and taking full responsibility for the outcome, both good and bad … There's a lot of life lessons to be learned through golf and many parallels with corporate life, so business shouldn't be shy in tapping in to what we have to say and what we stand for … That is why I think that companies can get more out of their sponsorship dollars and relationships with athletes. (*SBI*, 2011: 11) **"**

As a piece of communication this text seems to exemplify impression management and self-promotion strategies, and emphasizes values of individualism and capitalism in macho language that positions golf players as part of the commercial elite and members of the international business class.

These examples illustrate the way in which one particular sport (golf) intersects business, culture and society and functions communicatively and relationally to reflect and reinforce existing societal patterns and structures. Sport is therefore not a neutral social good.

Think Critically

Consider the way in which sport can 'open doors' or form a context for functional relationships in a variety of contexts. Has sport ever helped you form social bonds? Does sport necessarily exclude as well as include? In other words, can you identify how sport operates as a process of distinction and has done so in the context of your own life, relationships and those of your friends?

Corporate Hospitality

Corporate hospitality is a way of thanking business associates, but also employees and their families, children and friends for their work and commitment. It is intended as a bit of a personal 'thank you' and a treat, a chance to thank customers/partners (keeping existing customers is cheaper than obtaining new prospects). As a practice corporate hospitality is becoming less reactive and increasingly long-term and strategic as part of relationship-building strategies,

'
Businesses have tended to put even more focus on maintaining and retaining their clients and stakeholders. Hospitality is now central to long-term marketing strategies, and it's not something that brands just switch off and on in six to nine months … [major event packages] encourage strategic as opposed to ad hoc decisions. (Mike Burton Group quoted in Glendinning, 2008c: 10) **"**

At various times corporate hospitality has had a rather dubious reputation as conspicuous spending and lavish expense account culture, for example, the peripatetic F1 Paddock Club that travels with F1 for which the average price for a ticket was $3,600, bringing in $10 million in revenue to the Swiss owner Allsport Management International, visits 17 countries. The concept was developed by Irish entrepreneur Patrick McNally in 1984. Isabelle Kaufman, Paddock Club manager, explains:

'Our prime location above the pits where our guests are offered uninterrupted views of the start/finish and every pit stop, combined with genuine style, quality and pleasure makes the Paddock Club the ultimate in world-class hospitality ... [and in Monaco hospitality costs are] $5,000 per head where there is an open bar, champagne, gourmet lunch, fine wines and select boutiques (TAG Heuer, Hackett & Siemens) plus beauty therapists/masseurs. (Sylt, 2006: 43)'

However, following the world financial crisis there was some debate within sports business as to whether hospitality should continue as normal or show sensitivity by cutting back. Alternative perspectives emerged, both concerned with the potential impact on reputation. According to one commentator,

'The widely accepted view among marketers is that holding back on hospitality during tough times creates a perception that your business is having a bad time. (Fry, 2008c: 38–41)'

Nevertheless, some did revise expectations and activities, according to Graeme Muir the MD of Arena Structures,

'Corporate hospitality has not gone out of fashion. What has gone out of fashion is being conspicuous about it. I think the days of all-day liquid lunches could be gone. For the next 18 months at least corporate hospitality will continue to suffer this big image problem. Clients are asking for more business services at events and appear to be embarrassed at spending money on corporate jollies. (McCullagh, 2009b: 8)'

Hospitality has to be seen within the context of a relationship and communications ethics, for example hospitality offered during a tender process raises moral issues that, if exposed, are likely to be reputationally problematic. In the UK, regulation intervened in the corporate hospitality area in the form of the 2011 Bribery Act which requires that hospitality is reasonable and proportionate. This placed a burden of responsibility on organizations to develop guidelines on corporate hospitality and to ensure their executives and managers are aware of these and of guidance regarding limits.

Summary

This chapter has highlighted the importance of understanding the activities and techniques within the context of organizational policy and corporate objectives. Official communications had to take account of internal, intra-organizational politics as well as inter-organizational politics. The projection of organizational identities requires attention to organizational cultures and practices that both reflect and shape internal communications and their asymmetries.

The importance of environmental monitoring and issues management (both internal and external) as a central function of strategic PR practice has been emphasised along with risk assessment, noting that risks include communications and reputational dimensions that require specific assessment. Unmanaged issues and risks may develop into crises. Externally, the sports environment demands strategic-level investment to integrate risk analysis, issues management and CSR. The chapter has also drawn attention to organizational policies that intervene in society, specifically CSR programes and the ethical implications this has for PR professional practice. Sport itself can also be used directly as a medium for communication with key external stakeholders as well as employees.

Further Reading

Briassoulis H (2010) 'Sorry golfers, this is not your spot!': exploring public opposition to golf development. *Journal of Sport & Social Issues*, 34 (3): 288–311.

Highhouse S, Brooks M and Gregarus G (2009) An organizational impression management perspective on the formation of corporate reputations. *Journal of Management*, 35 (6): 1481–93.

Christensen LT and Cornelissen J (2011) Bridging corporate and organizational communication: review, development and a look to the future. *Management Communication Quarterly*, 25 (3): 383–414.

Godfrey PC (2009) Corporate social responsibility in sport: an overview and key issues. *Journal of Sport Management*, 23 (6): 698–716,

Inoue Y, Kent A and Lee S (2011) CSR and the bottom line: analyzing the link between CSR and financial performance for professional teams. *Journal of Sport Management*, 25 (6): 531–49.

Miller J and Wendt J (2012) The lack of risk communication at an elite sports event: a case study of the FINA 10K marathon swimming world cup. *International Journal of Sport Communication*, 5 (2): 265–78.

Reyson, S, Snider JS and Branscombe N (2012) Corporate renaming of stadiums, team identification, and threat to distinctiveness. *Journal of Sport Management*, 26 (4): 350–7.

Trendafilova S and Babiak K (2013) Understanding strategic corporate environmental responsibility in professional sport. *International Journal of Sport Management and Marketing*, 13 (1/2): 1–26.

Vos S, Breesch D, Késenne S, Lagae W, Hoecke J, Vanreusel B and Scheerder J (2012) The value of human resources in non-public sports providers: the importance of volunteers in non-profit sports clubs versus professional in for-profit fitness and health clubs. *International Journal of Sport Management and Marketing*, 11 (1/2): 3–25.

Waller R and Conaway R (2011) Framing and counterframing the issue of corporate social responsibility: the communication strategies of Nikebiz.com. *Journal of Business Communication*, 48 (1): 83–106.

Endnote

1. I am indebted to my colleague Magda Pieczka for her idea to use this framework as a student exercise.

4

Globalization, Culture and Sports PR

Introduction

This chapter aims to identify key issues that arise from the globalization of some sports and highlights intersections between sport, politics, and strategic communication to give examples of sports business perspectives and priorities. It begins with definitions of globalization and culture in relation to sport, sports business, international organizations and PR, drawing on appropriate literature. It draws attention to cultural and national identity work in sport and the role that communication plays in this and international communication more widely; the implicit tensions between nationalism and globalization; and public diplomacy campaigns. The chapter covers:

- PR, culture and globalization
- Sports globalization
- Sport business and global perspectives
- International communications
- Sports tourism
- National identity and nationalism
- Public diplomacy

Key Concepts

- Circuit of culture
- Corporate diplomacy
- Cross-cultural communication
- Cultural/national identity
- Cultural intermediary
- Cultural diplomacy
- Devotional-promotional communication

- Intercultural communication
- International communication
- International PR
- Globalization

- Public diplomacy
- Sports diplomacy
- Sports tourism

Globalization

Globalization is the term used to explain the impacts of easy travel and 24/7 communication connectivity. These include the homogenization of similar goods, services and economic rules. Globalization may be seen as modernism (Giddens, 1996) and homogeneity, or as having created spaces for 'heterogenous dialogues' in and between diasporic 'ethnoscapes', 'technoscapes', 'financescapes', 'mediascapes' and 'ideoscapes' as people confront the global disjunctures rising from global diversity and differences (Appadurai, 1996 see in Edwards 2012). Globalization as a trend is mitigated by cultural practice, ethnic ties and varied political and economic arrangements. The tensions between global and local practices are dynamic and fluctuating. Sport reflects these shifts and PR work is implicated in the diverse discourses that circulate around the phenomenon of its globalization.

PR's relationship with globalization is circular: it has benefited from, and played a part in, the stimulation of globalization processes and in transformational ideological and economic change that has facilitated the growth of consumerism; for example, PR consultancies were involved in the expansion of free-market enterprises in the former Soviet Bloc at the end of the Cold War. The role of PR in major global industries such as tourism, sport, and pharmaceuticals provide other examples of its linkage with processes of globalization. Critics have argued that PR is a global business activity linked to the power of capital which it seeks to protect and enhance partly through the promotion of consumerist ideology and practice,

> ❝ PR is global as a result of the globalization of capital and that PR has been instrumental in the globalization of capital. (Miller and Dinan, 2008: 193) ❞

PR develops and enhances relationships that drive sports business and promotes sporting images and spectacles that can be commodified for corporate interests. PR promotes the ideologies and discourses of sports business and corporate clients. It also works on behalf of aspiring nations that wish to gain worldwide status through hosting major events, and supports sports programmes designed to improve health, peace and development, so there are different possible readings of the PR relationship with globalization.

PR, Culture and Globalization

Sport's fluidity in global cultural contexts reflects an understanding of intersecting cultures that

'Exist in continuous flux, continuously interpreted and reinterpreted through human interactions and embedded within the context of the lives of the members of the cultures. Culture is both a carrier of traditions and a site of transformation … and within [the] tension between tradition and transformation that identities and relationships become meaningful. (Pal and Dutta, 2008: 163–8) '

The connection between PR practice and culture is fundamental (Edwards and Hodges, 2011). PR work responds to or instigates change and culture is 'a process by which meaning is produced, circulated, consumed, commodified and endlessly reproduced and renegotiated in society' (Williams, 1961, 1962; Hall, 1980 cited in Curtin and Gaither, 2007:35).

PR performs a role in the cultural processes in which meaning is created, modified and reinvented during processes of symbolization, representation, consumption and identity formation. This dynamic has been described as the **circuit of culture**, which emerged from British cultural studies. The circuit was introduced to PR by several scholars (Hodges, 2006; Curtin and Gaither, 2005, 2007; Terry, 2005). The circuit defines interlinked processes where meaning emerges and is negotiated. The moment of regulation comprises cultural expectation and convention reflected in laws and regulations such as those governing media law and rights, taxes, drugs and gambling. The moment of production describes the creative processes involved in envisioning and defining creative products and services, for example re-positioning and re-packaging a sport by creating a new World Tour or Series or elite circuit accompanied by new branding and sponsorship that helps to create a different value. The process of representation describes the effort of the creators/producers to 'encode' their meaning symbolically through advertising, branding and PR. These meanings are reinterpreted at the moment of consumption. Processes of identification create public identities associated with values and actions. Identification may be advanced through purchase, symbolic display or participation in certain activities so that identities are performed as part of a process of **distinction** between self and others. An example of this would be the basic decision to support one team rather than another. In a sporting context, PR operates as a **cultural intermediary** in symbolic meaning construction on behalf of sporting clients and stakeholders, including non-sporting sponsors. PR is part of the behind the scenes creative and co-creative meaning production, its communicative focus facilitating reflexivity and reinterpretations, while at the same time it aims to 'fix' meanings and identity at certain points to encourage engagement and identification. Curtin and Gaither (2005) explained the cultural turn in PR as a move from transmission models of mass communication to concerns around discourse and the cultural and political economies (2005: 93). They explained that the **circuit of culture** is helpful in viewing critically communication processes linked to power processes, knowledge use and exchange and the production of socially constructed knowledge. Such an approach assumes contested meanings, alternative readings and dialectical processes involved in the production of social meanings that inform the nature of the culture.

Cross-cultural comparisons are evident where people are on the move either individually or in groups. Athletes, coaches, amateur sports participants, spectators, officials, sports business practitioners and marketers contribute to the international sports dia-spora. Major sports events facilitate cross-cultural comparisons when national teams are accommodated in temporary global sports villages. **Cross-cultural communication** explores how specific cultural environments influence communication, for example communication practices in different cultures at weddings or at sports events – the 'Mexican wave' emerged during the football World Cup in 1986.

A cross-cultural communications approach to sports PR requires understanding of political, economic and social history and international relations which frame the emergence of sport in different cultural contexts. As Guilianotti and Armstrong pointed out,

‘ Football cultures in any location tell us much about the societies that play and under-stand the game in the distinctive ways they do … Colonialism, neo-colonialism and neo-liberalism … provide the circumstances within which African peoples make and remake their cultural identities and practices … Sport … has been destroyed, rein-troduced and refashioned through this interplay of historical, political, economic and cultural influences … fledgling European sports traditions were taught to young African males by Western missionaries, teachers, soldiers, administrators and busi-nessmen … some indigenous traditions did survive, notably the pan-African games known in southern Africa as *mancula* and *moraba-raba*. (Giulianotti and Armstrong, 2004: 1, 7, cited in L'Etang, 2010: 170) ’

Therefore sports PR practitioners need to understand the contextual histories of varied sports, their paths of globalization, and to take into account the way this will affect busi-ness and sporting relationships in specific local contexts, for example the side effects that the introduction and take-up of globalized sports might have on local traditional sports and communities and, crucially subsequent relationships.

Processes and Phases of Sports Globalization

- Internationalization – global navigation of sport and sport diasporas
- Liberalization – removal of cross-border barriers – fewer nationality quotas
- Universalization – harmonization/homogeneity – a small number of sports dominating globally with a tendency for the simpler sports to dominate because they are easier to assimilate
- Diminishment – local sports lose status and visibility due to international broad-casting
- Westernization – exclusion of developing counties – fewer facilities/resources
- Deterritorialization – fans shop around the global sports market for a cultural and sporting identity that they feel fits their personal brand. Increasingly states become less important and international bodies more important (Scholte, 2000: 67)

> ## Think Critically
>
> Identify sporting examples for each of the concepts in the framework that seek to explain the phases and processes of sports globalization. What are the implications of the framework for fans and fan relations?

Sports Globalization

Sports globalization creates 'super-sports' underpinned by corporate capital and ruled by powerful international bodies. Globalization contributes to homogenization of goods and services across the globe, and the dominance of some cultural products,

> ' The world is a far more homogenous place, something which is underscored by the ubiquity of global brands in everything from soft drinks and fast food to banking, motor cars and, of course, football. The top leagues have the pick of the world's best players. The market in labour is truly global. These polyglot clubs have become international brands. Thanks to TV and the internet, clubs like Real Madrid, Manchester United, Barcelona and Liverpool claim hundreds of millions of 'fans' outside their own borders. That there is a worldwide appetite for football's mega clubs and mega leagues is unarguable. It is the product of a process of globalisation which is likely to be irreversible. (Roberts, 2008b: 7) '

However, the successful internationalization of some sports can contribute to a decline in locally offered goods and services (sports is a service if defined as entertainment). For example,

> ' The Asian Football Confederation has been … arguing that fans in some parts of Asia prefer to watch the FA Premier League on ESPN Star Sports than attend a local league match or play themselves … the Chinese Basketball Association is worried about the talent drain to the NBA while the Japanese Baseball's ruling body is reluctant to let the USA's major league Baseball take too much of a lead in global development of the sport. (Fry, 2006: 44–6, cited in L'Etang, 2010: 175) '

Nevertheless, globalization is not monolithic and sports business has to pay attention to variable and partial uptakes,

> ' Golf is more or less universal among the people we need to be talking to … football works in most parts of the world, but not in North America or India, while cricket works in India, but not in markets like Brazil. Golf cuts through everywhere. (Roberts, 2006e: 19) '

Globalization, however, is more than just the creation of a global village of football teams and transnational transfers. The process emerges within historical, political, economic and sociocultural contexts. Not only does globalization raise questions over the national identit-ies and loyalties of players, it also impacts the role of national and international governing bodies and their power. This was illustrated when the FA Premier League proposed a series of matches around the world in host cities that would finance the operation (Roberts, 2008b: 7). The NFL's decision to locate some matches outside home territory is one over which that organization has full autonomy. But the political economy of football has developed quite differently, and, according to Roberts, it appeared that the FA had not consulted FIFA, UEFA or its fans, triggering hostile or indifferent responses, and suggested that

> ' The Premier League failed to realise just how big a grenade they were tossing into football's global administrative bunkers. (Roberts, 2008b: 7)   '

The row highlighted how existing power structures may be challenged by economic demands of globalization and raises questions over 'whether the structures which currently govern the global game will remain appropriate' (Roberts, 2008b: 7). In PR terms, the various organizational systems are operating in a context of environmental change, and failure to adapt may cause them to become irrelevant in a context in which, according to Giles Morgan, Head of Sports Sponsorship and Marketing, HSBC,

> ' Ultimate global events ... create true sporting legends ... the issue and the oppor-tunity to consider global leagues will not simply go away. There is simply too much money to be made. (*SBI*, 2008f: 37)   '

An inevitable business corollary of sports globalization has been foreign ownership and/or management, for example, that of the English football clubs Manchester United, Aston Villa, West Ham, Portsmouth, and Chelsea. These developments are examples of how globalization may override national structures and 'dilute' national identity.

Another feature of globalization is the gradual homogenization of services which cushion the more cautious travellers and those of the international business class, for example, Mayor Luzhkov claimed

> ' Moscow has grown into one of the best cities in the world: it has made multi-faceted progress, with rapid construction and an increase in the standard of living ... In the past, there was an uncertainty about Moscow, so people would prefer to go to a city like New York where they knew what to expect. But now Moscow has all the com-forts you would expect from a major international capital. (Glendinning, 2008b: 65) '

Matching this development was the fast growth of a new and ambitious class of Russian sports marketers who pushed the fledgling sports economy so that it was in a position to compete on the world stage, and a natural target for leagues such as NHL and NBA, should they go global (Roberts, 2008d: 66). However, the credit crunch impacted the class of super-rich Russian businessmen, whose wealth was based on energy resources and whose investments were financed by debt, according to the broker behind Roman Abramavoch's acquisition of Chelsea FC (*SBI*, 2009c: 8).

Accompanying globalization is the emergence of international business and emergent middle classes, whose aspirations are met by sports such as golf and tennis which have found new markets, for example, in China. However, while sports business practitioners often present these markets positively as an expansion of market size, the new markets are necessary economically because tennis is declining in its traditional base and some golf clubs in the UK struggle to recruit members (so there is another side to the story). In the case of tennis its traditional class base has been altered in the process of international marketing ensuring a much more economically viable market.

The ATP Men's Tennis Tour was re-positioned in Asia because, according to its CEO, Etienne de Villiers,

‘ There's no such thing as a one-size-fits-all tennis fan and the demographic differs hugely between the new markets of Asia and in the USA … In the traditional markets fans are getting older and in the US tennis has been challenged and is no longer a Top 10 sport. Yet in Asia the demographic is completely different. There tennis is considered a Now sport, it is not at all elite and is generally a sport of the masses. That, in turn, is different from the UK, America and France where it has always been something of a Middle Class sport which is not always a good thing. (Roberts, 2008c: 48)   ’

Likewise women's tennis is seen as having huge future growth for its sponsors as was made clear by Larry Scott, CEO of Sony Ericsson WTA Tour:

‘ The proposition is global and that dimension is very important to our sponsors. The Tour has significant local power as well as its worldwide profile. For example, our tournament in Hyderabad, India is particularly important to Sony Ericsson, and, as we are managing a global sport and competing against other sports in the global market place, we are very mindful of the significance locally of these events. Their local visibility and power is critical. In India we are building at a time when the local media market is exploding … China is another important market for our sponsors and we have a group of Chinese players making progress in the game. Our China Open draws a bigger audience within the country than Wimbledon. (Roberts, 2006h: 28–9)   ’

Globalization of the sports business requires sensitivity in terms of local markets, taking time with interpersonal relationships as part of PR initiatives. This has been particularly so in Asia, of which it has been argued,

‘ There are many obstacles to being commercially successful in the region … the number of financially active consumers is lower … growth is an urban phenomenon … 150 million Chinese live on less than 1$ a day … political goodwill in Asia is hardcore. Formula 1 and the ATP tennis Tour spent 10 years *pressing the flesh* before they began to make real inroads into China. (Fry, 2006: 44) (Author's emphasis.)   ’

Sports business practitioners constantly assess new markets for potential growth,

' The vision of sport as an economic driving force ... is being replicated right across the Asian land mass. In China, Japan, Korea, India, Malaysia, Singapore. Hong Kong, Qatar, Dubai and Bahrain, investment in sport has become one of the most visible symbols of the way economic power is shifting inexorably east. (Fry, 2006: 44–6) '

Sports business is quick to pick up on sports that cross cultures, such as baseball which attracted sponsorship from Anheuser-Busch, Gatorade, Mastercard Inc., MBNA, Benco Mercantil, Konami, and Tourism of Puerto Rico, as Judy Hector, director of Business affairs and Licensing for the major league Baseball Players Association said,

' 'The World Baseball Classic is a tribute to the global popularity of baseball – a fact that has not gone unnoticed by the international corporate community'. (Smith, 2006b: 10) '

Following the world financial crisis, sports business practitioners sought to find markets with longer-term development and solid growth potential, as was made clear by the shift by UCI World Cycling from Europe to China. Pat McQuaid, UCI President, explained,

' From a commercial point of view the European economy isn't in the healthiest of states, so there is much more opportunity for our teams to find sponsors in China and other continents ... as far as the teams are concerned the potential to attract new sponsors plus the chance for current sponsors to showcase their brands in China presents a wonderful opportunity ... That includes the bike manufacturers. China is a huge potential market for them and a lot are linked to the pro teams ... We are [also] in talks with Russia ... Brazil and India ... these four markets are extremely important for both current and potential sponsors, along with the wider development of the sport, owing to the huge populations in these countries. (Ridley, 2011: 24–5) '

However, opportunities and new territories also expose businesses to different and culturally specific forms of risk, for example to do with conventions over business ethics (bribery, for example) or tax regulation, as is apparent from the warning given by David Powell, Associate Director, Redmandarin in his comments on India in 2011,

' There's a confluence between corruption issues in Indian governance and a narrow range of available sports properties which has made it a challenging market for building differentiated sponsorship programmes ... the particular interwoven nature of politics, sport and major corporations in India has meant the tendrils of the current wave of scandals have shaken the sports world far more than conventional bribery or doping scandals – which can be blamed on the actions of rogue individuals ... the world's largest democracy is one of the most exciting markets in the world right now; it is rightly at the centre of many global expansion plans, but for those looking to enter the market through sponsorship ... tread with care. (Powell, 2011: 15) '

As these examples make clear, sports business is adventurous but strategically focused on capital growth and profits, and PR can help facilitate networking and relationships through business-to-business (B2B) PR that supports new business ventures in addition to reputation-building, stakeholder (B2B, investors) and media relations.

International Communication

International communication explores communications between countries and is part of international politics, state diplomacy and public diplomacy – largely studied within the disciplines of international relations, politics and political communications. This term also has a high degree of relevance to sport given not only its global scope, but its large-scale funding by political masters, and sport's role in the expression of national, racial, and ethnic identities. International communication 'Deals with power, politics and the process of influencing other nation-states. (Gudykunst and Mody, 2002: ix, cited in L'Etang, 2010)

Sport may be used for political ends, to bolster a nation's pride and confidence, enhance national identity, to unify a country in a common cause, to distract a population from political or economic crises, to improve health statistics and medical epidemiology. Hosting major events such as the Olympics represents a major opportunity for public diplomacy. For example, 'Asia's use of sport as a nation-building tool is important.' (Fry, 2006: 44)

International communication is grand scale analysis looking at nations 'world systems, groups and movements' (Gudykunst and Mody, 2002: ix). It also explores mass-mediated communication and is thus highly relevant to international PR and international sports PR in particular. International communication includes the use of sport for **public diplomacy** (communication with domestic publics of other nations, often about issues which have international and domestic implications – known as **inter-mestic publics**).

A more recent form of diplomacy and PR has arisen around cities, particularly those that bid for major international events such as the Olympics or the smaller-scale Asian Games.

' Cities have gained in importance in the study of global communications, culture and information: the notion of a 'world city' appeared … in the 1980s … and approaches to the study of the city now include those that look at urban centres as command and control sites for the intermeshing of global financial, production, and distribution systems … economic engines because they are dense in information resources … serving global functions because of their cultural creativity … as edges or links between nodes, rather than nodes in themselves … as symbolic sites. (Braman, 2002: 404)   '

It is not too far-fetched to describe this emergent form as **city diplomacy**, or **city PR**, and it has reached its apogée in the development of Sports Cities, such as Dubai, Doha, and Oman. A **sports city** can be defined from a sports business perspective as 'One which pursues a sustained programme of sporting events that are integral to the identity and economy of the city involved, with benefits that percolate from the elite to the grassroots levels'. (Glendinning, 2009a: 30)

A sports city is 'more than the sum of its parts' in that it is not simply a collection of facilities in co-ordination with media and sports business infrastructure. **Port cities** are those that are central to events such as Clipper Values races in which revenues accrue to the ports. Dubai Sports City is regarded as a benchmark, including,

> ❛ A state-of-the art futuristic indoor and outdoor multi-purpose stadia, dedicated cricket and hockey stadia and world class sports facilities and training academies … sited in a 50 million square foot area within Dubai-land, a 'biosphere' of leisure, tourism and entertainment. The Gulf States have positioned themselves on the global map for elite sport to provide an alternative income stream. In 2006 a number of sports academies had relocated or established training centres there, for example Manchester United Soccer School, David Lloyd Academies (leisure, spa and tennis), International Global Cricket Academy and the Butch Harman School of Golf (linked with Troon, Scotland). (Glendinning, 2006a: 50, cited in L'Etang, 2010: 172) ❜

Oman's 'Blue City' development was planned as a tourist destination with sports venues and academies, which was supposed to create thousands of jobs, important as all Gulf States seek to diversity their carbon-based economies (Glendinning, 2006a: 50). Bahrain, which made its name when it hosted the Formula 1 Grand Prix in 2004 has 'Khalifa Sports City' and Doha (Qatar) not only hosted the fifteenth Asian Games (bigger than the Olympics in terms of the number of sports) but 'is also one of the best places in the world for sports sciences … [which means] it could partner with the Australian Institute of Sports' (Glendinning, 2006a: 50, cited in L'Etang, 2010: 172).

Such cities are designed to attract **sports tourists** and offer an extraordinary opportunity for 'the tourist gaze' (Urry, 2002). In PR terms, these elite centres of population seek elite partners and strategic alliances to build brand and enhance their reputation.

These examples demonstrate the complexity and interconnections between sports business, national economies, tourism, and the cult of the 'mega'. PR in such a context is potentially political, promotional, propagandistic, and undeniably complicated in terms of stakeholder and community relations and corporate social responsibility where the PR function is likely to experience the global–local tensions.

Sports tourism is one of the fastest growing businesses in the world, both in sports and travel industries. It is often driven by political agendas according to Dr Lisa Delphy Neirotti, Professor of Sports Management and Tourism Studies, George Washington University,

> ❛ European cities have government backing for bids, but many are not very sophisticated in really understanding the business … They are throwing money at events that will never pay off, but they want to be in the business of sports tourism as it is …

somewhat sexy. So politicians often buy into it, especially if they have an interest in sport or want the exposure that comes along with a popular international event … when I consult with cities the first question to ask is: what are your objectives? … make sure that the people watching the event are the same target you want to reach. (Wilner, 2007: 62–3)

There are contentious debates over the longer-term economic benefit of sports tourism, for example, one report from the European Tour Operators Association said that 'there is no strong link between hosting events and increased tourism' (*SBI,* 2006e: 14).

National Identity and Nationalism

Sports is a subcultural or micro-cultural element of both national, ethnic and organizational cultures. National leaders use sport to enhance national identity and to endeavour to unify national culture and to capitalize on community allegiance.

'You have only to talk about rugby to a New Zealander to understand that sport has a different sort of power which is entirely unconnected to cash. It's to do with inclusivity, belonging, being part of a tribe' (Roberts, 2008a: 7).

Sport offers points of distinction for identity construction and the creation of insider and outsider groups. The issue of **national identity** is taken seriously within the business community as part of brand value, illustrated by the comments of Kevin Roberts, the Editor of *SBI*:

FC Barcelona … the sexiest brand of all … a club whose brand identity has been forged by history rather than being artificially inseminated in a boardroom specimen bottle … a rallying point for the people of Catalonia … A focal point for regional identity amid turbulent and often bloody periods in Spanish history and the most visible manifestation of Catalan pride … the club history provides many examples of the incidents that conspired to create the identity and its relationship with the community … It is a people's club – proud, independent, anti-authoritarian, stylish and successful … as the marketing men will tell you, these are very compelling attributes. (Roberts, 2006j: 22, cited in L'Etang, 2010: 168)

In conversation with Roberts, Esteve Calzada commented,

We kind of represent a nation here … [the fans] use the club to show who they are, how they feel … The brand is consistent around the world and when we play in China, Japan and elsewhere, you'll see Catalan signs and flags in the crowd. We work hard to leverage that uniqueness and to define ourselves as different … Our research suggests that the brand attributes are important to global growth and our research shows that they are attributes to which young people and women respond particularly well. (Roberts, 2006j: 22, cited in L'Etang, 2010: 168)

Indeed, Barça has been held to be the ultimate definition of Catalan identity, ahead of Picasso, Miró, Dalí and Gaudí (Salvador, 2004, cited in Xifra, 2008: 193). Catalan scholar Xifra suggested that,

'The array of rituals and devotions generated by Barça creates or recreates the national community, strengthens its cohesion and bestows on it a transcendental facet, while also helping to make the identification and mythological symbols of Catalan's imagined community and everything this signifies sacred. (Xifra, 2008: 195) '

Sports PR may be linked to national identity in a form of communication defined as **devotional-promotional communication** (Tilson, 2006) 'used by individuals and political or religious organizations in order to attract loyal and faithful followers' (Xifra, 2008: 194). From a relationship management point of view, PR is concerned with social and identity cohesion (Xifra, 2008: 195) and the formation of allegiances through events, celebrity icons, drama. Xifra argued that Barça,

'Can be seen as a type of civil religion and the role of PR is establishing, and above all, upholding this symbolically by using a devotional-promotional communication model ... 'civil religion' describes a form of social cement, helping to unify the state by providing it with sacred authority ... often practised by leaders within that society. (Xifra, 2008:192–3) '

Sport can be seen as an **institution** in society 'with unique ethical and rhetorical intricacies ... sport exists for the fans as a kind of secular religion [where] sporting contexts are mytho-religious rites' (Kruse, 1981: 283 cited in Jerome, 2008).

As Xifra demonstrated, civil religion is a very appropriate term to use in relation to Barça: during the election campaigns in 2006 the leaders of all three of the main Catalan parties each independently met Barça's Chairman for breakfast in a Barcelona street café (Xifra, 2008: 192).

In a globalized world, however, there is also the issue of personal affiliations and choice regarding national identity, for example, there have been a number of cases of sportspeople changing their national allegiance for various reasons, due to emigration, some opportunistic, for example Bulgarian Angel Popov became Said Asaad and Kenyan Stephen Cherono became Saif Saaeed Shaheen (Poli and Gillan, 2006) which may, from a sports business perspective, have brand implications:

'The more tenuous the link, however, the more sceptical fans will be. And it can be particularly difficult for fans to swallow when the athlete has previously represented another country ... New Zealand rugby player Shane Howard represented Wales on 19 occasions before rugby officials later discovered he was not qualified to play for the country as originally thought. It turned out he did not, in fact, have a Welsh grandparent. And he was not the only one. (Smith, 2006d: 70) '

Discuss!

What constitutes national identity? How can membership be claimed? Birthplace? Birthplace of parents, grandparents, great grandparents or earlier ancestors? Geographical location or upbringing? Language? Accent? Consider a range of sports and teams that are strongly linked with national identity – are these sports professional or amateur? What social standing do players have in their national or community context? What implications does national identity have for Personal PR?

Public Diplomacy

Public diplomacy is the term used to describe governmental communication that aims to reach the general public of another nation directly. Public diplomacy encompasses a wider range of activities to meet political policy goals. Cultural diplomacy is an element within this but focuses on person-to-person contact between citizens of different states, for example involving exchange-of-persons. Cultural diplomacy is long-term, soft diplomacy that aims to build relationships over the course of a generation. Sport is used by governments as a part of public diplomacy in order to signal a desire for closer relations,

' Sports contexts can be useful in that they betoken two countries' decision to rethink their relationships, they can also break the ice between officials on both sides. But sports contacts cannot, in and of themselves, lead to better relations. (Chehabi 2001:249) '

A frequently cited example of sports diplomacy is the 'ping-pong diplomacy' between the US and the People's Republic of China in the early 1970s during the Cold War. Since then there have been other examples, but care has to be taken that there is not too much risk of loss of face, so often sports are chosen that are played, but are not necessarily the national game, otherwise sport really does become an alternative scenario to conflict.

The 1972 Summit Series Between Canada and Russia

'At the height of the cold war, two hockey styles clashed: the swift, precise and contact-averse game of the Soviets against the dogged, rugged, punishing game of the Canadians. The series played out before a rapt audience on both sides of the Iron

(Continued)

(Continued)

Curtain. As it moved across Canada and on to Moscow, the games became increasingly desperate, although almost everyone had assumed the Canadians would win all eight games. The pressure drove the players to new heights of skill and, for the Canadians especially, questionable behavior ... The Canadians defended their actions, then and now, by comparing it to warfare. And indeed, the Summit Series was a more dramatic cold war clash than even the men's Olympic basketball final between the United States and the Soviets that took place that month in Munich, or the Fischer-Spassky chess championship of a month before ... Even today, the players look back on what they did and say it was a product of having to win to validate the kind of hockey they played, and their society's ideology.' (Klein, 2012)

Sports diplomacy encompasses development and development communication (Black, 2010) and nation-branding (Manzenreiter, 2008). The centrality of sport to politics has become more accepted, 'despite its strategic and enduring place within politics and international relations, sport remains an ambiguous, intangible and conspicuously elusive part of contemporary foreign policy' (Jackson and Haigh, 2008: 349). Although sport is regarded by both politicians and corporate leaders as a way of communicating with stakeholders, it also remains the case that there still exists the naive idealism that sport and politics 'do not, and should not, mix' (Jackson and Haigh, 2008: 349). Nevertheless the explosion of sport as a globalized industry requires it to engage with the global political agenda in relation to questions such as environmentalism and security, about which key stakeholders and governments have concerns (Jackson and Haigh, 2008: 350). Thus sport has become mired in politics, is used explicitly by political bodies such as the United Nations to achieve diplomatic goals and is a tool in governmental foreign policies. Sport plays a key role in the context of country branding and national identity (S. Cornelissen, 2008) often forming the basis of building communities (Spaaij, 2009) or negotiating relationships in divided communities or countries such as Korea (Merkel, 2008). Indeed, the involvement of sport in international and national politics is such that some have questioned the power-balance between sport and politics (Redeker, 2008).

Public diplomacy is employed by both sports and cities, often in conjunction, in relation to mega-events such as the Olympics. In practical terms this requires a huge effort to translate aspiration into reality via the competitive bidding systems, in which promotional rhetoric seeks to prove the long-term benefits to the country and city in question. As CEO John Tibbs pointed out,

' Bidding has become an extremely important part of the sports business sector because the stakes are so high for bidding cities and nations. Bidding today is not simply to do with staging an event for a few days or weeks but about driving re-development, social and economic change ... In some cases bidding campaigns are launched in order to forward the long-term ambitions of nations which have come to realize that they benefit from the global spotlight a major event delivers. This trend is underscored by the number of Heads of State who have become personally involved in bid campaigns in recent years … There is a growing understanding that the benefits of hosting are not confined to the Olympic Games and FIFA World Cup but that a range of other regional and sub-regional events have the potential to allow the host to realise specific goals. (*SBI*, 2007a: 114) **'**

Public diplomacy may operate as a long-term and ongoing programme or there may be specific campaigns to try and improve relationships with the general publics of other countries. For example in 2009 Denmark ran its Danish Year of Sport, and its Director, Lars Lundov explained this as a form of **cultural diplomacy:** 'We believe that, using sport, which is an international language, we can show guests and visitors the Danish qualities … efficiency with a smile … hygge … [the relaxed atmosphere] … when Danes are with family and friends' (McCullagh, 2009c: 24–5).

However, part of the programme did have a directly political intent – **public diplomacy**. The Danish Wrestling Federation was sent to Iran and Egypt, and, according to Lindov,

' This is just one programme among many to convince the Muslim world that Danes are not intolerant cultures … We want to illustrate that wrestling may break down cultural differences. We would like this journey to underline that, despite cultural differences, we humans are very much the same. One may say our journey is some kind of sport politics. (McCullagh, 2009c: 24–5) **'**

In China, the government has used golf to promote 'a dynamic new face to the world', not least through the 12-course Mission Hills complex developed by 'one of China's most astute sports politicians, Dr David Chu, one of China's emerging breed of super rich entrepreneurs' (Gillis, 2008: 65).

However, positioning sports starts as part of the diplomatic initiative, particularly if they are funded by the state, may highlight their debt to the public sector,

' In many countries throughout the world, there now exist full-time sportsmen and sports women whose activities are not funded by paying spectators. They are neither amateur nor professional … but state apparatchiks who exist to bring prestige to their nation and governments. They are products of a sporting étatisme which expects a 'medal return' for its investment, the political benefits of which are clearly located in domestic politics rather than in international relations. (Allison and Monnington in Allison, 2005: 24) **'**

For this reason some business people have controversially suggested that state-funded sports stars, even though they may be national ambassadors, should be obliged to give back to the state in some form to recognize the benefits they have received.

Although there are a number of specialist areas developing that consider specific contributions to public diplomacy efforts, it is important to retain an overall sense of the political motivation to forge relationships with overseas citizen publics. When reading some sources on sport and politics it is possible to detect a greater focus on the relationship between sports/tourism elites and political elites as opposed to those who consume the intangible services of sport (the marketing approach). Practice varies in different cultural contexts, depending on economic resources and political priorities, but in some countries there exist umbrella organizations that cover all activities that operate as public and/or cultural diplomacy, such as The British Council in the UK, which includes sport within its ambit (see www.britishcouncil.org).

Corporations may use sport as a means of **corporate diplomacy**, as a way of enhancing relationships with external groups in areas of strategic business or marketing interest, for example through **corporate hospitality** that can create a space for subtle lobbying. Both public diplomacy and corporate diplomacy are terms that describe a strategic form of PR – where PR action is driven by management policy to prioritize reputation management and embark on 'hearts and minds' campaigns. It is a term that also implies a quasi-diplomatic status for the PR practitioner. PR has been compared to diplomacy, public and cultural diplomacy by a number of scholars who argue that these two types of strategic communication overlap in terms of concepts and practice (Signitzer and Coombs, 1992; L'Etang, 1996, 2009a).

Think Critically

Describe and discuss the key features of three different types of sports culture. If possible, go and observe friends participating in sports you do not play yourself and socialize with them after they have completed their activity. You might want to choose one sporting activity that is completely different to your own sporting activities (climbing or orienteering compared to ball sports), and one that is closer (football compared to rugby). Take observational notes about the way people dress, speak, behave and relate to each other.

Summary

From this survey of some cultural issues in sport, it can be seen that popular elite sports fuel a major global economic activity that is tied in to other sectors, especially travel and tourism. PR is an activity which follows economic activity and economic policies, and is present at all levels: even though it may not be recognized as such, it should be clear that sport is both entertainment (promotion) and politics (diplomacy). PR necessarily supports sports international marketing, although it is not limited to this role, and it is required to engage and communicate with culturally different media, stakeholders, audiences and publics. Key points that have arisen from this chapter include:

- To practice PR in sports business requires a close knowledge of sports business and international business and not just of sports.

- Globalization demands cultural sensitivity, competences and training. PR practitioners specializing in sports need to be able to understand a variety of sporting cultures, organizational and corporate cultures and ethnic and national cultures.
- Sport is used politically for cultural and policy purposes.
- PR is closely linked to cultural and public diplomacy practices since all of these are fundamentally concerned with building relationships and communicative action.
- Sport may be used to repair fractured communities in a variety of international contexts.
- Notions of national identity are central to sport but may be open to interpretation in a globalised world.

Further Reading

Garcia C (2012) Nationalism, identity and fan relationship building in Barcelona Football Club. *International Journal of Sport Communication*, 5 (1): 1–15.

L'Etang J, Falkheimer J and Lugo J (2006) Public relations and tourism: critical reflections and a research agenda. *Public Relations Review*, 33: 68–76.

Merkel U (2008) The politics of sport diplomacy and reunification in divided Korea: one nation, two countries and three flags. *International Review for the Sociology of Sport*, 43: 289–311.

Redeker R (2008) Sport as an opiate of international relations: the myth and illusion of sport as a tool of foreign diplomacy. *Sport in Society: Cultures, Commerce, Media, Politics*, 11 (4): 494–500.

Rowe D (2012) Reflections on communication and sport: on nation and globalization. *Communication & Sport*, 1 (1/2): 18–29.

Rowe D and Gilmour C (2010) Sport, media, and consumption in Asia: a merchandised milieu. *American Behavioral Scientist*, 53 (10): 1530–48.

Sarver Coombs D and Osborne A (2012) A case study of Aston Villa Football Club. *Journal of Public Relations Research*, 24: 201–21.

Tang J and Gregg E (2010) Sports public figures in China: an historical analysis of media images. *International Journal of Sport Communication*, 3 (2): 137–48.

Thibault L (2009) Dr Earle F. Zeigler Lecture Globalization of Sport: an inconvenient truth. *Journal of Sport Management*, 23 (1): 1–20.

Wong L and Trumper R (2002) Global celebrity athletes and nationalism: fútbol, hockey and the representation of nation. *Journal of Sport & Social Issues*, 26 (2): 168–94.

Xifra J (2009) Building sport countries' overseas identity and reputation: a case study of public paradiplomacy. *American Behavioral Scientist*, 53 (4): 504–15.

5

Sports Business and PR

Introduction

This chapter explains the scale, scope and indicates the communication needs of sports business. It explains connections to the sports media complex and the main elements of sports business including ownership, media rights, sponsorship, hospitality, and regulation. The chapter characterizes sports business as driven by networking and opportunism. In defining key structures and disciplines within sports business, it considers the implications of sports business functions and structures for the practice of PR. It suggests that PR may fall between marketing, promotion and media relations. The chapter covers:

- Definition and scope of sports business
- The dynamics and drivers of sports business
- Key features of sports business
- Sport business, converged media and technology
- Entertainment
- Ownership and structures
- Sports marketing
- Brand management
- Sponsorship
- Media rights

Key Concepts

- Commercialization
- Entertainment
- Evaluation
- Hospitality

- Marketization
- Relationship marketing
- Sponsorship
- Sports business

- Sports marketing
- Sports media complex
- Sports property

Definition and Scope of Sports Business

Sports business is the term used to describe commercial activities that aim to make a profit, or create wealth by selling sports events, services, products and **properties** that can generate income through sponsorship. Sports business intersects satellite industries and is a central feature of contemporary economies. Ticket sales are but a single aspect of sports business, and specialist sports marketers seek to maximize value through branding, sponsorship, merchandising, and corporate hospitality that reach a diverse range of customers and stakeholders. The term **sports property** is used in sports business to describe a facet of sports practice that can be sold, for example, sponsorship and media rights. Valuable properties may include individual sports stars, specific single events (as varied as an FA Cup Final or a round-the-world yacht race) or an ongoing tour (Association of Tennis Professionals ATP or Women's Tennis Association WTA in tennis). Such properties undergo extensive brand management and evaluation, so as to maximize their saleable value in a competitive and increasingly crowded market. PR is involved in the **activation** of sponsorships, hospitality and event management, and supporting the branding process through a range of stakeholder communications, media relations, and web management.

Sport has become an investment opportunity, funded through a mixture of private and public – state, national or local government – finance. The focus of sports business is revenue-generation through exploitation of popular elite sport. However, as sports business has developed, so have its practitioners, who have seized upon a much greater variety of sports that can deliver different audiences in various cultures. Sport is a tool for a wide range of non-sports businesses, to enhance relationships with a range of consumer, corporate and business stakeholders. For example, the International Paralympic Committee (IPC), the governing body for Paralympic sport acquired sponsorship revenues from worldwide partners Visa, Ottobock, Samsung and Atos and international partner Allianz (Glendinning, 2012: 15). Likewise, the ATP World Tour (men's tennis), which attracted nearly 4.4 million spectators in 2009 and 2010 in 62 tournaments in 32 countries gained blue-chip partners including Corona Extra, FedEx, Ricoh, South African Airways and Barclays. ATP's Europe CEO Laurent Delanny explained the attraction:

The Tour is unique in the way it combines the consistency and coherence of a global platform with the flexibility to activate locally … we can provide partners with access to all the major territories they want to target. If they want to increase their activity at specific events we can work towards that with the event organisers … partners can leverage the aspects of the ATP World Tour that are most relevant to their business and their brand. The versatility of the ATP means that it can be harnessed by both consumer and B2B brands. It offers both widespread media exposure and top-class hospitality opportunities … [it is] an opportunity for consumer brands to trial their products and services on upscale, engaged fans … Corona and FedEx … view ATP as a valuable partner in helping to develop their businesses outside the US. But for Corona, the appeal of ATP is that it is a lifestyle brand – premium, fun, fresh. For FedEx, which targets a business-to-business audience, the emphasis is on scale, speed, timing and delivery. The beauty of ATP is that it offers so many ways for marketers to express themselves. (Fry, 2011: 52)

These examples show how sport has become central to national and international economies as well as cultures.

Sport is seen as a way of connecting at a deep level with consumers and stakeholders beyond the natural or transitional fan base, and the alignment of non-sporting products and services with sport can highlight key brand values that resonate with groups of importance to an organization. As Ralf Hansman, Head of BMW Sponsorship, pointed out,

The basic appeal of sport marketing still lies in its 'emotional' component and the ability to engage customers emotionally … The first is the image dimension and the issue there is, does it fit? The second is whether the sport connects with the premium car customer group and the third is whether the sport is global enough to give us the reach we need into Europe, American and Asia … after that there is a fourth filter which is a consideration of the possibility of including our core competencies into the sport itself … it is easy to see how that is achieved in motorsport … [but] our other properties work in the same way. Sailing is a naturally high technology environment [which] has allowed us to inject our engineers into the boat building team … Professional golf clothing certainly provides a platform for engaging those who were likely to buy a BMW. (Roberts, 2006i: 14)

The work of sports business is often described and justified by its practitioners as 'making profit from passion'. The term 'passion' is used frequently by sports business practitioners who often describe their relationship to the business as a vocation rather than a career, typical comments being 'not just a job but a passion'; 'I'm a passionate fan'; 'I have a passion for the sport I represent'. The term 'passion' was also employed to communicate and promote their businesses as emotionally involved, for example,

Perfect Motion is passionate about sport and fitness across all levels dealing with the marketing of health issues, active recreation and Olympic performance. (www. perfectmotion.org)

Business creativity combines entrepreneurialism and technological innovation to generate new markets based on relationships forged and deepened through that passion. A good example of entrepreneurship and creativity was the formation of the Superleague Formula in summer 2008, when 'Football branded cars … [competed] in a series designed to win the hearts and minds of football and motor racing fans alike and deliver a significant new audience for broadcasters and sponsors' (*SBI*, 2008c: 50–51).

The Dynamics and Drivers of Sports Business

The dynamics and drivers of sports business are economics and profitability.

' One of the most visible aspects of modern sport is its strong links to commercial enterprise. Stadiums and arenas bear the names of businesses that pay to buy the naming rights to these venues. Commercial sponsors' logos appear on athletes' clothing and equipment, on the facilities in which they play, and in the titles of the events in which they compete. Media companies spend vast sums of money on the rights to broadcast sporting events and advertisers pay to promote their products and services in the commercial break during the screening of these events, cities invest large sums of money, often at the expense of other more important social projects, to stage major sporting events or to attract professional teams to their area. Star athletes are transferred for millions of dollars or pounds and professional sport franchises are sold for sums that are higher than the Gross National Domestic Products of some countries. (Slack, 2004: xxii) '

Sport's role in contemporary cultures has arisen as part of the rise of consumerism, which has been explained in various ways, often drawing on critical theory and neo-Marxist perspectives. PR has been, and continues to be, part of this process, and in the UK the PR industry expanded alongside the development of new consumer products in the 1950s and 1960s that then had to be marketed to virgin markets. Consumers had to be educated about product benefits and subsequently, as competition increased, educated about their choices between competing sets of 'brand values' used to reclassify a mass market. The purchase of particular products and brands subsequently became part of the symbolic expression of an individual's identity and contributed to the emergence of the 'lifestyle' concept. Consequently, it seems that PR contributes to a substantial sociocultural change in the way that sport is perceived, it is no longer a 'playful space' (Featherstone, 2007; 84) but a capitalized industry that demands expansion of products, consumption and markets, and at the same time articulates symbolic communication that speaks to distinctive and self-conscious groupings and individuals. Thus sports business, and its PR and marketing practitioners, have contributed to significant cultural shifts in terms of making available style choices that are perceived as relevant and significant in symbolically marking consumers as part of a particular group, elite or class. For example, polo is an expensive sport associated with international elites and royalty, whereas football has a much more inclusive scope. However, sports do not necessarily map directly on to traditional class structures, but operate a separate field of **distinctions**. This concept and its relevance to PR and sport in society is discussed in the final chapter. PR and advertising operate as **cultural intermediaries** to generate discourses and symbolic communication that communicate relevant meanings for consumer and demographic groupings identified by marketers.

Consumerism changes the relationship between participants and their sport:

' The satisfaction derived from goods relate to their socially structured access in a
zero-sum game in which satisfaction and status depend upon displaying and sus-
taining differences … [There are] different ways in which people use goods in order
to create social bonds or distinctions … [then] there is the question of emotional
pleasures of consumption, the dreams and desires which become celebrated in consumer cultural imagery and particular sites of consumption which variously generate direct bodily excitement and aesthetic pleasures. (Featherstone, 2007: 13)   '

In other words, sport business and the communications around it create and emphasize
brand identities that connote values, emotions, micro-cultures and class that offer consumers choices that assist them in their own identity construction projects. As sport increasingly crosses traditional boundaries, branding becomes a more competitive and complex
affair. For example, sportswear increasingly crosses into fashion and high street styling, and

' As the market for sports apparel becomes more fragmented and more competitive –
with most of the manufacturing taking place in the BRIC countries [Brazil, Russia,
India, China] – the established players are constantly on the look-out to up their
game. (Adler, 2011: 16)   '

Adidas developed a relationship with designer Stella McCartney and she designed the
athletic kit for the London 2012 Olympics and Paralympics. Kit was made commercially
available to fans through supermarkets and tourism organizations. Adidas had plans to
expand into the US and targeted the 14–19-year-old age group, hoping to build lifelong
relationships with this generation (Adler, 2011: 16). Integrated communications, blending
PR and marketing, is central to that process. Overlapping spheres of interests are reflected
in business and organizational scope and structures, for example IMG presents itself as
'Global leader in sports, fashion and media' (www.img.com)

Brands can be extended beyond their primary function. For example NASCAR-branded
car washes were launched to take advantage of NASCAR fans' loyalty using existing facilities but re-branding with emblems, shields and a particular style of customer service under a
20-year agreement for exclusive rights in North America and parts of the Caribbean. Grand
openings were accompanied by driver appearances to garner publicity. Entrepreneur Dan Dyer
sought marketing partners for sublicenses and is aiming for 25 per cent of the market. Car
washes sold NASCAR products and customer service were to be unique, as Dyer explained,

' The people who work there all wear NASCAR uniforms and t-shirts. And if the
customer gets full service, the guys swarm around kind of like a pit crew when they
come out and do everything they do. (Wilner, 2011a: 19)   '

Different sports have varied potential for capitalization depending on participation, cultural resonance, tradition and historical roots, and spectator appeal. Cross-country skiing, for example, has been seen as a northern European sport, and while a staple event
in the Winter Olympics, has been found 'commercially lacking'. The development of a

> ' Season-long World Cup into an integrated product complete with a family of spon-
> sors and impressive growth in TV ratings, has at last brought cross-country into the
> modern era' (Hill, 2012: 18–19). Success of national elite performers has spiked
> interest in Slovenia, Czech Republic, Poland and Switzerland, and there are hopes
> that a German success could act as a tipping point for the sport, especially since
> innovations such as urban races and the 'Tour de Ski' contemplating 'virgin territor-
> ies such as London, Paris and Rome. (Hill, 2012: 18–19) '

In such a competitive environment, communications and advocacy are central.

Over-commercialization?

Even within the sports industry itself, reservations have been expressed about
over-commercialization, for example Eelco van der Nohl of FIFA noted that in
managing the expectations of, and relationships with, the most prestigious corporate
brands who supported the FIFA World Cup in 2006

> ' One of the issues we have is finding the balance between partners' exercising their
> rights and the integrity of the sport. We certainly don't want to turn it into one big
> commercial enterprise. (Roberts, 2006b: 24) '

Commenting on the same issue Shaun Watling, Associate Director, Strategic Sponsorship
at Redmandarins argued that

> ' The biggest … challenge for the industry as a whole is commoditisation … While there
> is no problem with commercializing sport … Commercial relationships are, generally,
> a lot healthier than relationships driven by ego. But commercializing changes all the
> dynamics: with commercialization, rights owners and sponsors owe it to consumers
> to deliver the highest quality of experience. But all too often, what happens is that the
> consumer is considered to be the lowest common denominator, and the consumer
> experience is leveraged and exploited far more than it is enhanced. Generosity of spirit
> tends to be associated with the days of amateur sport, but it's a critical part of success-
> ful commercialisation as well. (*SBI*, 2006b: 54) '

This suggests that sometimes priorities are weighted in favour of the sponsor rather
than the consumer, and also hints at some lack of authenticity. Brian Sims, Manager of
the South African Grand Prix Circuit, put this much more bluntly:

> ' I think that is the way in which sport is being dominated by money. In other words,
> greed! Too many people are taking money out of sport, money that could be used to
> generate better value for sponsors and the paying public. (*SBI*, 2005a: 62) '

This cultural commercial shift has impacted on sport and its elite performers in many
ways, particularly in terms of its professionalization and industrialization – sports stars are
increasingly a product of physiological management and promotional communication,

media trained and image-aware. Sport has risen on the public agenda because it is seen as a powerful form of communication, and that power has been transformed into economic power. Not only do individual consumers enjoy watching the unfolding drama of sporting events, they can identify themselves more closely with their chosen sport by 'buying-in' to products and services that enable them to display their affiliations. Therefore football clubs can make money through the sale of frequently redesigned and very expensive football shirts for adults and children. However, this is a strategy that can backfire, as Adidas discovered in relation to their rugby shirts for the New Zealand All Blacks just as New Zealand hosted the World Cup,

> The All Blacks are one of the most iconic brands in sport and Adidas has paid royally over the years to be their kit suppliers. But the company has pulled a defeat out of the jaws of victory by showing complete disregard for the All Black fans in New Zealand itself. Fans are furious that replica All Blacks jerseys on sale in New Zealand cost significantly more than in other countries if purchased on the internet. Adidas clearly over-estimated elasticity of demand and under-estimated public fury having refused to budge on pricing. The result: the brand has become one of the most unpopular in New Zealand at a time when it should be milking its relationships with the All Blacks for all it's worth. (Roberts, 2011: 7)

Sport's political and socio-economic currency has led to it becoming heavily mediatized. Although the media have always been involved in the advertising and reportage of events, technological change and diversification of media formats means that a complex media market has developed in which media organizations compete for the rights to broadcast events either in real time or for later online delivery. The sports media environment has been described as the **sports media complex** (Rowe, 1999), a term that describes the intertwined nature of 'sporting organizations, media conglomerates, and transnational corporations' (Maguire, 1999, cited in Scherer et al. 2008; Jhally, 1989; Maguire, 1993; Rowe, 1999).

Sport, Converged Media and Technology

The **sports converged media complex** not only comprises the intersections among different forms of media, its dynamic social spaces, specialized forums and blogs, but also the sports business's ongoing entrepreneurial relationship with technological innovations. Communications opportunities and practice continue to change, with increasing levels of live sport consumption across social media, though the proportion varies globally, highest take-ups being China (63 per cent), Russia (46 per cent) and Brazil (43 per cent) (compared to the UK around 25 per cent) (*SBI*, 2012e: 23). Technology continues to offer new modes of engagement that appeal to fans, drawing in other stakeholders and networks and enhancing the revenue-earning potential of social media. The sports business challenge is how to realize commercial value and leverage broadcast rights from social media (Lott, 2012: 8). Sport is a competitive arena for the social media, particularly between YouTube and Facebook. YouTube won a deal to stream all 26 matches of South America's premier international football tournament, the Copa America, and the rights to broadcast the Indian Premier League (IPL) with consequent user gains. Facebook, however, offers more interactivity, for example the Ultimate Fighting Championship computer game (*SBI*, 2011: 20).

Sports business has been fast to capitalize on the opportunities offered by the fact that early adopters of social media were in a lucrative demographic. Consequently, by early 2011, major names were beginning to shift their emphasis to the promotion of their Facebook pages rather than their websites and to use these as a focus for their ticketing campaigns (Ledwith, 2011: 20). In a competitive market, however, new ideas for increased interactivity are needed to engage and retain fans. The GigaPixel FanCam takes a 360-degree image of an event crowd (within which video content, sponsors logos and hyperlinks can be added). When it is uploaded to the Internet it allows fans to tag themselves and link to their Facebook pages and share the photo, a product that has viral potential (Ledwith, 2011: 20). FamCam was used by the 2011 Rugby World Cup, at Real Madrid's Santiago Bernabéu Stadium, and in 2012 to the English Football League by Sports Entertainment Intelligence who hold the UK licence for FamCam and whose London director explained,

> It is a platform for really integrated brand messaging. When you have people's attention for six minutes there is a lot you can do to create dialogue including competitions and discussions and creating links to a host of brand websites. There is a fundamental move towards the use of technology and social media and one of the key drivers for social media engagement is to allow people to share their experiences right here and now. FamCam does precisely that. (Roberts, 2012b: 13)

Integration, fluidity and flexibility are essential to maximize converged media opportunities but require investment in time and resources. A siloed approach to social media is too rigid with the flexible media on offer. Sports Event Denmark (SED) used a 'mash up' combination of Twitter, cross-platform provider Chatroll, Facebook and Flickr to engage audiences in the Professional Windsurfers Association Cold Hawaii World Windsurfing event, a much more complex communications campaign than the simple use of Facebook they had employed in promoting Challenge Copenhagen, an Ironman triathlon (*SBI*, 2012b: 20).

The company PlayUp specializes in mobile-based sports/social gaming apps. Its downloadable free app PlayUp provides statistical data in real time during match play and a platform for fans to interact with, either publicly or with subgroups in 'private rooms' (Evans, 2011: 19). One revenue stream is generated from the development of the same principle in which premium paid-for content gains access to more intimate superior discussions including athletes and celebrities; a second stream, built on the first, consists of advertising and sponsorship that can be attracted once there is a sufficient membership (Evans, 2011: 19).

But it is not just sports business that can benefit financially from converged media, sport starts can also take control of their digital assets by monetizing their social media followings (Harman, 2012: 21). Cloozup is a tool that integrates athlete content produced via social media offering enhanced information via an athlete's Cloozup personal page that can double-up as their website, and where advertising space can be offered to sponsors. Co-founder and former Dutch international footballer, Ruud Gillit, explained,

❝ From their Cloozup accounts athletes can manage all of their activity from one site. They can push content to Facebook and Twitter and this content will drive traffic back to Cloozup, creating a space where we can develop a deeper relationship between athletes and fans … For those athletes that don't share the popularity of footballers it is a good opportunity to earn a bit more money and expand their social media presence i.e. a skier or a volleyball player. (Harman, 2012: 21)   ❞

Nevertheless, converged media is not all burgeoning positivity and interactivity can cut both ways, as demonstrated in the vignette beneath.

McDonald's

McDonald's had held sponsorship with the Olympics since 1976 and this was renewed in 2012 until 2020. The company decided to invite its customers to tweet their customer experiences, expecting positive messaging in the build-up to the Games. Their hopes were dashed by a stream of pithy negativity that was publicly visible and available for escalation via re-tweets. Open communication channels such as Twitter cannot be edited and can easily spiral, not least for their entertainment value, which was added to in this case by various comedians. The campaign acquired notoriety as 'McFail'.

A number of concepts and principles are illustrated in this case. McDonald's ongoing issue analysis should have shown that the obesity crisis, marketing to children and environmentalism were ongoing challenges for their business. Public opinion polling (as opposed to consumer research) would have picked up the extent of this problem and the potential threat to reputation. Positive association with the Olympics could not outweigh reputational challenges that arise from the nature of the core business. In fact reverse damage was possible.

A strategic approach to communication would have been monitoring these broader trends in relation to the company's ethical and CSR principles before and considering from all points of view how the initial tweet might be seen and how the company could realistically respond to negative comments, prior to the post.

The nature and form of communication also matters. As media guru Marshall McLuhan pointed out many years ago, 'The medium is the message'. In this case Twitter is open, informal synoptic communication and establishes expectations with regard to conversational responses in that setting. Consequently, 'Attempting to quell the onslaught with sanitized corporate messaging only adds fuel to the fire, incites further negativity and exacerbates the problem' according to Scott Minto, Director of the Sports Business Program at San Diego State University.

In short, companies should be careful what they wish for. If they invite dialogue they must be prepared for a range of responses, some of which will be embarrassing or negative. Dialogic forums raise expectations about the communication relationship as to the form of subsequent communication, so retreating to a safe position and attempting to communicate from behind the corporate veil will only exacerbate the existing problem.

Source: Wilner B (2012) McFlurry of abuse. *SBI*, 176: 17.

The flows of capital and power intermingle through processes of cultural intermediation that opportunistically enhance and combine these elements with sporting talent to enhance its desirability and potential for further commodification and financial exploitation, on a trajectory that ranges from the local to the global in the quest for revenue streams and business growth. However, as Scherer et al. pointed out, 'there is a danger in simply viewing the media sports cultural complex as one of seamless economic synergy and untrammeled affinity between interest groups' (Scherer et al., 2008: 49).

> **Think Critically**
>
> In the light of this incident, consider how you would develop a communications strategy for McDonald's to build towards Rio and a renewed contract.

Research into the relationships between the New Zealand Rugby Union, media conglomerate News Corporation, and transnational corporate partners, especially the main sponsor, Adidas (Scherer et al).

Communications was central to 'the complexities and uneven power relations between the NZRU, Adidas, and News Corporation: the interest groups that exemplify the media sports cultural complex within New Zealand'. There were contested strategies regarding the national game, for example, a former coach John Hart argued for a commercial model to structure the game's future, prioritizing the needs of sponsors so that the sport would be 'Driven by the marketing imperatives and neo-liberal philosophies of these businessmen, the commodification of the game and players who have emerged as junior brand managers.' Rugby administrators from New Zealand, South Africa and Australia collaborated to construct a Southern Hemisphere rugby organization that became aligned with Murdoch's News Corporation and warded off the threat of a Kerry Packer-backed initiative to gain control over leading players and the international game. Relationships were shaped by organizational commercial and political power in the context of global financial ambition that essentially changed a game deeply embedded in New Zealand's cultural heritage and a central part of its national identity. Its marketing globalized a sports product that at points risked alienation from at least some of its supporters, who could no longer access international games on state broadcast television, but had to pay for the privilege. In this case cultural intermediaries took a sport and reproduced it into a new form with loudly

(Continued)

(Continued)

articulated 'brand values' to enhance its saleability and global meaning but this led to tensions at the national level.

Source: Scherer et al., 2008

Key Features of Sports Business

In the remainder of this chapter key functional and structural features of sports business are briefly sketched, providing a range of definitions illustrated with examples and giving linkages to PR in the following areas:

1 Entertainment
2 Ownership and structures
3 Sports marketing
4 Brand management
5 Sponsorship
6 Media rights

1. Entertainment

Sports business practitioners identify their competitors as those supplying leisure goods and services including technology, music, and gaming. Retaining market share for sport is a concern on the sports business agenda as well as for sports administrators.

❛ IOC President Jacques Rogge ... gives voice to a concern, shared by many world sports leaders, that the very future of sport is on the line because too many youngsters are getting their kicks ... from the PC and games console rather than the playing field. The fear is that a generation will emerge which may watch a bit of sport on TV and play sports-based computer games, but will never shed a drop of sweat or dirty a knee in pursuit of a ball or just the boy or girl ahead of them. Rogge fears for the health of this generation and its successors. He worries that if the sports habit is lost now, it is unlikely to simply skip a generation and will be gone forever. (Roberts, 2008e: 7) ❜

The connection between sport business to the entertainment business is strong, but the constant comparison to the traditional entertainment industry was criticised by the then editor of *SBI*,

❛ The most over-used phrases to appear on the pages of *Sports Business* would certainly be ... '*Sport is big business. Sport is now part of the entertainment business. Sport is the ultimate theatre*'. Sport is essentially unlike other forms of entertainment because it is all too often, not particularly entertaining ... [but] dull and repetitive ... you never know exactly what you are going to get ... fans are prepared to put up with the tedium because they understand ... [the] broader context ... we love the unpredictability

[that] every sports week is unique [that] we may be watching history being made ... sport is not theatre. Theatre demands a script. (Roberts, 2006a: 5)   **'**

Sports business competes with other sectors for sponsorship, as Kevin Roberts, editorial director of *SBI* pointed out,

' This may be a period of opportunity which will shape the future of sports consumption and revenue patterns ... If sport gets it right, there's every chance that a far greater share of the world's marketing communications budgets will be spent on sports properties, and that even niche sports will thrive as a commercial bridge between sponsor brands and highly targeted audiences. (Roberts, 2006a: 5)   **'**

The implication of this is that sport has to continue to commodify itself and present new and exciting opportunities with which business people can align their products and services. One example of **brand extension** in relation to sport is the growth of video games and **fantasy sports** which might be regarded as competitors, especially in relation to the younger generation (where the issue of fitness and obesity is high on the agenda) but which are attractive to business because they are a growth industry that also incorporates **product placement** opportunities (Wilner, 2011b: 16). The very definition of 'sport' is being renegotiated. For example Marc Ganis, president of Chicago-based consultancy company SportsCrp, claimed that,

' Another 'sport' that has huge potential is on-line poker if the US government alters the law and allows it ... a number of major companies are poised to exploit that sport is they receive the green light from the feds. (Wilner, 2011b: 16)   **'**

Boundaries between sport and other forms of entertainment have blurred, for example big sports events may be preceded by music or dance acts. Some organizations marry sport and other forms of entertainment. A prime example of this would be ESPN Inc. that not only pioneered the X Games in 1993 but extended ownership over the whole media event so that ESPN created, marketed, promoted, staged and broadcast the Games (Pedersen et al., 2007: 26). The blurred boundaries can also offer sport business creative opportunities, for example in gaming. (Harman, 2011: 17)

2. Ownership and Structures

'Professional sports utilize different ownership and governance models in order to regulate and manage their businesses effectively' (Hoye et al., 2006: 61). Sports business practitioners may work in-house in specialist firms that deliver sports products or services; for professional sports clubs or leagues; for publicly funded government sports associations; for regulatory or legal bodies; for diverse national or international specialist sports

> ### Discuss!
>
> What PR issues arise from associations with betting and online gaming? How might lobbying and public affairs be employed?

associations such as those that exist in the UK for sports including angling, archery, association football (several associations), athletics, ballooning, basketball, biathlon, boccia, boxing, canoeing, cricket, croquet, cycling, darts, equestrian (several associations), Gaelic football, gliding, golf (several associations), gymnastics, horse racing, ice hockey, ju jitsu, kendo, luge, microlight, motorsport, mountaineering, netball, orienteering, parachuting, pétanque, polo, pool, rugby league (several associations), rugby union (several associations), tennis, triathlon, weightlifting, wheelchair sports, and wrestling.

The agency structure is a major feature of sports business. These vary in terms of the range of services that are offered, as Ben Nicholas, IMG's senior vice-president UK and new media sales pointed out,

> ' An agency with many departments can offer legal, accounting, international and new media expertise with production built-in. Most importantly, it can offer creativity. (cited in Sherlock, 2006: 42) '

As in PR, there are some outstanding major players who dominate the market, for example IMG which positions itself as encompassing sport, entertainment and media (www.imgworld.com) and which claims it is 'the most powerful sports and entertainment agency in the world' (*BritSport* 09: 102) and whose portfolio includes strategic planning and evaluation, sponsorship activation, international brand management, exploration of emerging markets, Olympic consulting, and rights negotiation as well as mass events such as the Sony Ericsson Run to the Beat (www.runtothebeat.co.uk), Etape Caledonia (www.etapecaledonia.co.uk) and the Stockholm Triathlon (www.stockholm.triathlon.org).

Agency mergers, acquisitions and re-branding are common as managers seek greater effective and return on investment (ROI) for their clients. Agencies continue to survive for the same reason that PR agencies survive: services can be bought in when needed, and they can offer an 'outside perspective'. According to Miriam Sherlock, then deputy editor of *SBI*,

> ' Agencies remain critical to the business of sports TV and … they will continue to grow. If anything their role will expand and become more important because of the increasing complexity of the TV marketplace. With the redistribution of audiences and content in this multi-channel world, come multiple commercial opportunities that agencies are in a unique position to help rights holders maximise. (Sherlock, 2006: 42) '

Agencies face challenges, however, as Philipp Grothe, joint CEO Kentari agency pointed out,

> ' Even for the best agencies, margins are shrinking, so you need to come up with really good reasons to keep clients. In our business the average length of a contract is let's say three years. That means that on average, an agency is renegotiating a third of its portfolio of rights every year – that is a lot of work. And you need new business if you are to grow. That means you have to come up with 40 per cent to 50 per cent of new entrants each year. If you stop either having creative ideas or a strong business model, you are going to be out of the market within two or three years. The

growth rate of the sports business and the pace of change mean that an agency has to reinvent itself every six months. (cited in Sherlock, 2006: 44) **,**

There are clearly major opportunities for those with education or experience in PR because communications is central to sports business at all levels. However, PR as a specialist named area does not seem to have great prominence in sports business, tending to be subsumed into sports marketing or brand management or simply as media relations and publicity, as is discussed in the final chapter of this book.

Agency Services

Agencies offer a range of distinct particular services: advertising, PR and sales promotion; general sports specialist consultancy (integrated communications, education programme development, research, seminar and conference organization, licensing, brand positioning, IT infrastructures for events, graphics, event bidding and management); design, licensing and branding; capital projects (architects, construction and engineering, service and equipment providers including property and cost consultancy), ticketing, smart cards (linked to hospitality, ID and security); events (conferences, exhibitions and venues, event management and corporate hospitality, security); leisure (facilities, fitness and training which also lists non-agency organizations such as national sports centres); media (statistical data and information suppliers, media owners, new media, website design, media training); professional services (athlete management, financial services and accountants, insurance and risk management, lawyers, management consultants); properties (rights holders, export support from UK trade and investment, destination marketing and promotion); sports television (distribution and syndicators, production companies, service and equipment providers such as stadia and support services to maximize revenue or the manufacture of synthetic sport surfaces); travel and tourism (logistics, air, coach and rail, tourist boards).

Sources: *SportBusiness Marketplace: the global sports services directory* (2010, 2011 and 2012); *BritSport 09: the definitive sports industry guide.*

---

3. Sports Marketing

Sports marketing has been defined as the 'application of marketing principles and processes to spot products and to the marketing of nonsports products through association with sport' (Shank, 2002: 2). Marketing is based on consumer research that provides sociological and psychological understanding; buyer behaviour; an understanding of market segmentation and positioning; branding; promotion and distribution. Sports marketing as an academic area has tended to be functional and somewhat conservative, based on the notion of 'exchange' between buyer/consumer (spectators, participants, sponsors) and seller/producer, and applying the standard 'marketing mix' comprising of the key elements of product, price, promotion and distribution to sports products and services (Shank, 2002: 30–31). A simple definition of key exchanges is given below, but as Shank points out, sports exchanges are multiple, overlapping and complex,

❛ Sports spectators exchange their time, money and personal energy with sports teams in exchange for the entertainment and enjoyment of watching the contest. Sports participants exchange their time, energy, and money for the joy of sport and the better quality of life that participating in sport brings. In sponsorships, organizations exchange money or products for the right to associate with a sporting event, player, team, or other sports entity. (Shank, 2002: 31–32) ❜

Yet there are exchanges between spectators and owners; spectators and licensed product vendors; venue owners and governing bodies; media and governing bodies; product sponsors and team owners (Shank, 2002: 32). The emergence of **relationship marketing** emphasizes that 'exchange' is based on interpersonal and inter-organizational relationships, and this approach overlaps with PR, particularly the relational approach.

4. Brand Management

Branding is the process of combining concepts, language and design to create a distinct brand identity and associated values that is authentic and clearly differentiates a product or organization from its competitors by bestowing a fictive but credible 'personality'. Key features that contribute to the brand and its marketplace effectiveness – **brand equity** – are quality, brand awareness, brand associations and brand loyalty. Major companies that have benefited from their sports sponsorship include Vodafone and Samsung.

PR contributes to brand management by helping to align brand images with brand and organizational realities; by promoting brands through integrated communications and promotional activities; and by generating reputational capital for a brand, as well as defending a brand, for example, at times of crisis. Furthermore, PR may be involved in re-branding or re-positioning a sport, as in the case of yachting where efforts have been made to establish,

❛ An acceptable distance from its overwhelming association with wealth and prestige, partly because many of its stars are neither wealthy nor privileged … racing attracts brands from sectors from finance and business consulting to auto manufacturing, fashion and retailing. (Roberts, 2005: 62) ❜

Brands can dominate a sport's image, for example the Ironman brand that markets distance triathlon events is iconic, and even though events of the same length are run by other organisations, they cannot be described as Ironman events.

5. Sponsorship

The essence of sport sponsorship is the establishment of an alignment between qualities associated with a product or service and a sporting skillset, event or elite. A virtuous circle can reinforce the core values associated with the sporting and non-sporting elements of the partnership in a mutually beneficial way that enhances the positioning of both elements in their respective markets. The relationship between sponsorship and branding strategies is key:

❛ We see more commercial messages than ever before but most of the time we don't believe them or are so fatigued by them we block them out. Brands … need to engage with us then demonstrate how they will improve or enhance our busy lives. This is where sponsorship comes in because it is all about the brand in action. A good sponsorship gives brands multiple opportunities to connect with consumers. This shift in attitudes to sponsorship has had far-reaching implications for agencies and consultancies. From the perspective of media and ad agencies, it has forced them to take sponsorship seriously as a discipline rather than viewing it as a poor relation. (Fry, 2008a: 16)

Creative and imaginative sponsorship strategies can also be aspirational in making a clear statement about the direction, vision and wish-images (desired identity) of the commercial backer of the sport concerned.

All England Tennis Club Wimbledon Tennis Tournament

Wimbledon is an interesting case in terms of sponsor relations because it has 'official suppliers' rather than sponsors, which connotes a more regal presence (Roberts, 2006g: 16–17). Of those suppliers Slazenger has been involved with the event for more than a century and Robinsons (barley water) for more than three-quarters of a century (Roberts, 2006g: 16–17). Rolex is one of only two brand names visible on court (the other is IBM on the speed gun). These restrictions mean that new ways have to found to deliver commercial opportunities for suppliers while 'keeping the brand as pure as possible' (Ian Ritchie cited in Roberts, 2006g: 16–17).

The All England Lawn Tennis Club (AELTC) CEO, Ian Ritchie, offered his reflections on the Wimbledon brand on his appointment,

> The first thing that comes to mind is the tradition ... grass is very important ... we are differentiated ... Having started in 1877, it is a great thing to have the history and tradition. Second is style. By that I don't simply mean stylish as a tennis championships but as an event as a whole. The third element is quality in everything about the event and the way it is run ... These are the elements that shriek at you but I think that they have to be seen alongside innovation ... We have tradition but we are not living in the past ... [We seek] really significant relationships. ... because we are a long-term player, not a public company with short-term pressure from shareholders – even though we want to deliver a decent surplus to the LTA for the development of British tennis. (Roberts, 2006g: 16–17)

One interesting trend has been for sponsors to take more control by creating their own events, such as the Prism UK Brand activation company which helped both Land Rover to establish their G4 Challenge and Standard Chartered their Greatest Race on Earth (a team event marathon series) located in key territories (Nairobi, Singapore, Mumbai and Hong Kong) (Smith, 2006c: 20). According to one commentator,

> With a degree of saturation in the sponsorship market, especially among the major sports, potential sponsors will inevitably turn their attention to creating their own events … [which] can open up some very strong lines of communication with consumers. (Smith, 2006c: 20)

One example was the month-long Land Rover G4 Challenge involved the use of the 4×4 in-between cycling, climbing and kayaking because,

> We want our customers to understand what the Land Rover brand is all about; we want them to associate Land Rover with the adventure that can be realized with our vehicles. We want the event to create, deliver and inspire adventure … an event that would be an extreme test for man and machine. There is not an event in existence that combines the elements we required to deliver against our objectives – therefore, we created our own. By having control of each element of the Challenge we can ensure it is a true reflection of what the Land Rover brand stands for. (Smith, 2006c: 20)

6. Media Rights

Sports media rights form part of a broadcaster's brand identity and therefore central to PR and marketing practitioners working for broadcast media. The business discipline of media rights is based upon the sale and purchase of rights to view in various technological formats. It includes media law, intellectual property (IP) and copyright (including trademarks). Digital technologies have thrown up new challenges for the control and policing of intellectual property rights and raise fundamental questions regarding the flow of information in society, democracy and freedom. 'Issues of power and control are at the heart of understanding contemporary struggles between governments, regulators, trade bodies, media corporations and consumers of media content' (Haynes, 2005: 5).

Media rights are central to the creative and cultural industries in terms of economic outputs and the generation of wealth, yet it can be argued that the expansion of intellectual property systems privileges the rights and profits of global media corporations while erecting barriers to entry for innovators and thus limiting wider cultural innovation (Haynes, 2005: 9–11).

Deals are complex and the principle of sale of rights has diversified into image rights and stadium-naming rights. Legal specialists have extended their expertise into image rights which, in the era of celebrity recognize,

> The increasing power of sports personality in the marketing mix … helping athletes to establish, protect and realise the value of their personal image rights, an area which has grown tremendously … as awareness of IP rights grew and the concept of 'athletes as brands' developed. (SBI, 2006d: 24)

Piracy has considerable implications for the regulation of the industry in order to protect capital investments and also exclusivity and reputation. PR specialisms of public affairs and lobbying to protect industry interests would be very relevant in this context.

The growth of Internet piracy has risen up the agenda because, unchecked, it could lead to falling investment in stadia, facilities and grass roots sport, as one Premier League spokesperson pointed out,

> The ability of rights-holders to monetise content is critical to investment models that have seen sport flourish over recent years … There does need to be some education of the public … this is something governments and other agencies should share responsibility in. (McCullagh, 2009a: 18)

Sports law is a specialist area that deals with issues such as match-fixing – an issue that has often arisen in the first place via a **media sting operation,** as in the case of the Pakistan cricket team and snooker's John Higgins in 2010, with consequential reputational fallout (Domingues, 2010: 73). In addition to these high-profile cases,

> Sports as diverse as greyhound racing and lawn bowls have also been forced into a very public debate about their relationship with the betting industry and how they protect the integrity of their competitors. (Domingues, 2010: 73)

Media rights are not solely commercial but are of interest politically in terms of access to national sports for citizens. The government's interest and motivation in this case will be a form of public diplomacy, and they may intervene in the economy in order to obtain a favourable outcome for themselves and the wider population, which may have a negative impact on the commercial gain to be made, as in the case of the Indian Government, which in 2006,

> Forc[ed] all broadcasters to share coverage of major sports events with the state-run broadcaster … It leaves sports channels facing an uncertain future and looks set to force down rights fees for key events, notably those involving the Indian cricket team. (*SBI*, 2006b: 10)

The global picture is diverse and the Asian TV rights market has some distinctive features that depress its commercial value: lack of competition in terrestrial free-to-air broadcasting; monopoly players in India (Doordarshan), China (CCTV) and Vietnam (VTV); collusion between networks to control rights inflation (Korea and Japan); and inefficiency of Asian PayTV due to piracy and poverty (Fry, 2008: 30). Exceptions are the positive impact of cricket on Indian PayTV where competition has been fierce for a decade, and which has benefited the International Cricket Council and the Board of Control for Cricket in India 'which has rapidly emerged as one of the richest rights-owning federations in the world' (Fry, 2008b: 30).

Technological developments have revolutionized media and continue to have a dramatic impact on sports business, in terms of multiplying media rights opportunities, but also in terms of developing innovative products and services such as fantasy sports, iPod podcasts and interactive services through digital platforms.

Sports Entrepreneurship and Financial Capital

The top twelve sports investors and entrepreneurs according to SBI are:

Larry Ellison, worth $39.5 billion, co-founder and CEO of Oracle, leading enterprise software company, USA-funded Oracle Racing, the sailing syndicate formed to compete for the 2003 America's Cup.

Mukesh Ambani, India, worth $27 billion, inherited Reliance Industries from his father and bought the Indian Premier League (IPL) franchise the Mumbai Indians in 2008 for $113 million. He entered a collaborative 50:50 partnership with global sports marketing company IMG in December 2010.

Sheikh Mansour Bin Zayed Al-Nahyan, Abu Dhabi, worth $20 billion, invested more than £1 billion in Manchester City and is planning a training complex costing in the region of £100 million. He is Chairman of the International Petroleum Investment Company which acts as investor for the Abu Dhabi government.

Mikhail Prokhorov, Russia, worth $18 billion was the first non-American to own a NBA franchise and also challenged Vladimir Putin in Russia's presidential race.

Roman Abramovich, Russia, worth $13.4 billion took over English Premier League's Chelsea club in 2003, and triggered a sharp rise in transfer fees.

Paul Allen, USA, worth $13 billion. The co-founder of Microsoft bought NBA's Portland Trail Blazers in 1988 for $70 million, now worth in excess of $350 million, and bought NFL franchise the Seattle Seahawks in 1997 for $194 million, worth $900 million a decade or so later.

Ernesto Bertarelli, Switzerland, worth $10 billion, inherited biotech firm Serono and funded the yachting syndicate Team Alinghi in 2000, winning the America's Cup in 2003.

Silvio Berlusconi, worth $7.8 billion is majority shareholder of broadcaster Mediaset, and has been owner of AC Milan since 1985.

Suleiman Kerimov, Russia, worth $7.8 billion, an oil tycoon who bought FC Anzhi Makhachkala in 2011 attracting a number of high-profile footballers. His other investments include a club stadium, hotels and a football training centre that is part of a $1.5 billion project on the Caspian Sea.

Philip Anschutz, USA worth $7.5 billion. The Anschutz entertainment Group (AEG) is the sports and entertainment division of privately owned Anschutz Corporation and owns sports venues worldwide.

Xu Jiayin, China, worth $7.2 billion, owns Evergrande Real Estate Group which has injected funds into Guangzhou FC who became Chinese Super League Champions. In 2011 Xu came to an agreement with Real Madrid to build China's largest football academy in Guangzhou.

Micky Arison, USA, worth $5.9 billion, took over the cruise empire Carnival from his father. He owns NBA franchise the Miami Heat.

Source: *SBI*, 2012k: 31–5.

Summary

This chapter has provided a tour d'horizon of the sports business industry and identified the key elements that intersect with PR work. The key points are:

- Sport is a vehicle for income generation, investments and venture capital
- In sport business sponsors, investors and shareholders are the most important stakeholders
- Sports business seeks to commodify sports and sports practitioners for commercial gain
- PR supports sports business through networking, business-to-business relationship-building, publicity and promotion, media relations, branding, and integrated communications (with marketing)
- The boundaries between marketing and PR in sports business appear blurred
- PR does not have a high profile as a specialist strategic discipline within sports business: it tends to be seen more as media relations. However, those with public relations education/experience have many opportunities in sports business – it may, however, be sensible for them to rebrand themselves as 'sports communication' specialists as this is more likely to encompass strategic scope and skill levels

Further Reading

Clement A (2011) Intellectual property and the media: an examination of copyright, trademark, and right of publicity in sport. *International Journal of Sport Communication*, 4 (1): 82–98.

Garcia C (2011) Real Madrid football club: applying a relationship-management model to a sport organization in Spain. *International Journal of Sport Communication*, 4 (3): 284–99.

Whiteside E, Hardin M and Ash E (2011) Good for society or good for business? Division I sports information directors' attitudes toward the commercialization of sports. *International Journal of Sport Communication*, 4 (4): 473–91.

Williams J and Chinn S (2010) Meeting relationship-marketing goals through social media: a conceptual model for sport marketers. *International Journal of Sport Communication*, 3 (4): 422–37.

Pichot L and Tribou G (2008) Scholarly commentary: Sport sponsorship, internal communications, and human resource management: an exploratory assessment of potential future research. *International Journal of Sport Communication*, 1 (4) unpaginated.

6

Sports Spectacle, Mega Events and PR

Introduction

This chapter aims to explain strategic intention and promotional imperatives in event management, highlighting their ideological aspects and connections to nationalism and propaganda. It explores concepts and promotional communication around events drawing on insights from events management literature, sport, media and cultural studies. The chapter covers:

- PR and event management: functional perspectives
- Mega-events, sports spectacle and media events
- PR, sport and politics
- Evaluation, impacts and legacy

Key Concepts

- Bids
- Critical incidents
- Event management
- Legacy planning
- Media events

- Mega-events
- Pseudo-event
- Side effects
- Spectacle
- Triangulation

Event Management

Event management is a specialist field of management that designs, oversees and implements all the processes, people and logistics required to create, plan, market, brand,

and evaluate an event in liaison with multiple stakeholders, sponsors and communities. Events take place at a specific time and place and are culturally grounded, for example linked to heritage and tradition, even though they may be international in scope. Opening and closing ceremonies perform significant symbolic moments for cultural diplomacy and intercultural communication. Events intersect sports business, and the leisure and tourism industries entwined with corporate hospitality and largely mediated mass entertainment. The events business intersects with a wide range of other businesses (construction/equipment) in its role as co-ordinator and commissioner of what is known as **event overlay** – equipment and temporary structures.

Events take place in a globalized world, and while they are partly a driver of globalization and deliver to globalized expectations in terms of entertainment and standards of service delivery, they may also be seen as efforts to distinguish cultural and geographical locations and identities that resist globalization. Thus events are enigmatic and contested sites of cultural interchange. They may also be used as functional micro-political 'policy tools' to promote cultural development, assuage social tensions and to foster inter-group understanding (Salem, Jones and Morgan, 2004, cited in Yeoman et al: 17). They may be motivated by desire for prestige, branding opportunities, media publicity, business and social development. However, their sociocultural significance goes beyond their strategic goals and can deliver multiple readings. For example Tony Bennett (1988) drew on Foucault to describe the emergence of an **exhibitionary complex** in the nineteenth century that employed,

' Organized spectacle as a device for building a **public culture** of conformity and consent … By identifying with the generosity and numificence of the state, the people take it upon themselves to administer policing roles, in respect of emotional restraint in national obedience and groups identity, that were formally the reserve of the public bureaucracy. Pride in the event therefore becomes a branch of **moral regulation**, no different in principle from schooling or policing. Thus, exhibition spaces operate finally to reinforce social hierarchy and *engineer consent*. (Rojek, 2013: 107; author's italics) '

The language used here is particularly interesting for those in PR, since *Engineering consent* was the title of an essay in an article published in 1955 by the US publicist and self-styled 'PR Counsel' Edward Bernays (double nephew of Sigmund Freud). 'Engineering consent' connotes rather precisely the sort of image of behind-the-scenes manipulation that has plagued PR practice for decades. Indeed, it was this that led many first-generation PR academics to seek theoretical frameworks and concepts that could justify the practice morally.

From an historical point of view, the emergence of international expositions or expos in the mid-nineteenth century were not only the production of public culture but also acted as 'a business opportunity for entrepreneurs and a means of expressing civic pride and boosting the local economy through tourism' (Rojek, 2013: 107). PR practitioners were part of that story, organizing exhibitions and establishing commercial and personal relationships.

Events are constructed symbolic festivals, corporate and political playthings, that are for those who can afford it,

> ❛A status symbol, both for super-rich individuals who have acquired a taste for football clubs, motor-racing teams and thoroughbred stables, and for governments who see hosting sport's leading events as sign of their national virility and position in the global pecking order … it drives a multi-billion dollar global media, marketing, events and real estate business. (Roberts, 2009a: 7)❜

Events are central to PR practice, since PR activity both creates and responds to events (some of which may be **critical incidents** or crises). All events have effects, some planned, some unintended (**side effects**) and action triggers reactions, immediate, short and longer term. **Critical incidents** are those that are significant moments that mark a shift in relationships or orientation of subtle, but notable, balance of power. However, critical incidents may not be fully recognized for their significance at the point of occurrence, it is only retrospectively that their historical importance may be understood. On the other hand, crises are obvious and require immediate attention. Therefore we need to distinguish between planned and unplanned events. Planned events, which may be planned specifically as media events, are strategic and driven by institutional or policy logics and intentions. For example, they may be devised with the aim of forming or enhancing communities, conflict resolution and peacemaking or as a distraction from political or economic problems. In this way they act as symbolic constructions intended to communicate messages, values, even behavioural change. For example the 2012 Olympics was suffused with **discourses** around the event as a stimulus for mass citizen participation in sport as the key intended legacy of the Games. A year after the Games it was proving hard to evaluate and quantify the uptake of participating citizens and British Olympic amabassadors were instead claiming a positive impact in 'how we see ourselves'. Thus events may be **rhetorical** and sites of struggles for **legitimacy**, authority or power (over **regulation** for example) or **jurisdiction** (for example between various different versions of some sports such as taekwondo, some of which have higher status than others). Events are therefore not just about practical logistics but deeper meanings concerning cultural practices, conventions, values, rites and rituals.

Events take actual place at a particular time and in a particular place, in other words, they are **bounded spatially** and **temporally**. This makes them ideal as **case studies** that can be researched using multiple methods, exploring a variety of alternative perspectives from different actors in the event (the technical term for this is **triangulation**). It may help to think of an example or two:

- Nike is not in itself an event or suitable topic for case study research; Nike pulling sponsorship from Lance Armstrong is an event suitable for case study research;
- global media sports events are a category of events but London 2012 was a particular event or case study.

However, events 'take place' through multiple media platforms in varied global locations and viewed not just in 'live time' but retrospectively. They are also created and viewed not only through media constructions by salaried journalists but through eyewitness images (YouTube) and accounts. Events can therefore be described as **decentred** (Volkmer cited in Anstead and McLoughlin, 2011: 1341) and **event time** 'stretched',

❝ The one-off interruption to routine brought by an international sporting tournament is extended over a number of weeks. During and after the tournament, footage of the matches is available to watch in real time at convenient, asynchronous moments. The tournament's spatial distribution is temporally uneven, inevitably: some audiences will witness games live, others in 'real-time' delayed broadcasts, others through abbreviated highlights packages on television or online. Spectators in stadiums with large media screens will witness replays within the game time. Online audiences may read about the latest game before then watching the highlights. Tournaments depend on a temporal oscillation: most games are engaged with through routine, everyday media rituals; 'big' games involve audiences interrupting or reorganizing their daily routines to 'make time' and 'make space' to watch the game. (Anstead and O'Loughlin, 2011: 1342) ❞

PR and Event Management: Functional Perspectives

Event management blends a number of management disciplines including PR, and require considerable investment in both strategic and micro-management. There are several key phases for event management and PR (according to Yeoman et al 2004) (see below):

- the emergence of the idea and interested parties – conceptualization, imaginization, fantasy, excitement;
- formalization – politics, policy formulation, mission, vision and short-, medium- and long-term objectives networking and evaluation strategies, lobbying, persuasion, creative concepts, feasibility studies and schedules;
- decision to bid – stakeholder and relationship management, networking, community relations, issue management, impact assessments and legacy considerations, pro/anti lobby groups – for example there may be arguments over the benefits such as controversies that occurred over the opportunity costs of the Major League's Baseball's Tampa Bay Rays proposal to construct a facility on the St Petersburg waterfront which led to extensive public and media discourse regarding notions of the public good (Mondello et al., 2009);
- bid process – event concept and themes, pitching in political and economic contexts, sponsorship and branding strategies, scheduling, corporate hospitality;
- event preparation – sites, building, hardware, transport, risk assessment, crisis planning, contingency planning, financial control, IT/communications, crowd management, security, environmental impact, waste management, ticketing, signage, marketing and merchandizing (Salem et al 2004);
- event delivery – issue management, media relations;
- evaluation against short-, medium- and long-term objectives – event evaluation will focus to some degree on effectiveness and operational delivery as well as policy objectives (for example London 2012 specifically identified mass participation in sports) but evaluation should include short-, medium- and long-term evaluation of stakeholders and relationships and reputation (evaluation should include political and economic objectives such as public diplomacy and societal goals defined by power elites).

PR needs to be embedded into event management at all levels and at the outset because of the multiple stakeholder relationships and potential reputational impacts. Events offer opportunities for PR work because they lie between 'populism and the market' (Rojek, 2013: 109). Events comprise many practical products and services that need to be integrated into a single timetable: logistical and project management skills are central to event delivery since time is finite. There are many aspects of event delivery that can cause PR problems, for example sliding schedules, contracting processes, and business ethics might become a matter for public debate and reputational threat. Throughout the whole process, PR is a central part of expectation management and the reputational risks of hosting an event are considerable. For example, Ghana was criticised for its hosting of the 2008 African Cup of Nations because of its 'chaotic accommodation, ticketing and accreditation arrangements' and it is thought that the country will struggle to utilize the four new stadia in Accra, Kumasi, Sekondi and Tamale. 'Economists have questioned the wisdom of staging the tournament in such poor countries … and point to Burkino Faso and Mali who hosted the 1998 and 2002 tournaments' (Sannie, 2008: 31).

Bidding is both a national and international political process in which the PR process of lobbying is central. The specialized nature of this work means that some build their careers purely as event-bidders and never stay to see their event realized.

The Bid Professionals

Those bidding for events are becoming sophisticated specialists though many do not stay to work at the event itself but move on nomadically. This category of workers are always in the advance guard:

> [They] have built significant businesses around the bidding process. They are the consultants who help cities and nations to create a bid rationale against their specific objectives and develop and implement bidding strategies. It is a sector of the business which has grown significantly in the last 15 years, both in size and sophistication. Today's bids in sport are akin to major political campaigns, involving the same sophisticated research, evaluation, lobbying and communications techniques. It is a highly specialist area which continues to evolve in line with the changing bidding environment, ambitious clients and available communication technologies. (Roberts, 2012d: 39)

The Event Junkies

The group of workers who travel the world from one sports championship to the next one are often described as event junkies … [many volunteers] interviewed [after Sydney] claimed it to be the most exciting and fulfilling thing they'd done. (Roberts, 2006f: 45)

> It gets into their blood and their social and personal lives can become entwined with the events they work on and the people they work with ... you do have to have a particular mind-set. In many ways it can be like an international club. Mary Keegan, Project Director for event specialists Rushmans. (Roberts, 2006f: 45)

Mega Events, Sports Spectacle and Media Events

The notion of **performance** is also central to sports spectacle and has become embedded in the notion of elite sport conducted for entertainment – performance sport. Sports psychologists have to counsel some athletes on performance anxiety. Performance is linked to ideas of artistry and creativity (Conquergood, 2002 cited in Madison and Hamera, 2006: xii) and one of the attractive aspects of spectatorship can be watching the accomplished making the difficult look smooth and easy. Watching an athlete under-perform or perform badly can be deeply uncomfortable, although for those who support the opponent there can be the element of *Schadenfreude* (pleasure from the discomfort of others).

Researchers from various disciplines have sought to define and explain mega-events and media-events (Dayan and Katz, 1994; Scannell, 1996; Marriott, 2007). Mega-events can be defined as events that are touchstones which individuals (ordinary citizens in everyday life) may use as structural tools in making sense of their own lives but which also have greater significance culturally and politically, such as expos and the Olympics. In his detailed examination of these phenomena, Roche defines mega-events as

> Large-scale cultural (including commercial and sporting) events which have a dramatic character, mass popular appeal and international significance. They are typically organized by variable combinations of national governmental and international non-governmental organizations and thus can be said to be important elements in 'official' versions of public culture. (Roche, 2000: 1)

Mega-events are a tool, used by governments, both to promote nation-states and to forge a sense of national identity in an international arena. Such events may be part of a broader strategy to reposition a nation not just within the international political and economic classes, but with their citizens as part of a public diplomacy initiative and **inter-mestic** communications, a term created by international relations specialists to explain international, politically inspired communication targeted at overseas domestic citizens.

Events offer communication power through rhetorical and performative constructions whose underlying ideological values may be obscured by idealistic expressions. Sport is political in itself and intersects politics because it is a source of communication power.

> ❝ Sport itself operates in an inherently political environment. Its very foundations are based upon structures which require institutions to be elected to various positions of power and influence from local to global level. Those at the top have significant, perhaps even enormous influence, and like any other politician their journey to the summit has turned on promises, pledges, deals, bargains, compromises and cop-outs … Think about the way that sports governing bodies present the opportunity for nations and cities to host their major events. Sure there's lots of vitally important stuff about social and economic legacy but one of the clinchers is the role that sport plays in nation-branding … simply being selected as a host of a major event … lends the host status and legitimacy … that's why people worry about the potential of hosts using their associations to airbrush out domestic issues such as human-rights abuses, corruption and inequality. (Roberts, 2012a: 7) ❞

One example of mega events which are clearly public rituals are the opening and closing ceremonies of Olympic Games, described by some as 'kitsch' (Bale and Christenson: 11). These ceremonies promote Olympism as a sacred ideology that can transcend barriers, thus contributing a sense of solidarity and community, achieved through an emotional and symbolic ritual display (Bale and Christensen op cit). These ceremonies are somewhat akin to a postmodern pagan festival, fusing local mythologies in a dramatic construction combining magical and unexpected formations and smaller events to cultivate an atmosphere conducive to a solemn mysticism designed to encourage meditative reflection on Olympic ideals. There are also predictable elements that reassure: the lighting of the torch, the parade of athletes, the cliché-ridden and boring speeches by Olympic administrators and local politicians. **Atmospherics** is an important part of event management and well understood by event managers, entertainers, politicians and propagandists alike, for example the Nazi rallies at Nuremberg, party political rallies, and pop stars.

Attempts to create other events off the back of the Olympics concept can be seen in the creation of Paralympics, Special Olympics, Transplant Games and the Gay Games, although these can also be read as political acts that promote inclusiveness and diversity. All of these have worked to create and celebrate identities in an international context and reinforce their legitimacy and capabilities.

However, despite the social imperatives, these newer events are both aspirational in marketing terms and viewed as market potential. Suzi Williams, group marketing and brand director of BT explained,

> ❝ The Paralympics have travelled an incredibly long distance in a very short period of time. The courage of these athletes has really inspired us, but by coming in to sponsor the Paralympics there was courage shown by BT as a business too. BT believes the power of communications helps make a better world and the Paralympics make that tangible in a world in a world where it is quite hard to find anything else that does that quite so well. ('Summer of two halves' *SBI*, 2012c: 14) ❞

In other words, the Paralympics opens up a new market and highlights 'courage' as a characteristic for the BT brand. However, this is not in itself uncontroversial. Common descriptions of Paralympians and other disabled sports people frequently emphasize their courage and, by so doing, treat them as different and 'other' than able-bodied athletes.

Mega-events are status events serving many political and economic ends at different levels. Despite the aura of glamour, mega-events still need to be sold to host communities, implying the need for PR to manage issues and work with communities to discuss and resolve social responsibilities, as Roche points out:

> Mega-events typically tend to be produced and imposed by urban elites who nonetheless need to attract the support of local citizens to legitimate, attend, work on, and help pay for them. (Roche, 2000: 157)

Indeed, the significance and meaning of mega-events may well be challenged, as was shown by analysis of the 2007 Pan American Games held in Rio, which positioned 'investment in sporting infrastructure and the success of athletes as a response to long-standing issues of violence, crime and inequality' through 'a neo-liberal development policy of speculation, construction and privatization' to achieve economic liberalization (Darnell, 2012: 873).

This example illustrates the behind the scenes cultural intermediation of PR activity that shapes expectations through dominant discourses that also get replicated in professional media and dominate the public sphere. There was dissent, but it was that of a few activists whose contribution to debate may well be framed as marginal.

Rising Like the Phoenix after Losing a Bid

Event bidding has become a publicity strategy for international positioning, and bid failure simply part of city PR.

- Manchester failed to win bids for the Olympic Games in 1992, 1996, and 2000 but won the 2002 Commonwealth Game bid.
- Madrid failed to win bids for the Olympic Games in 2012 and 2016 but subsequently integrated its national and regional policies in order to bid for the 2020 Olympics.
- Istanbul failed to win the bid for the Olympics in 2008 but its new stadium meant that it won the UEFA Champions League final in 2005.
- Chicago failed to win the 2016 Olympic bid but benefited from its job creation scheme.

Source: Evans 2012b: 27.

The term **media-events** emerged directly from media studies (Scannell, 1996; Marriott, 2007) and refers to the mediated version of mega events including a range of sporting and cultural events, although it goes beyond such pre-planned activities to include unscheduled events such as natural disasters, war, and major acts of terrorism such as 9/11. Media events are broadcast live, are international and globalized, sufficiently spectacular and dramatic that they are a focus not only for stakeholder or policy agendas, but which involve and mobilize viewers into social commentators, thus transforming them from 'mass' to 'public' or even to 'crowd'. From a purely functional perspective media events may also be PR crises or rhetorical opportunities for **primary definition**. Important concepts in analysing media events are the notions of **spectacle**, **ritual analysis**, **framing**, **eye-witness**, **documentary**, **audience research**, and **media effects**. Events are part of cultural heritage, identity and country branding and an opportunity to explore a culture's mores, values and self-understanding through its self-conscious self-presentation and media interpretations of official promotion. For example, opening and closing ceremonies are televised live but pre-event secrecy and hype means that broadcast media are necessarily dependent on media briefings into which positive self-congratulatory messages may be inserted and subsequently reproduced.

PR and Pseudo-events

PR work is inextricably linked to the notion of events in popular culture and in some nation-states, such as the US, this arises from the fact that early PR work was dominated by publicists focused on gaining media attention. Within the then Institute of PR (IPR) UK in the 1950s there was often debate about whether events organized by practitioners were in 'good taste' and fears for the respectability of the occupation. Sociologist Daniel Boorstin conceptualized those fears in the early 1960s in his term 'pseudo-events' – events created specifically to attract media attention – and later media sociologists have built on this critique to argue that 'the professionals of PR have become the image-builders, manipulators and event manufacturers' (McNair, 1996: 51). Debord's pessimistic (and somewhat existentially inspired) critical political and cultural theory, popular in the 1960s, continues to provide justification for concerns regarding authenticity,

> ' The whole life of those societies in which modern conditions of production prevail presents itself as an immense accumulation of spectacles ... All that was once lived directly has become mere representation ... reality unfolds in a new generality as a pseudo-world apart, solely as an object of contemplation ... The spectacle appears at once as a society itself, as a part of society and as a means of unification ... The spectacle is not a collection of images; rather it is a social relationship between people that is mediated by images. (Debord, 1994: 12) '

Within the Olympic context, it is worth reflecting on the nature of the Olympic torch relay which, while it has on occasions provided an opportunity and focus for public and media debate about human rights and civil liberties, can also be seen as a rather anodyne pseudo-event. Spaaij and Burleson (2012: 906) note that the decision to focus the London 2012 torch relay domestically was supposedly 'inspired to bring the torch to people's doorsteps ... but could be seen as a missed opportunity for promoting peaceful internationalism ... [or to] open ... up spaces for global participation and dialogue'. Although the torch relay filled broadcast space, and certainly provided a vehicle for people to feel involved, it is questionable as to whether much of the UK coverage met news values. Spectators invited to comment on the event frequently commented that 'it is a wonderful opportunity' (especially where children were involved) but apart from appearing on the media the nature of 'the opportunity' was not very clear. The torch relay could be seen as an artificial and constructed media event created for PR purposes in order to generate some coverage that appeared to meet public participation and engagement objectives. This contrasted with the Beijing torch relay, which was the focus of political dissent drawing attention to Chinese policy in Tibet.

As with much else surrounding Olympic ideology and hype, the torch relay is intended idealistically to promote a form of intercultural humanism. However, depending on the geopolitical location it may offer opportunities for the expression of alternative perspectives, including of the Olympics itself. Such protests may be marginalized as political activism or anti-globalization (especially where protestors have the temerity to challenge the Olympic movement). Nevertheless, some argue that such conflicts open up spaces for debate,

> ' Although at first glance the anti-Olympics movement may be seen to disrupt rather than promote the IOC's aim of advancing peaceful coexistence, in reality the movement plays a vital role in fostering global dialogue and communicating alternative forms of knowledge and action, including in relation to questions of what a more peaceful and ethical world should look like and how it can best be achieved. The anti-Olympics movement has reinvigorated transnational activist networks and has led to a strengthening of transnational communities of resistance. The Olympic Games thus provide a global platform for both advocates and opponents to voice their ideas and concerns regarding the promotion or erosion of peace and human rights. (Spaaij, 2012: 766) '

PR, Sport and Politics

Sport is embedded with political systems worldwide because of its cultural significance and meaning, which means it can become an important 'carrier' for ideological meanings. Thus sport has long been used by regimes to communicate national values, to unify populations and win support for political regimes. For example, the Olympics are a **mega-event** used by governments for political ends, even though the Olympic movement's ideological aim is 'to use non-discriminatory sport to educate the world's young people in the values of peace and justice ("fair play") mutual

understanding and international friendship' (Roche, 2000: 195), ideals rather consonant with PR ideology. Probably most famous example of the political appropriation
of the Olympics of these has been the 1936 Berlin Olympics. The Berlin mega-event
served functional ends achieved through

> Mass pageantry and festivity … the organisers … were concerned with fashioning a
> persuasive image of Nazi Germany and projecting it as much as possible in concur-
> rence with the internationally sanctioned image of the Olympic festival … [they] …
> apparently succeeded in their aim to make of the event a vehicle for the image of a
> powerful but peace-loving Germany. But this image was a mask. (Byrne, 1997, cited
> in Roche, 2000: 18–19).

At this distance it could be possible to underestimate the lasting impact of the 1936
Olympics, not solely because of the careful impression management orchestrated by
Hitler and Goebbels but because of the paradigmatic film made by Leni Riefenstahl,
Olympiad. Previous Olympics had not produced anything more than 'scrappy newsreel'
(including the Los Angeles Games where geographical location might have stimulated
some interest from Hollywood) (Salkeld, 1997: 4). Reifenstahl's promotional film was
technically artistically innovative (underwater cameras, slow motion, travelling cranes,
hydrogen balloons, catapult camera) and she always saw it as an opportunity to show

> The drama and ritual significance of the Games … the modern Games would be
> linked to their Greek origins … she would film the Olympic flame being lit and
> carried on its long path to the Games – the first time this had become part of the
> Olympic ritual. (Salkeld, 1997: 8, cited in L'Etang, 2006)

Reifenstahl's focus on human endeavour, tension and drama produced a glorious sports
film which, however, cannot be separated either from the regime from which it sprang,
or from the other film for which she is most remembered, and never forgiven, *Triumph
of the Will*.

Other Olympics that have been used explicitly to promote regimes include the
Games held in Mexico City (1968), Moscow (1980) and Seoul (1988). The Olympics
have also been arenas for political confrontation, for example, during the Cold War
or for rehabilitation (Italy, Japan, Gemany) (Maguire: 1993: 53). Olympic hosts (and
politicians) use the Olympics as a major promotion for their nation, as public diplomacy
and to generate national unity and pride in a campaign to celebrate national values and
identity. The 'feelgood factor' is often employed as politicians navigate their way around
ideological arguments regarding state versus private funding of major events, as the following example from France illustrates,

> Listen to Jean-Luc Rigaut, Mayor of Annecy, France's choice to bid for the 2018 Winter
> Olympics and you could be convinced that the benefits to his town of the Games are
> so self-evident that voters are pleading with him to invest their money in the project.

Yet, when pressed, Rigaut was simply not able to articulate economic rationale beyond the somewhat nebulous benefits of feelgood community spirit and the chance to explore the wonderful harmony between sport and nature. (Savage, 2009: 46) ❯

Politics and indeed terrorism have famously invaded the international sporting arena in protests over apartheid in South Africa, the murder of Israeli athletes at the Munich Olympics in 1972, and the British Tory Government's attempted boycott of the Moscow Olympics. In the run-up to the London Olympics 2012 and coinciding with the thirtieth anniversary of the Falklands War between the UK and Argentina, the coach of the Argentine hockey team, Fernando Zylberberg, released a video apparently filmed secretly, that showed him 'running and exercising in the Falklands' capital Port Stanley'. Described by the BBC as 'a political advert' the video ended with the catchline 'To compete on English soil we train on Argentine soil' (BBC News, 2012). Somewhat naively, the UK defence secretary Philip Hammond was quoted by the BBC as saying, 'I … think it's a breach of one of the fundamental principles of the Olympics: that politics is set aside, that nobody should exploit the Olympic logo, the Olympic message, for political purposes.' It is precisely around such critiques that PR is enacted, often in crisis mode, and yet the issues will have been developing over a period of time.

The examples discussed in this section show how sport is politically implicated, often motivated and financed to communicate internationally on behalf of nations, politicians and the corporate class. From a Marxist perspective, sport is the opium of alienated workers whose labour underpins the expansion of international capital.

This critique of mechanistic approaches to sport and its endless commodification highlight the ideological role that is necessarily performed by communicators in normalizing specific practices of sport business in contemporary promotional culture.

Olympic Ideals Tarnished?

Edelman PR were awarded the communications contract for Live City, Vancouver's celebration sites for the 2010 Winter Olympics. Outreach included extensive use of social media. There was an extensive legacy programme focused on environmental, social and economic opportunities. All went well until the eve of the Games when Professor Christopher Shaw published a critical analysis of the Olympics, Vancouver's decision to host and its evaluation methodology. Furthermore he alleged IOC profiteering and argued that discourses of peace, harmony and unity were used to inhibit the civil liberties of those who wished to question the Olympic movement. He singled out PR as the root of misleading communication about stakeholders whereas various business, government and NGO organizations were privileged above the local community. Shaw

(Continued)

(Continued)

added his voice to those of earlier critical analysts who have questioned claims of the 'economic multiplier effect'. A number of activists in a loose coalition, the Olympic Resistance Network (ORN) endeavoured to counter official sources that dominated media frames.

Shaw was subjected to institutional pressure, and interviewed by plainclothes officers from the Integrated Security Unit, an Olympic operation led by the Royal Canadian Mounted Police.

Source: Rojek, 2013: 83–8.

This case goes some way to illustrating the connection between power, ideology, language and PR.

Evaluation, Impacts and Legacy

Sports business shares many of the ideals concerning the social and economic benefits of events and there are regular specialized events (Barbados in 2008 and Vancouver in 2009) focusing on legacy at which the positive impacts of a major event are highlighted. For example, Peter Mann, Chairman PMP Legacy summed up the Legacy Lives conference as follows:

> ' We can continue to look to legacy to help deliver many tangible and intangible benefits for those cities that take up the challenges of bidding and staging a major event – elevating the city's profile and status on the world; unifying the city and region around a common purpose; accelerating the pace of change; promoting collaborative working between organizations that hitherto did not even communicate with each other; building confidence in our disenfranchised communities and empowering them to be involved and of course, delivering benefits across a broad canvas that goes way beyond sport and culture. (*SBI*, 2008a: 46) '

The concept of legacy has become central to events, bidding, hosting and to sports business. In many ways it has become a pious hope or ambition that is employed rhetorically in order to deliver the opportunity to generate economic capital. The dominance of this discourse means that other questions, such as why not invest the money to be spent on events directly on the social and economic problems they are supposed to contribute towards, do not necessarily get asked or given the same depth of consideration. The events cycle has become an inevitable cultural punctuation. Sports circuses circulate in infinite combinations and cycles as consumptive combustion for economic growth, but also produce environmental impacts. In a sense legacy has become a form of corporate social responsibility that is integral to large sports events and a moral justification for the expense entailed in their hosting. However, the promises and claims have been subject to scrutiny, highlighting methodological challenges in monitoring and evaluating legacy in international contexts and deeper problematics such as the power balance between donors and recipients of international aid (Kay, 2012: 888). In fact these moral problems are in fact very similar to issues in corporate social responsibility programmes in which rhetorical claims made by corporate donors have a tendency to univocality and tend to dominate discourse (L'Etang, 1994, 1996) Kay (2012), building on Coalter (2006, 2007, 2009, 2010a, b) goes further in suggesting that the very monitoring and evaluation (M + E) processes themselves reinforce those inequalities,

‘ Despite the rhetoric of 'partnership' that surrounds sport in development and Olympic legacy programmes, M + E systems play a major role in constructing the donor–recipient relationship as hierarchical. M + E procedures are shaped by funders' information requirements, emphasize external accountability, limit local programme learning, compromise data quality and impose burdensome forms of data collection and reporting that undermine relationships. (Kay, 2012: 888)   ’

Such findings have major implications for PR practice and the sorts of grand claims that may be made at many stages of event management. If PR is about advocacy then it needs to be sure that it can supply sufficient evidence that will stand the scrutiny of the legally and morally inclined critic, or risk being condemned for flackery.

Evaluation, impacts and legacy are linked terms that connote varied motivations, aspirations and ideals. Evaluation is a managerialist term imbued with accountancy values and language such as 'metrics', often focusing on the issue of economic benefits of events, a contentious field. While evaluation is initiated by the sponsors of events (public and/or private) the idea of impacts is somewhat more dispassionate, since it acknowledges positive and negative impacts and the inevitable **side effects**. Legacy on the other hand is a somewhat pious term, presented to the public as a gift, whereas the reality is that events are hugely expensive and often subsidized by the public purse. Thus language is used as a cloaking device to obscure the real beneficiaries. The complexity and multiple variables of economic costs and benefits allows many claims to be made, but

‘ One of the difficulties of accurately quantifying the economic impact of a sporting event is that the indirect benefits, and costs, are often difficult to identify and owing to the lack of a standardized measurement model, the criteria for analyzing economic impact is often inconsistent from one case to another. (*SBI*, 2013b: 69)   ’

For example, a 2005 PricewaterhouseCoopers study sponsored by the UK government in 2005 predicted that the 2012 Olympics would boost the UK's gross domestic product (GDP) by £1.9 billion between 2005–2016. However, Lloyds Banking Group, one of the partner's of London 2012 and therefore with insider interest, predicted £16.5 billion between 2012–2017 (*SBI*, 2013b:70).

In advance of the Games, the London Mayor Boris Johnson highlighted what he saw as the key features of the 2012 Games legacy:

' We are using the Games to generate other long-term benefits across the whole capital, including employment and training, participation in sport and promoting volunteering. The Games have prompted unprecedented investment in homes, jobs, parkland, venues, infrastructure, and transport in east London, which is vital to London's continued growth and competitiveness, and will be the basis of a much wider burst of activity in the area. Our long-term plans for the Olympic park have been carefully made, ensuring that the mix of housing, employment space, parkland and sports facilities is matched to London's needs. London is already a leading global centre for financial services, media, education and much more. Our ambition is quite simply for London to be the Digital Capital of Europe. The real boost to London's economy will be seen over a period of 20 years or more as London's improved global profile, and our investment in infrastructure pays off. The precise sale and timing of this is impossible to predict, but we do know that the Games are already generating a benefit to London's economy. (SBI, 2012a: 78–9) '

There are a number of things to note in this quote. The emphasis in volunteering linked to the Conservative Party's much lauded, but ill-defined 'Big Society' (possibly inspired by communitarian ideals). The claims for economic benefit were conveniently far into the future, and long after any of those in power could be held accountable.

London's ambitions in with regard to legacy were inevitably set against the historical backdrop of Barcelona's contested and controversial transformation, Athens's apparent failure (unused, derelict facilities), Sydney's slow growth, and Beijing's fading structures (Roberts, 2012b: 81), but one major societal legacy was that of substantially increased surveillance.

Sports event legacies are usually articulated in terms of societal benefits. London's legacy was supposed to be that of a healthy-fitness orientated society, particularly centred on children and teenagers who would, it was hoped, be inspired to take up physical challenges that would turn them into healthy disciplined citizens. However, disciplinary societal tendencies were state-sponsored in the form of security measures that included

' The deployment of more troops than the war in Afghanistan, unmanned drones, surface-to-air missile systems, a thousand armed US diplomatic and FBI agents within an Olympic zone divided from the rest of London by an 11 mile, £80 million 5000 volt electric fence, a new range of scanners, biometric ID cards, number plate and facial recognition CCTV systems, disease tracking surveillance and checkpoints. (Graham, 2010, 2012 cited in Rojek, 2013: viii) '

Although values of openness, dialogue and engagement are frequently highlighted as important values in PR, issues and crisis management functions at major events are necessarily implicated in a rather different form of communications agency. Increased surveillance is a consequence and perhaps an unintended side effect.

Bid narratives, and the PR efforts that accompany them, have to incorporate not only the facilities, infrastructure and environmental policies but their narratives of 'what the Games can do for the communities that will welcome them' (Walmsley, 2011: 34). Key stakeholders and beneficiaries have to be identified and the levels and extent of change and contribution specified. However, sports business commentators acknowledge that,

❛ Success in the field of social impact is still about outputs rather than outcomes – about hosts' ability to deliver programmes aimed at creating community benefits rather than the demonstration of clear linkages between individual events and long-term improvements in health, skills, self-image. There is a clear consensus in the field that social impacts are difficult, time-consuming and expensive to measure, and subject to a range of influences wide enough to make causality hard to establish with the degree of certainty required. (Walmsley, 2011: 34) ❜

Think Critically

Develop a legacy proposal for a bid in a medium-sized city with which you are familiar, identifying the key stakeholders, beneficiaries and the rationale for your choice. What sorts of event would be suitable for your chosen city and why? What rhetorical strategies would you deploy and why?

Discuss!

Does Olympism offer unique ideals for humanity? What can Olympism deliver? How are Olympism ideas different to moral values that can be found elsewhere in spiritual, religious or moral philosophical writings? Has Olympism simply re-branded pre-existing ideals? And finally, how do the proclaimed ideals of Olympism square with the apparent yielding to commercial gain and profiteering?

Summary

This chapter has argued for the integration of PR practice and concepts into event management practice and highlights the significance of PR in public culture, heritage and politics. It suggests that bid professionals encompass public relations within their skill sets and shows how all phases of event management require reputation and expectation management dealing with a range of stakeholders. Finally, attention has been drawn to the rhetorical politics of legacy and the importance of evaluation supported by research.

Further Reading

Carey M, Mason D and Misener L (2011) Social responsibility and the competitive bid process for major sporting events. *Journal of Sport & Social Issues*, 35 (3): 246–63.

Sze J (2009) Sports and environmental justice: 'Games' of race, place, nostalgia, and power in neoliberal New York City. *Journal of Sport & Social Issues*, 33 (2): 111–29.

Giulianotti R (2009) Security governance and sport mega-events: toward an interdisciplinary research agenda. *Journal of Sport & Social Issues*, 34 (1): 49–61.

Hautbois C, Parent MM and Séguin B (2012) How to bid for major sporting events? A stakeholder analysis of the 2018 Olympic Winter Games French bid. *Sport Management Review*, 15: 263–75.

Matheson CM (2010) Legacy planning, regeneration and events: the Glasgow 2014 Commonwealth Games. *Local Economy*, 25 (1): 10–23.

Matheson CM and Finkel R (2013) Sex trafficking and the Vancouver Winter Olympic Games: perceptions and preventative measures. *Tourism Management*, 36: 613–28.

Misenor L (2012) A media frames analysis of the legacy discourse for the 2010 Winter Paralympic Games. *Communication & Sport*: 1–23

Real M (2013) Reflections on communication and sport: on spectacle and mega-events. *Communication & Sport*, 1 (1/2): 30–42.

Lee H-S and Cho C-H (2008) Mega events, fear, and risk: terrorism at the Olympic Games. *Journal of Sport Management*, 22 (4): 451–69.

7

Promoting Sport for Social Goals

Introduction

This chapter introduces the concept of social PR and discusses the ways in which sport is used for social goals. It describes the role of PR and sports business in promoting sport for peace, development, and health and the implicit and explicit ideological implications of their role. It explains how sport is used internationally for development and peacemaking, and to promote healthful living and the role of PR work in such contexts. PR has rhetorical and relational roles in such work. Practitioners and academics from sport and health promotion suggested that sport should be promoted specifically to combat growing levels of obesity and sedentary living. Claims have been made that major sporting events such as the Olympics have a positive impact on participation and the rhetoric and legitimacy of such claims is sometimes contested. Sport and physical activity are incorporated into health campaigns but there are difficulties in reaching some demographic groups, some of which are under-represented in sports media.

The chapter covers:

- Social PR
- Sport for Peace
- Olympism: ideology and rhetoric
- Sport for Development
- Sport for Health

Key Concepts

- Development
- Economic colonialism
- Empowerment
- Health promotion
- Lifestyle

- Media imperialism
- Participatory communication
- Social marketing
- Social PR

Sport as a Driver of Change

Because sport is both international and a part of every day life it shapes relationships at every level: diplomatic, cultural, economic, organizational, community, and inter-personal. Sport has come to the fore as an international, national, and regional communication tool, and as an arm of public and cultural diplomacy. There are ambitious global initiatives as is apparent from initiatives such as the Sport & Peace Conferences (www.peace-sport,org) and the Homeless World Cup (www.homelessworldcup.org). There are historical and contemporary links between Olympism and peacemaking reinforced by Jacques Rogge, the President of the International Olympic Committee (IOC), when he confirmed that 'building a peaceful and better world through sport, practised without discrimination of any kind and in the Olympic spirit' (Spaaj, 2012: 761, 765).

Sport has been increasingly depicted as a key driver of sociocultural, economic, and political change and the following quotes illustrate how sport is seen as a societal intervention that can achieve policy goals, mend political and religious rifts and improve health.

Sport as Societal Improvement

'The power of sport is far more than symbolic. You are the engines of economic growth. You are a force for gender equality. You can bring youth and others in from the margins, strengthening the social fabric. You can promote communication and help heal divisions between people, communities and entire nations. You can set an example of fair play.' (Louise Frechette, UN Deputy Secretary General at the World's Sports Forum in 2000 cited in Coalter, 2007: 68)

'In Qatar our leaders believe that sport is the best possible tool for building society and that it is our best ambassador, both internally and worldwide.' (Secretary General of the Qatar Olympic Committee QOC Sheikh Saoud Bin Abdulrahmin Al-Thani)

'Today, [sport] is at the heart of global development and education programmes, it helps provide a focus for disaffected youth, it is the catalyst for regeneration and construction projects and is at the heart of just about every health-programme world-wide.' (*SBI* Editor Kevin Roberts, 2009a: 7)

'Turkey is in a good place just now and its Olympic narrative [for the 2020 bid] is sure to be strong. With a fast-growing economy, a young population and a relatively sophisticated infrastructure in some professional sports, the country is likely to appeal to IOC members with an eye for taking the Games to new territories. Equally important is the symbolism of Istanbul itself, the city where east and west meet. At a time of continued underlying tension between the Muslim and non-Muslim worlds, it appears ideally placed to represent the power of the Olympic Games as a unifying global force.' (Roberts, 2011: 7)

Think Critically

To what extent has sport contributed to societal improvement in your community/region/nation? How have communications contributed to any initiatives? What obstacles or resistance have been faced (and why)? What more could have been done (and why)? Which key stakeholders should be brought together to address issues and why? What negative side effects have arisen and to what extent have they been articulated in the public sphere?

Ingrid Beutler, from the United Nations Officer on Sport for Development and Peace, stated that 'Sport, as an international language, can build bridges between people, help overcome cultural differences and spread an atmosphere of tolerance' (Beutler, 2008: 359) and then went on to explain how the idea of sport as a tool for development and peace became institutionalized at the UN,

> Since the appointment of the first Special Adviser to the United Nations Secretary-General on Sport for Development and Peace in 2001, the United Nations has promoted sport as a cost-effective tool to accelerate the achievement of the Millennium Development Goals and to promote peace. It has been proved that the systematic and coherent use of sport can make an important contribution to public health; universal education; gender equality; poverty reduction; prevention of HIV and AIDS and other diseases; environmental sustainability as well as peace-building and conflict resolution. (Beutler, 2008: 359)

In her article, Beutler explained how physical activity had been used as therapy for trauma by humanitarian aid workers for many years and how ideas had developed within the UN, initially from concepts around child rights. A UN Task Force co-ordinated a range of agencies to formulate a strategic plan and international programme. The PR technique that was chosen to launch the new direction was the International Year of Sport and Physical Education in 2005 which,

'Sought to emphasize the role of sport and physical education as additional tools to assist in the overall efforts to achieve the MDGs, economic and social development, improve public health and peace at the national and global levels (Beutler, 2008: 361). A Special Adviser was appointed as a gatekeeper and conduit into the UN. This function represents the UN at global sports events and acts as an advocate and a facilitator. In fact the role of the Special Adviser can be seen as that of PR, since the role includes the promotion of understanding and support for sport as a tool for development and peace and to encourage dialogue, collaboration and partnerships around sport for development and peace between actors from different sectors of society and within the UN system. (Beutler, 2008: 364)'

The UN Special Adviser's Role

- Raise awareness about the role of sport as a cost-efficient tool in the attainment of development and peace objectives amongst all stakeholders, including sports organizations, athletes, multilateral organizations, governments, bilateral development agencies, non-governmental organizations (NGOs), the private sector and sports industry, research institutions, the armed forces and the media.

- Encourage the regular use of sport to address education, health and development issues and to increase understanding, peace and tolerance within and between communities.

- Support systematic, co-ordinated and coherent approaches to using sport as a tool to address locally identified needs.

- Develop networks and foster international co-operation and co-ordination to ensure the inclusion of sport on development agendas and the inclusion of a social development perspective on sports agendas worldwide.

- Ensure due attention is accorded to cultural and traditional dimensions, respect upheld for the principles of human rights – especially youth and child rights – human diversity, gender equality, social insertion and environmental sustainability.

- Advocate for the continued assessment of progress achieved and difficulties encountered in promoting the use of sport as a development tool through research, monitoring, and evaluation.

Source: Beutler, 2008: 364.

A Call to Action in 2005 directed attention to a group of priority stakeholders: sports organizations, athletes, multilateral organizations, bilateral development agencies, governments at all levels, armed forces, NGOs, research institutes, and the private sector, especially the sports industry. In addition the media were identified as crucial and the Call argued for 'editorial strategies that ensure the coverage of social and political aspects of sport; train journalists; and raise awareness of the possibilities of sport for development and peace' (Beutler, 2008: 368).

> **Think Critically**
>
> Critically evaluate the mandate of the Special Adviser and specify the elements that are central to PR practice.

Thus it can be seen that the idea for sport for peace and development emerged from within international bureaucratic organizations as a consequence of grass roots experiences in areas of conflict. The formalization of the idea into programmes and the creation of special posts to take forward these ideas progressed the idea of sport for social ends as a social movement. The involvement of sports business provides additional resources and offers business opportunities for CSR.

Social PR

The concept of social marketing has flourished since the 1980s and is used to describe initiatives that employ marketing techniques but for social (often health) rather than commercial ends. Social marketing approaches are used in health campaigns across the world, for example in anti-smoking (such as the successful Australian campaign for plain packaging) and safe-sex campaigns. Curiously, there has been no complementary development in PR, yet reflection on this term has the potential to redirect our thinking about PR towards a rather different type of instrumentalism. Rather than the traditional and dominant models that focus on organizational interests, and argue that the ethical practice of PR resides in the marketplace of ideas and the court of public opinion, the concept presented here of social PR repositions the function as possessing the potential to serve societal goals, possibly through the interventions of a variety of societal agents and stakeholders. By focusing on multiple rhetorical efforts and discursive formations, this approach to PR links it more clearly with the theories and concepts of social movements. The UN programmes relating to Sport for Peace and Development (SPD) are an outcome of, and a stimulus for, an emerging social movement. Social movements are relevant to sport and sports business in terms of PR and reputational issues, for example in relation to environmentalism and sustainability, alcohol, tobacco.

Social PR can be conceived of as those interventions that employ PR concepts and techniques to create discursive spaces where issues and social goals can be debated to produce deliberative social goals. As with social marketing, however, this is not a panacea. Social marketing has sometimes been criticised because it has focused on rational choice approaches and failed to acknowledge sufficiently where health problems may be the consequence of social inequities. Social marketing has been influenced by its parent discipline in terms of quantitative approaches and tendency to individualize problems, failing to take account of the broader context, and has sometimes also failed to take sufficient account of ethnic and micro-cultures. In some contexts social marketing has been over-focused on technique, rather than political, economic and sociocultural contexts, historical chains and inheritance, strategic and policy intentions and societal side effects, in short, the bigger picture. Likewise, PR also needs to straddle understanding, relationships and intrinsic and extrinsic linkages and connections between the small-scale and the large-scale.

Despite these issues, considering PR as a form of social action is in my view beneficial, and certainly more honest than the retreat behind organizational skirts. Acknowledging and assessing societal impacts is in any case long overdue and under-researched. Social PR links the practice explicitly to advocacy, activism and social movements (as mentioned above), it highlights the necessity to ensure that the occupation is transparent, subject to societal inquiry and employed in societal interests. Of course what counts as societal interests is debateable, but at least there should be societal transparency and accountability about, for example, PR agents operate on behalf of tobacco, alcohol, moneylenders and gambling organizations, all of which have had or do have relationships with sport. While social PR in health contexts might seem indiscernible from social marketing, the distinction lies in its reputational and relational focus, and its commitment to dialectic and the creation of discursive space as part of its remit.

Sport for Peace

In his 1996 book *Peace by peaceful means: peace and conflict, development and civilisation* Johan Galtung discussed some key definitions of peace:

- Peace is the absence/reduction of violence of all kinds
- Peace is non-violent and creative conflict transformation
- Peace work is work to reduce violence by peaceful means
- Peace studies is the study of the conditions of peace work (Galtung, 1996: 9).

Galtung argued that peace required understanding of, and engagement with, conflict in order to transform it. He likened peace studies to health studies, applying the triangle diagnosis–prognosis–therapy. Although he did not write about sport in any detail, it is clear that for some, sport can act therapeutically among groups where there has been violence and conflict. Galtung did, however, allude to sport very briefly when considering the relationship between the flowing of processes that change over radically different types of time: he refers to the speed at which mountains crumble and glaciers move in comparison to biological and human biographical time in relation to events, speech and tipping points,

' If something changes gradually (continuously) and something else does not change at all, and the two are coupled together, then something will happen, sooner or later. One of them has to yield … martial arts start here. (Galtung, 1996: 19) '

The idea that sport may be part of the process of healing also requires exploration of sport that ruptures, that is, a cause of violence or reflects or represents societal or international conflicts. Sport as a contributor to peace needs to be seen as part of peace-keeping and not as a single technique.

However, Perry (2012) suggests this is a fallacious position, because it fails to

'Distinguish between conflict and competition … However, I would rather suggest that aggression in sport presents opportunities for moral education and moral development. When playing sport we exercise our potential for aggression, and we may also be tempted by the attractions of violence in pursuit of our aim … So sport is not about conflict but competition; not about violence but controlled aggression; neither is it amoral and value-free but is itself a moral enterprise. Of course, sport is not a cure-all, and if sport programmes can be useful in peace-building, then they must be implemented as part of a wider set of peace-building strategies. I have tried to argue that the very nature of sport lends itself to the task of interpersonal understanding and respect, and that the nature of cooperative striving in rule-governed competition can lead towards civilized and peaceful resolutions. I have claimed that it is this peacemaking capacity of sport that informs its peacekeeping potential. (Perry, 2012: 777, 779)'

There are various peace through sport initiatives, some sponsored by elite figure-heads, whose interest may lie in their own personal PR and reputation management to ensure support and goodwill for their elite social positioning. In other words, their acts may be somewhat akin to Victorian charity, that allow the donor to feel good about themselves and to promote themselves as ethical and caring, but do not in any way address the inequities or hegemonic structures that are at least partly responsible for problems such as poverty, deprivation and lack of opportunity in the first place. However well-meant, such initiatives may not succeed in achieving longer-lasting impact.

Sport for Peace Initiatives

- Generations for Peace is an initiative spear-headed by HRH Prince Faisal Al Hussein of Jordan.
- Peace and Sport was founded under the High Patronage of HSH Prince Albert II of Monaco and it co-ordinates efforts among international organizations, NGOs, corporations (in relation to their CSR campaigns), 57 sports 'champions for peace' (only 14 of them women though), national Olympic Committees, sports associations, academics and civil society (www.peace-sport.org).
- The Peres Center for Peace was founded by Nobel Peace Prize Laureate and former Israeli Prime Minister Shimon Peres in 1996. It focuses on a range of issues affecting the Middle East, including the provision of sport and youth activities. The Sports Unit implements sports projects that facilitate peaceful coexistence and understanding between Israeli and Palestinian children (www.peres-center. org).

A range of examples where sport has proved helpful in building relationships can be cited, for example Tassell and Terry, who examined the case of the two Koreas and argued that,

> More than 50 years of complete social and political separation and maintenance of divergent political systems and ideologies have inevitably created social and political gaps between the two states and their people, and sport serves as a mechanism to aid in bridging that gap … By marching together at international sports events, as they did at the Olympic ceremonies in the 2008 Beijing Games, the 2004 Athens Games and the 2000 Games in Sydney, North and South Koreans are able to build a sense of cohesion and oneness among them. This unity is not only meaningful for the team members who are able to march jointly, but also for the spectators and the fans of both North and South Korea who, while cheering for their own state, also find themselves cheering for the state that was once their greatest enemy as was witnessed by the international community at the ceremonies of the Olympic Games in Sydney and Athens … sport provides a less threatening environment for North and South Koreans to interact on two levels. On the political level, the issue of sport has generally been a non-threatening area for co-operation between the two states. Thus, discussions about unified teams and marches are relatively non-con-frontational and provide a framework for later discussions that may regard more serious or critical issues. Also, discussion of sport-related topics provides a basis for the establishment of regular meetings and talks among top and lower level leaders in the two Koreas, allowing increased frequency of opportunities to build personal relationships and ties between the states. (Tassell and Terry, 2012: 816; Sports and Development, n.d.)

Nevertheless, politics and power are likely to trump sport initiatives, even those instigated as a form of sport diplomacy.

Olympism: Ideology, Rhetoric and PR

Peace is specified as one of the main goals of the Olympic movement in the Olympic Charter, the UN endorses the Olympic Truce (which is supposed to last three months prior to an Olympic Games and three months after it finishes) and it is historically embedded in the instigator of modern Olympism, Pierre de Coubertin's 'Ode to Sport':

> O Sport, you are Peace!
>
> You forge happy bonds between the peoples by drawing them together in rever-ence for strength which is controlled, organized and self-disciplined. Through you the young of all the world learn to respect one another, and thus the diversity of national traits becomes a source of generous and peaceful emulation. (Cited in Martínková, 2012: 788)

Olympism is an ideology that endeavours to educate and promote values that improve the human condition, so it incorporates a moral compass. Specifically it highlights 'excellence, joyful striving, harmonious development of the human being with respect to the self as well as others, and last, but not least, peace' (Martînkova, 2012: 789). Important values are self-discipline, self-knowledge, respect for others, and internationalism. Olympism is promoted in a persuasive way that promotes certain ideals but also the movement itself and its institutional base as a global force for good. However, some of de Courbertin's ideals are increasingly hard to maintain in a promotional age, such as amateurism, excessive competition aimed at material gain and self-promotion and that led to jealousy, envy, vanity and mistrust and amateurism (Martînkova, 2012: 790). The Olympic movement may be understood as a social movement that has discursive strategies and tactics to ensure its ongoing survival, while at the same time its promotional work clearly embeds it in commoditization and consumption.

Another difficult area to negotiate is that of politics, particularly with regard to peacemaking which is necessarily entwined with human rights and also entails understanding and engagement with the roots of conflict, otherwise Olympism's claims may remain 'motherhood and apple pie' ideals (Lederach, 1997 in Spaaij and Burleson, 2012). Indeed, the Olympic Movement has been criticized for its 'delusional belief' and seen as 'show-business internationalism' (Hoberman, 2011, 1995 cited in Spaaij, 2012: 767). Peacemaking requires integrative relational networks working with a wide range of politically focused organizations and it has been argued that the 2016 Rio de Janeiro Olympics will raise 'oppositional voices … in the ongoing struggle for development, equality and the building of peaceful relations in and through Olympic sport and the hosting of the Games' (Darnell, 2012 cited in Spaaij and Burleson, 2012: 911). In any case, others have argued that the Olympic Movement is necessarily situated within 'the broader global political order' despite its self-positioning as an apolitical organization (Stockdale, 2012: 840). This conundrum is exemplified by the fact that the IOC bestows political legitimacy on new sovereign states arising from decolonization or self-determination following the collapse of major power blocs, and seen as politically significant by those powers as an exercise in nation branding and national identity (Stockdale, 2012: 841). National identity is also performed rhetorically by Olympic hosts in extravagant opening and closing ceremonies, where,

❛ Particular symbols can be deployed and manipulated to construct an image of the host cities/states as bastions of human achievement and cultural richness while simultaneously serving to explicitly obscure the less savoury practices of local sovereign authorities. (Stockdale, 2012: 842)   ❜

Olympism is promoted, if slightly reinvented by its high priests, according to the issues of the day. For example IOC President Jacques Rogge emphasized youth participation and the successor generation in response to the obesity crisis,

' The legacy will be for the Olympic Games and the Olympic movement. The Games are fundamentally a response to the threat to sport. At the same time we are entering a new era where people communicate differently, we have to talk the language of today, to hire young people to talk to young athletes. This is not just about sport but about education and providing opportunities to learn about lifestyle, social responsibility, respect for the environment and, from a sporting perspective, the lessons of anti-doping. Our challenge is not so much organizing the Games as developing the educational language (to deliver the programme). The most difficult thing is effective trans-generational communication. (Roberts, 2008f: 34–35) '

Sport for Development

Development communication explores communication structures and practices in developing regions, both in relation to the developed world, but also, more reflexively, in terms of how communication contributes to processes of change and development such as nutrition, health, literacy and sport:

' Development communication is the study of social change brought about by the application of communication research, theory and technologies to bring about development – defined as a widely participatory process of social change in a society, intended to bring about both social and material advancement. (Rogers and Hart, 2002: 9–10) '

An example of this can be cited in relation to the **sportification** of Africa and the work of the Mathare Youth Sports Association (MYSA) which, since 1987, has grown to become the largest youth organization in Africa, focused on football as a way of strengthening self-esteem and belief and to alter distorted images of Africa (Hognestad and Tollison, 2004: 211). It has entailed the ambition of an international media campaign, as well as utilizing sport as a form of communication that can bestow individual and community confidence. While optimists have claimed societal benefits as a consequence of sportification others have pointed out that 'many African leaders have turned to sport as a lifeline to provide some credibility for their failing regimes' (Allison and Monnington: 17).

Historically, 'development' was seen as an international rather than an internal domestic issue partly as a consequence of colonization (that contributed to underdevelopment); of economic and political expansionism during the Cold War; and of privatization and neo-liberal capitalism that facilitated marketplace solutions (Mody, 2002: 415). Sport for development purposes raises some interesting challenges in terms of sports colonization and the extent to which communities are able to set their own agendas and participatory communication and relationships. There are questions to be asked about the extent to which sport for development empowers communities or whether, inspired by modernization, it creates markets for international sports business capital.

There have been four main ways of conceptualizing and practising development (Melkote, 2002: 420), and these can be usefully applied to sport development (see box beneath).

Approaches to Sport Development (Melkote, 2002)

1   Modernization

Based on neoclassical economic capitalist values, modernization promotes Western models of economic expansion, consumption, and technology. These ideas also drew some influence from social evolutionary theory and implied that there needed to be attitudinal and behavioural changes in Third World countries. Mass communications and the media were used to propagate key messages based on the belief that the media produced powerful effects. Young academics were taken to the US for their advanced academic training and thus acculturated into Western approaches. Globalization retains a connection to modernization and both are historically linked to colonialism. The concepts of electronic colonialism (McPhail, 1981, 2006) and media imperialism (Boyd-Barrett, 1977, 1998; McPhail, 2009: 26) are relevant to the global operation of the sports business.

2   Critical perspectives

These challenge economic and cultural expansionism and what is seen as the 'imperialism of modernization', arguing for political and economic restructuring to distribute resources within and between societies more evenly (Melkote, 2002: 420). This paradigm also challenged assumptions that development was equivalent to material possessions as well as inherent ethnocentrism and patriarchy. Furthermore, the media are affected by power imbalances.

3   Liberation or monastic

These perspectives are developed from Freire's liberation theology and argue that personal and community freedom from oppression leads to autonomy. Freire promoted dialogic communication in which 'Being dialogic is not invading, not manipulating, not imposing orders. Being dialogic is pledging oneself to the constant transformation of reality' (Freire, 1973: 46 cited in Huesca, 2002: 502).

4   Empowerment

This perspective reflects upon issues of power and control in development theory and practice, for example participatory programmes.

Source: Melkote, 2002: 420.

The field of development evolved from a top-down mass approach to diffusion of innovations developed by Everett Rogers in the late 1960s. His ideas were influential on US and UK PR practice in which ideas were communicated through particular channels among opinion leaders within a social system, through the stages of: awareness, interest, evaluation, trial and adoption. This was subsequently overtaken by the social marketing approach, which took more account of audience perceptions and feedback in undertaking behavioural change, such as campaigns related to family planning, or adult literacy. The use of entertainment-education in which information was embedded into media products as a way of setting social agendas was a slightly different approach to change. Essentially one-way flow of information from Western nations to less developed countries (LDCs) was challenged in the 1970s and the 1980s in debates about the New World Information and Communication Order (NWICO) in UNESCO, and this remains a live issue in terms of the protection of indigenous media systems (McPhail, 2009: 10).

Participatory communication programmes have proved challenging because they require change agents to step back and allow the marginalized the opportunity to take social and political action to facilitate conscientization, which allows them the autonomy to identify their own needs, goals and constraints. Participation may involve representatives, local experts, and audience research outreach. Finally, it is important to highlight the concept of empowerment, which in the development literature includes the following elements:

- increasing community control over consequences that affect them
- autonomy over personal and community projects/direction/policy
- ongoing process involving mutual respect, critical reflection
- symmetrical relationships between actors
- grass roots organization.

It is against these criteria that sport for development initiatives need to be reviewed, alongside a critical review of the sponsors of such development with a consideration of power dynamics and an assessment as to relative benefits.

Sport Business Involvement in Sport for Peace, Development and Health

- Peace and Sport, Monaco, 'works with a range of companies, some of which sponsor Peace and Sport and others of which contribute to particular initiatives. However, the Peace and Sport partners, although investing significant amounts of money choose to give money without any publicity and retain a certain amount of discretion' (*SBI*, 2009d: 68).
- 'Generations for Peace' founded by HRH Prince Faisal Al Hussein of Jordon, organizes school camps in 23 countries in Africa and Asia. It has a range of partners

including NBA and Samsung, but 'Unfortunately, we have been affected by the global recession. We appointed a world-leading marketing agency to assist us with our commercial partner acquisitions. It proved to be an expensive exercise which did not produce success ... [but] the fact that Samsung and NBA [joined us] makes us optimistic of using sport as peace-building tools despite the economic crisis' (*SBI*, 2009d: 70).

• WhizzKids United (Africaid) is part of a project to tackle HIV across sub-Saharan Africa. Football is used as an analogy to teach life skills required to prevent HIV infection.

While optimism and hope is expressed by those from sports studies about the emancipatory and development potential of sport, caution is also present:

' There are heartening success stories in SDP. The evidence is that, when conducted in responsible, culturally appropriate ways, with community support, SDP has enhanced the education, health and well-being of participants. Yet despite the plethora of programmes, international conferences and endorsements, international SDP is still in its infancy, woefully underfunded, completely unregulated, poorly planned and coordinated and largely isolated from mainstream development efforts. None of the programmes has been able to address the overwhelming need. Whenever a successful programme is launched, the organizers are bombarded by requests from others in the region that they are unable to meet. Moreover, while the entrepreneurial spirit can be a plus, it has also led to a multitude of competing NGOs, and a complete disregard (in this writer's view) of the over-arching need to restore and strengthen state programmes of health and education. In fact, in the competition for donors, photo ops, and placements for volunteers, NGOs not only compete against each other but against state schools. (Kidd, 2008: 377)   '

Community-based Games

Special interest games have also emerged that foster bonds in particular sports, for example The Transplant Games, Gay Games and the World Leisure Games. The World Leisure Games's theme is 'Improving the quality of life through leisure experiences', because leisure is 'integral to social cultural and economical development' and is designed to 'drive social change and improve society through participation in non-Olympic ... popular leisure pursuits' (Evans, 2012c: 28–9). Fifteen thousand participants from 50 countries attended the World Leisure Games in South Korea in 2010 to compete in a variety of sports such as jokugu, inline skating, skateboarding, sport climbing, sport fishing, paragliding, billiards, model aircraft, powered paragliding and B-boy dancing. The World Leisure Games are also a business opportunity and vehicle for companies to break into emerging markets while proclaiming community and CSR values.

The SPD movement has a diverse approach and track record in its efforts to mobilize sport for social development, including health and sexual responsibility in AIDs-torn east Africa; information campaigns in the former Yugoslavia about landmines; facilitation of communicative and cooperative relationships among those from different ethnic or religious backgrounds in Israel, Northern Ireland and South Africa; gender equality; environmentalism – 'all part of a rapidly mushrooming phenomenon, the use of sport and physical activity to advance sport and broad social development in disadvantaged communities' (Kidd, 2008: 370).

In some cases, however, interventions have led to 'muscle drain' in which the best athletes and coaches acquire skills and opportunities that lead them to leave their countries, meaning that SDP has no deep impact on the target communities for which it was devised. There is also a clearly colonial and exploitative dimension where developing countries are identified as workers for the sports business. Sport imperialism is funded by multinational sponsors that do not address the infrastructural and underlying problems of poverty, hunger and illiteracy (Andreff, 2008).

Even from a limited sport perspective there are disadvantages to SDP initiatives:

> It diverts the most talented athletes, those few who have had the opportunity to benefit from the rare domestic coaches and sport facilities. In some cases, it erodes the capacity of the home country to use its most talented athletes in international competitions. (Andreff, 2008: 6–7)

Cautionary and critical views of Development through Sport (DTS) or Sport for Development and Peace (SDP) have been offered by a political scientist, David Black, who warned that 'developmental ideas inevitably bear the imprint of those who have articulated them, and are therefore inclined to empower some and disempower others' (Black, 2010: 125). Black cautioned against international sports rhetoric and the lack of accountability of private capital interests interventions,

> The boundaries between institutions, ideas and interests have become blurry, and key development buzzwords, like empowerment, partnership, and poverty alleviation, have become profoundly ambiguous in their meanings and implications. For example, how much significance and optimism should be vested in the growing movement towards Corporate Social Responsibility (CSR) among private sector actors – a trend that bears on DTS through the role these corporate actors play in funding various initiatives? (Black, 2010: 125)

This has direct implications for PR practitioners who operate on behalf of companies as well as those who work for activist organizations and governmental or international organizations. They have to find a common language as well as strategies and solutions that can make impacts that meet participatory requirements (Black, 2010: 126), and yet they have to remain authentic. Stakeholder communication and the ability to communicate across ideological divides is of central importance in such a situation, in addition to inter- and cross-cultural communication challenges.

Sport for Health

Sport development *per se* is an outcome of national and international policy-making processes, often overlapping with health and education and understood as an enabling process of facilitate participation or improved performance, but also as sports advocacy, designed to intervene and improve the take-up of sports activities. Inevitably there are tensions for many governments in both developing and developed countries between participation and performance objectives in terms of resource allocation (highlighting the PR role for lobbying).

A recent example of political usage, which is partly directed towards the national health agenda in the UK, has been the launch of the first School Olympics which took place in 2006 as a way of talent-spotting for the London Olympics in 2012. Despite the British tradition of non-intervention in sport the state has begun to infiltrate this area, influenced perhaps by the World Health Organization ideology that 'sport is positively correlated with health and is a means to the achievement and maintenance of health' (Roche, 2000: 197). The IOC has collaborated with WHO and also with the International Labour Organization (ILO) over a variety of health and social issues related to world sport, including concerns over sports corporates and trafficking of talented under-age youngsters (David, 2005). The shift towards defining health as sport-related was enshrined at the policy level in the UK in a Department of Health White Paper Choosing Health, which declared,

❛ Sport's unique contribution – sport and active recreation make a significant contribution to overall physical activity levels in the population ... today's busy lifestyles and the availability of a wide range of sedentary pursuits are increasingly creating competing pressures. (Cd 6374 November 2004 p. 91) ❜

Hence in the UK the evolution of development through sport has been linked to the welfare state system (including issues such as child protection) and ideological shifts between state and private provision and discussions over the degree of emphasis on competitive school sports (Houlihan and White, 2002). Sport became linked in the 1980s to urban policy following a series of riots throughout the summer of 1981 and thus embedded in social policy (Coalter et al., 1986 cited in Houlihan and White, 2002: 35). Consequently, communications around sport are ideological, politicized and strategic, concerned with lobbying and interest/action groups that see sport as an instrument of social change linked to moral values but are challenged by financial pressures and limited resource.

There is some overlap between the goals of 'sport development, humanitarian sport assistance and SDP [which] are often blurred in rhetoric and practice' (Kidd, 2008, 373) and the goals of development and health. For example:

❛ Whereas 'sport development' is largely a project of sporting organizations, SDP is increasingly pursued by NGOs in partnership with government departments of education and health. The best example to make this point is the Aerobics for Pregnant Women Program in Zimbabwe. It was begun by Commonwealth Games Canada in 1994, financed by the Canadian International Development Agency (CIDA) and continued by local women after Canadian foreign policy required CGC to leave Robert Mugabe's Zimbabwe in 2002. The idea is to strengthen maternal health and combat infant mortality through aerobics combined with education about nutrition, effective parenting and other social services available in the community. Few of the participants have ever competed in organized sports. (Kidd, 2008: 373)   ❯

Multiple goals and stakeholders therefore require strategic co-ordination and communications between and among the agencies involved (inter-organizational communication).

Think Critically

How can PR contribute to improved inter-organizational communications? Consider which organizations would be relevant to a development programme in a locality of your choice (it could be your local community), identify the core stakeholders, and develop a strategic plan for inter-organizational communication for the programme that you develop.

Who are the key sports stakeholders in your community? Who drives sports policy and what different interest groups can you identify? What discourses emerge around sport regarding its social role?

Public health communication campaigns that focus on physical activity and sport share many of the same features and issues discussed in relation to development campaigns in relation to their early beginnings as one-way transmission, behaviour-change and persuasion to community and culture-centred approaches (Dutta, 2008). Within Western societies such campaigns may be designed to increase physical activity in sedentary urban settings or with less active groups. In particular efforts have been focused latterly on young girls and women. Public communication campaigns have struggled with impact and effectiveness.

There are challenges in access and take-up among different groups and maintaining life-long activities. In particular, it has been argued that there is a problem in retaining young girls and women in active sport in the UK. The charity Women's Sport and Fitness Foundation (WSFF) (initiated in 1984) has been endeavouring to address this issue by working with key stakeholders to develop a social marketing and research-based approach (www.wsff.org.uk). They aim to increase female participation as their research suggested that 80 per cent of women do not do enough exercise. They have run conferences and seminars and published a series of reports analysing a range of issues and contributory factors such as body image, school experiences, media representations of female sport, inequitable investment into male and female sport, and inequitable media coverage of female in terms of content. They have also taken up public issues such as,

❝ The Sky football sexism row and the BBC's Sports Personality of the Year contro-versy, when no women featured in the final award shortlist. The BBC subsequently agreed to review the way the shortlist is compiled. (WSFF Impact Report 2012) ❞

Their research reports and conferences provide a focus for media comment and reflec-tion upon a range of fitness barriers for groups such as young mothers and older women. In 2012 its project *Faith and Action: Born to Succeed* tackled low numbers of Muslim women in sport, exploring options such as basketball and futsall through outreach projects.

However, the societal and environmental barriers cannot be played down, as Roberts and Brodie pointed out,

❝ If it was just matter of persuading young people to participate ... the task of sport promotion would be relatively easy. The reality, however, is that there is intense com-petition for everyone's leisure time and money, and, as we have shown, sport makes heavy demands, especially on time. (Roberts and Brodie, 1992: 48) ❞

The problem of time and competing activities is well recognized by those in sports busi-ness who fear a longer-term threat to the sector,

❝ I think the sports business faces the same challenges as sports participation. Fewer kids play sport because of major competition from other sources of entertainment. The business of sport – media, spectators, TV, sponsorship, licensing – face a sim-ilar challenge from more consumer choice. The solution may come from working more closely with the competition of choice, rather than ignoring it or trying to fight it. (John Tibbs, CEO, quoted in *SBI*, 2007a: 114) ❞

However, some sports business practitioners still seemed to believe that dissemination and advocacy and media campaigns could solve the problem of obesity and sedentary lifestyles. For example, Pippa Collett M/D Sponsorship Consulting argued,

❝ Strong leadership with a coherent strategy that targets parents as well as children is critical to increasing activity levels and this is where the media could offer invalu-able support. Mass communication of obesity agenda messages in informative and entertaining formats would make a significant contribution to changing social per-spectives on diet and activity. (*SBI*, 2008f: 36–7) ❞

The involvement of some products as sponsorship has begun to be questioned, although some sports business practitioners such as Nigel Currie Brandrapport defended their involvement,

❝ Fast food, fizzy drinks and alcohol brands all face the enormous challenge of bal-ancing their promotion of sport and encouraging healthy outdoor activity while at the same time defending 'unhealthy' products. Many have developed innovative 'insurance' sponsorship programmes designed to get youngsters playing sport and becoming involved in grass roots coaching and sports development programmes. Some might argue that this is hypocritical but I am sure that most people would prefer that their children be encouraged to take part in sport even if it is as the result of a significant financial support from fast food or fizzy drink brands than being allowed to stay indoors watching TV and playing computer games. The positives of getting our youngsters playing as much sport as possible far outweigh the negatives and sponsors have a major part in this. (*SBI*, 2008f: 36–7)

Think Critically

How convincing is Nigel Currie's argument? Which stakeholders are affected by the reputational issues underlying his argument and how should they manage this issue, and why? Should any potential sponsors be banned from sport sponsorship and, if so, which and why?

Theorizing SPD Initiatives

Scholars have employed a number of theoretical frames looking at sport as development, as bridging and bonding social capital, as postcolonial critique. Of these, social capital and postcolonialism are already present in PR literature and can be blended to explain the purpose and value of sports PR initiatives in this context. Indeed PR can be understood as a powerful resource that is utilized to change relationships and to redress and respond to imbalances,

❝ Sport could be viewed as a venue in which conflicting groups engage across power differentials ... Fields operate on the basis of uneven distribution of various forms of capital: social, economic and cultural. In consequence, the different actors in sport must be viewed as possessing unequal resources; systemic challenges would then include transcending these inequalities through consistent attention to relational change. (Schnitzeret al., 2012: 12)

Summary

This chapter has introduced the concept of Social PR in the context of sport used as a policy tool for positive social outcomes. It has explored Olympic ideals in relation to peace, development and health objectives outlining key challenges. Key points include:

- Sport development is derived from policy initiatives and needs to be understood as politically motivated.

- Communicators in the area of sports development, whether it is national or international, and whether it is private or publicly funded or a combination, need a detailed understanding of political interests and a background in debates over the role of sport in society.

Of wider significance to those in public relations is that for many theorists PR is seen as a way to achieve social goals through dialogic communication and collaborative relationships, thus aligning with many of the goals espoused by those in the peace and development movements.

Further Reading

Black DR (2010) The ambiguities of development: implications for 'development through sport'. *Sport in Society*, 13 (1): 121–9.

Coakley J (2011) Youth sports: what counts as 'positive development'. *Journal of Sport & Social Issues*, 35 (3): 306–24.

Darnell S (2010) Sport, race and bio-politics: encounters with difference in 'Sport for development and peace' internships. *Journal of Sport & Social Issues*, 34 (4): 396–417.

Hartmann D and Kwauk C (2011) Sport and development: an overview, critique and reconstruction. *Journal of Sport & Social Issues*, 35 (3): 284–305.

Kaufman P and Wolff E (2010) Playing and protesting: sport as a vehicle for social change. *Journal of Sport & Social Issues*, 34 (2): 154–75.

Levermore R (2011) Evaluating sport-for-development: approaches and critical issues. *Progress in Development Studies*, 11 (4): 339–53.

Misenor L and Mason D (2009) Fostering community development through sporting events strategies: an examination of urban regime perceptions. *Journal of Sport Management*, 23 (6): 770–94.

Skinner J, Zakus DH and Cowell J (2008) Development through sport: building social capital in disadvantaged communities. *Sport Management Review*, 11 (3): 253–75.

8

PR for Minority and Lifestyle Sports

Introduction

This chapter explores 'minority' or 'lifestyle' or 'adventure sports', their underpinning ideologies, relationship with commerce, the extent of their marketization, and implications for PR. The sports in question are quite varied in that some minority sports are quite traditional, and others modern or postmodern. Terms applied to these sports are not employed consistently and sometimes overlap, as in 'adventure' and 'lifestyle'. Reference is made to key developments in the sector, in particular the emergence of specialist organizations, media and events to service this sector. The way in which such sports are represented is considered. PR is relevant to the creation, circulation, commodification, reproduction, consumption, and reinterpretation of meanings about 'lifestyle sports' in contemporary society.

The chapter covers:

- Definitions
- Commercial perspectives
- Functional PR perspectives
- Lifestyle, adventure and ideology
- Lifestyle, adventure and the 'circuit of culture'

Key Concepts

- Adventure
- Challenger brand
- Circuit of culture
- Distinction
- Edgework
- Extreme

- Freerunning
- Lifestyle
- Minority
- Parkour
- Risk
- Traceurs

Definitions

Minority sports have been defined by the PR industry as those **challenger brands** that are at something of a crossroads or tipping point in terms of their profile, recruitment and government funding, such as handball, taekwondo, or triathlon in the UK. Some of these sports are beginning to develop their PR capacity either in-house or through the recruitment of agencies in order to capitalize on their visibility and viewing figures acquired during London 2012. As M&C Saatchi Sport and Entertainment MD Jamie Wynne-Morgan pointed out,

❛ Many sports will never have a better platform than this, and now governing bodies have to communicate what makes their sport different and interesting. (Owens, 2012b: 3)   ❜

PR tends to be seen as useful marketing support in terms of gaining media profile and collaborating with sponsors,

❛ PR will be one of the key ways for minority sports to maintain momentum as they won't have big marketing budgets and will have to use the assets they have imaginatively. A good sponsor will play a key role in helping with these campaigns, and they often need an agency to help create the right work. (Eddie May, co-founder of Threepipe consultancy, in Owens, 2012b: 3)   ❜

However, there are many sports that have not yet reached the dizzy heights of challenger brand and some struggle to survive, for example korfball whose national association has relied upon volunteers who,

❛ Do a bit of PR, basically emailing the nationals, the local papers, trying to get on national TV, fact-finding and compiling lists of the national newspapers, trying to establish contacts within the television companies, the media, the radio stations and the newspapers.   ❜

Lifestyle is a term used colloquially to determine behavioural, attitudinal, and stylistic patterns of an individual or group. The term has been operationalized by marketers as a way of conceptualizing and measuring coherent categories of consumers about values and associated ways of living. It is an important concept for all the promotional industries (advertising, marketing, PR and design) and to cultural theorists who focus on consumption. Lifestyles produce and are the consequences of subtle distinctions between identities and therefore actualize social difference. Economic growth has led to consumer culture and the availability of goods and services, which allow for individual choices to mark identity.

Lifestyle sport is one of a number of terms used to define unconventional and risky sports. Terms used include 'adventure sports', 'extreme sports', 'action sports'. They are 'alternative', seen as sub- or micro sporting cultures. They have been defined as challenges to dominant sporting cultures, and are sometimes rather crudely defined by media as 'extreme'. But as Wheaton pointed out in her review, 'it became evident that a particular style of life was central to the meaning and experience', in other words, culture. Lifestyle sport is one of a number of choices that individuals may take in defining their identities and determining their life courses and as such, is part of the processes conceptualized by Bourdieu as **distinction** (discussed in more detail in the final chapter. Lifestyle sports embrace a particular orientation to life wherein the activity is not specifically competitive and may merge with the notion of play, for example Brazilian **capoeira** (a cross between martial arts, gymnastics and dance), skating (skateboarding) and other urban sports such as **parkour** or freestyle BMX. Many lifestyle sports are highly visual and acrobatic, such as **coastering**, and become points of cultural reference in ads and films to connote freedom and the unconventional. Others have a weirdness and artificiality such as **zorbing** (or **sphering**) or **aquasphering**, and **bungee-jumping**.

Windsurfing, kayaking, rock climbing and ice climbing are good examples of international lifestyle sports possessing globalized subcultural formations. The strength of the subculture can be measured by the ability of its members to travel to various parts of the globe and be recognized by those from other ethnicities primarily as 'a snowboarder', 'a white-water rafter', 'a climber'. PR can help a subculture to realize, celebrate and symbolize its features, values, ideologies and ideals in a coherent way so that it can be more visible and better understood among the wider public, including governmental sporting bodies. Lifestyle sports may tempt participants to adopt a nomadic lifestyle to 'follow the weather' and seasons to experience surf, mountains, rivers, and air currents at the most propitious time. Whether lifestyle itinerants see themselves as tourists or travellers is an interesting question, for their existence necessarily impacts local economies and cultures, raising questions of social responsibility and sustainability. These are lifestyles of lived fantasy and adult play. Fantasy is linked to the concept of escape, of 'Enchanted spaces created for the purposes of marketing consumer goods, spaces that attract people and their money because they offer an escape from the institutional constraints of modern social life' (Lyng, 2005: 3).

Fletcher noted the phenomenon of the dominance of the professional middle class (PMC) in risk sports, a consequence of 'Such sports' capacity to simultaneously satisfy and provide a temporary escape from a class habitus demanding continual progress through disciplined labour and deferred gratification' (Fletcher, 2008).

Thus lifestyle sports and their ability to deliver an individual human experience of living in the moment that is constrained by regulatory society. The distinctive difference between these sports and others is that risk-taking and survival are intrinsic to the experience at a profound level, in a way that a competitive game of football or tennis is not. Lifestyle sports are typically in the natural world, compared to the unnatural world of 'normal' sport that is ruled by artificial and arbitrary conventions. Lifestyle sports are not so concerned about punishing training programmes or body shape that require dedication and self-monitoring in physiologically obsessed conventional sports (although power-weight ratios may still be crucial in adventure sports).

The lifestyle identities that are created from such ways of living are of defining importance to the individuals concerned:

> For many of these subculturalists, particularly the very committed, subcultural statuses and identities were seen to be more important than other spheres of these lives or identities. (Wheaton 2004: 10)

A sport which becomes a lifestyle becomes a major motivation for the individual, a central, if not defining feature of their identity, and their social world is defined by the activity. But lifestyle subcultures are not necessarily strongly bounded; social worlds of related disciplines overlap; and in any case some individuals participate in diverse activities, often according to the season, the weather, or simply whim. For example, it would not be unusual to meet some of the same people at an orienteering event, a fell race and a mountain marathon. Such overlapping worlds are interesting to those in PR because they illustrate the fact that 'publics' may be loose and dynamic formations. Issues over the rights to access land might primarily be of interest to hillwalkers, but is highly likely to resonate with kayakers (who wish to access water) and others whose sport is rural (and natural) rather than urban (arguably artificial). However, some groups might also clash (fishing community vs. open water kayakers) in some cultural contexts and merge in others (**lifestyle kayak fishing**). In some cases lifestyle sports may be involved in public affairs, lobbying and activism – as in the case of the Long Live Southbank campaign group of skaters and BMX riders who managed to delay the Southbank Centre's £120 million development plan that sought to re-locate 'the much-loved Undercroft skatepark' (Dawson, 2013: 32).

A further aspect of lifestyle sports that has been commodified is that of **adventure tourism**, part of **sports tourism**. Companies package together a variety of **extreme** experiences for **adrenalin junkies** and construct a risk context for consumption that is very different to individual exploration. In short it commodifies an experience into a tourism experience that can be purchased by consumers who are attracted to the identity and would rather buy than just try. There is an important distinction to be made between those who 'go it alone' and those who purchase commercial lifestyle or adventure sports holidays. Here the illusion is created of extreme sport marketed as a challenge and unique experience for the individual, even though many have been given the opportunity to purchase the same trip. Controversy has arisen over guided trips up Everest and to Antarctica, both in respect of environmental damage and the ability and competence of paying punters. The ethics of the free market in relation to such commercial opportunities is a PR challenge that some companies have been unable to navigate. It is almost inevitable that some such demanding adventures will resulting accidents and fatalities – only a company that had undertaken scenario and crisis planning would stand a good chance of surviving the media backlash that would inevitably follow the wake of any disaster.

Promotional aspects of PR work need to create discourses that titillate and meet the fantasies of those who seek to add 'extreme' to their persona. Yet simultaneously, they must reassure. Risk must be safety-netted by organizations, and PR walks a tightrope between the allure of thrill and the threat of death. PR work in this context is that which negotiates publicly aspirational and risk components through discourse work.

Commercial Perspectives

SBI touted women's professional tennis on one of its front covers in Issue 114, June 2006 as 'Girls on Tour: how the Sony Ericsson WTA Tour is putting lifestyle into marketing'. The story was that the sponsor's products (Sony Ericsson's mobile phones) could be marketed with downloads of the Tour and personal details about the players, such as their shopping habits and preferred brands. In 2007, *SBI* described triathlon as 'the ultimate "lifestyle" sport [which] in the word of the International Triathlon Union ... exudes vitality and charisma ... its social side is very important ... has some of the world's biggest brands onboard as sponsors ... a very attractive demographic ... Its main age group is 30–39' (Sherlock, 2007: 52). These examples show that branding and commercialism can dilute or appropriate terminology. More conventional definitions when it described lifestyle sports as emerging markets as evidenced by Iolo Jones, Chief Executive of Narrowstep's comments that,

' Sports such as windsurfing are accessible globally now to a new audience and can attract better sponsorship and stage better events as a result. It's been good to see the growth in popularity and events for the Professional Windsurfers' Association. The definition of a clear market has the power to attract sponsors, which can in future capitalize other lifestyle sports and give them a presence in mainstream culture. (*SBI*, 2005b: 16) '

PR plays a crucial role in 'activating' sponsorships and gaining media coverage and publicity. PR becomes a necessity as events grow in status, as evidenced by a media release issued by the iconic Southern Traverse Adventure Race on 11 January 2008 announcing that Fairydown was a new sponsor of the multi-day event (there are also shorter 14-hour and 8-hour events), and stating that,

' It is an endorsement of the Traverse's standing as New Zealand's premier adventure race to have attracted sponsorship from the internationally recognized brand ... [while Fairydown director said that Fairydown] 'has a history of being involved with adventure racing since the sport began and our mantra is "adventure for life" and fits well with the outdoor community. By supporting the Southern Traverse we are expanding our involvement with the athletes who take part in adventure racing. (Hunt, 2008) '

Bull-riding

Some extreme sports capitalize on their spectator value, such as Professional Bull Riders Inc. (PBR) which have 'generated an incredible buzz around bull riding, creating mainstream attention for America's original extreme sport' (Sherlock, 2009: 58). The PBR was formed in 1992 when 20 rodeo riders broke away 'because they wanted more attention and more cash for professional bull riding' (Sherlock, 2009: 58). Each of the riders invested $1000, each is now a millionaire in recognition of their mainstream status which includes a circuit of 225 events, a partnership with IMG that delivered 25 broadcast partners, reaching 57 territories and major markets in Australia, Brazil, Canada and Mexico (Sherlock, 2009: 58),

> 'The fastest growing sport in the US currently is **professional bull riding** which is now experiencing real global growth ... More than 100 million viewers annual watch prime time programming on various networks around the world. Nearly two million fans attend events each year and Professional Bull riders – the international professional bull riding organization based in Colorado – was nominated as the 2010 Sports League of the Year alongside the NFL, NBA and MLB.' (Zak Brown CEO of Just Marketing International cited in Wilner, 2011c: 17)

As budgets have got tighter and markets saturated, sports business practitioners have turned to explore the potential of minority sports to generate some lost income and supplement strained budgets (it is recognized that these alternative sports are not going to outrank the traditional sports). In so doing, practitioners are recommended to follow the cliché 'think outside the box', in other words generate creative and unusual sponsorships in new areas.

Other sports are **mixed martial arts** (Ultimate fighting championship), **competitive dancing** and the Olympic sports of **gymnastics** and **figure skating** for women. These sports are nibbling away at the declining sports that apparently include 'any women's professional sports ... some motor racing series ... tennis and golf' (Wilner, 2011c: 17). As mentioned elsewhere, tennis and golf are marketing very hard in China as a consequence of their decline in the US. It will be interesting to see whether the lifestyle sports will also be marketed more strongly in Asian and/or BRIC countries once saturation has been reached with the core conventional sports.

Parkour or **freerunning** developed in Paris in the 1990s with an image that the Director of Parkour Generations, Dan Edwardes, describes as **extreme** and trendy. Most parkour practitioners or **traceurs** are based in the UK, and despite its short history it has already acquired some myths and negative imagery which Parkour Generations are working to correct with reputational capital derived from community work as part of a wider campaign to establish an international association, as Edwardes explained:

' Parkour myths relate to the dangers and the sense that it is practised by youths using it to refine cat burglary techniques. To set the record straight, at Parkour Generations, the world's leading group of instructors, we are welcomed with open arms by schools and leisure centres for the simple reason that we motivate children and teenagers to take part in physical activity and reduce offending rates ... our coaching programme is now recognised across Europe as a vocational qualification and has members from Brazil to Russia ... we are working towards building an international community which will develop parkour within its true spirit ... the ultimate goal is to create a world governing body. (Edwardes, 2010: 9) 〉

The article quoted here has a clear subtext related to sponsorship and clearly trails the brand values of the sport to those sports business readers who might be interested in a rather more unusual sponsorship,

〈 We believe that we can offer a powerful platform for the right brands because we can help them to tap into some very positive attributes. Not only are we seen as cutting edge extreme sport but our ethos is about putting back into society. Wherever we train, we ensure that we leave the environment as we found it, or we improve it by removing sharps, broken bottles and litter ... Aside from our CSR initiatives that parkour can help to deliver, it is also able to tap into the digital media phenomenon. For example when parkour was the theme of YouTube's home page for the day, it was the most popular ever run ... True to our ethos, however, we only want to talk to brands that are serious about their responsibilities so alcohol, fast food, caffeine-based energy drinks and big oil are all a firm 'no'. (Edwardes, 2010: 9) 〉

> ### Think Critically
>
> Which brand would be suitable sponsors for parkour and why from a PR perspective? How would you persuade your chosen brands to sponsor parkour and why?

Functional PR Perspectives and Adventure Sport

Adventure sport is not solely comprised of recreational or competitive activities in the field but to some degree is industrialized as part of the leisure or tourism industries. Although individuals take themselves off to sea-kayak or climb a rock face, they need to purchase equipment (from commercial companies) and will need to learn basic skills from more expert practitioners, who are often based in clubs. For example, membership of the Scottish Mountaineering Council or an Alpine Club gives access to facilities such as huts. Such organizations represent the interests of those who participate in such activities, for example, lobbying for access to private land. Thus commerce and markets, as well as bureaucracies and regulation, are realized through organizations. Organizations are necessarily communicative, and communication is intrinsically organizational.

Regardless of whether or not adventure sports have access to professional or formal PR, PR issues are there to be faced by adventure sport. In other words, even if no-one is taking responsibility for the image or reputation of a particular sport, stakeholders and the wider public may still have views about adventure sports depending on their own experience or those of peers or on their media consumption, for example negative views of skateboarders. It is notoriously difficult and time-consuming to turn around negative perceptions or media coverage, although it is often the realization that there are negative perceptions that could be detrimental to the long-term survival of the organization or activity in question that concentrates organizational minds on PR. Much better, however, is to take a proactive strategic approach to PR and to invest time in identifying key stakeholders and building ongoing relationships with those communities by facilitating feedback.

The very idea of 'PR' might seem too 'mainstream' for some lifestyle sport exponents, and ideologically questionable given twentieth-century PR's symbiotic relationship with capitalism and free market values. This was partly acknowledged by one journalist, who commented,

> ‘ We cut the PR people out of the equation … I guess we're embedded media, so to speak, within the scene, so we don't need a lot of highly paid people telling us how to take photographs of events … PR companies are a function of the way large brands operate and they're required because I'm sure they deal with a lot of media that don't really know anything about skateboarding. ’

Yet in the privileged globalized and networked world, the ability and willingness to communicate and discuss issues is central to collective organizational and individual identity formation and maintenance – and PR work, whether recognized as such or not, is part of that (often unseen) process. In promotional culture, such work is necessary, and, in any case, may be performed knowingly or unknowingly by representatives of those sports. PR happens, whether or not there is an organizational function that is made responsible and accountable for its management. In other words, organizations need to communicate with a variety of individuals and groups, and these parties, consumers and the wider public will form impressions about an organization, whether or not PR activity is a managed function. That is why PR is as relevant to lifestyle sports as it is to heavily commercialized sports such as football or basketball. Indeed, a better understanding of PR work in practice across a variety of lifestyle and traditional sports could reveal the extent to which PR activity reinforces power imbalances between different sports through domination of the public sphere resulting from political, economic and cultural capital.

Gender and Race Issues in Skateboarding

It is not a girls' sport. It's too hard and there is too much pain involved. There are lots of cuts and bruises even learning basic tricks. They hurt themselves a lot. They fall on handrails and get split testicles. (Skater)

(Continued)

(Continued)

> I get grief all the time, only from gnarly ragas though ... It's only narrow-minded people who say stuff though [and] would think that skateboarding is a white boy's thing. (*Haunts*, 2005: 076)

> There are female skaters but they're very, very few and far between. (Journalist)

There are some generic issues intrinsic to adventure sports that require a PR focus. Given the nature of adventure sports, particular areas of concern relate to safety and risk-management practices. Adventure sports organizations need to plan in advance for the handling and communication of possible accidents involving adults and children in both recreational and competitive situations. Adventure sports organizations may need to collaborate in their crisis management planning with other adventure sports organizations, local government and emergency services. The nature of responsibility and alternative rhetorical strategies and tactics need to be considered in advance of any incident. Whose is the legal liability and who is to apologize, if apologies are to be made? If there is an apology, who represents the organization and what form does the *apologia* take?

The Original Mountain Marathon (OMM) 2008

The fortieth anniversary of the OMM unexpectedly turned into a media frenzy when bad weather caused organizers to cancel the self-supported orienteering event halfway through the weekend. As the weather was exceptional the media were already writing bad weather stories and the OMM fell into that category. Coverage was exacerbated by the media's ignorance of mountain sports and consequently shock-horror reports of hundreds missing, casting the organizers into a poor light even though the nature of the event is that competitors are self-sufficient, choose their own route and therefore are not traceable. As one participant commented,

> It's a weekend event and people are self-sufficient so people are never accounted for on the Saturday night. It was a very poor area for telephone reception and you can't use a mobile. There was one phone line for emergency numbers but that was given to the media and the organizers couldn't do their job properly because the media kept coming through on it. Once the decision was taken to abandon the event, volunteers had to leave the base to start accounting for people which meant that it was even harder to deal with the media.

Source: L'Etang, 2009b: 62–63.

> ## Think Critically
>
> Given the nature of this event, how could organizers best be prepared in terms of crisis communications planning so that the media did not frame them as incompetent and irresponsible?

Lifestyle, Adventure and Ideology

PR can help 'sell' lifestyle sports for companies, as one specialist PR practitioner commented, 'We can educate companies … getting sponsorship for the Mountain Bike World Cup was like pulling teeth' largely because the sport cannot deliver media coverage that traditional sports do. However, this very opportunity throws up a dilemma for lifestyle sports participants, since engagement in PR managerial activities, concepts, values, discourse, runs counter to espoused 'alternative' values, and can clearly be seen as part of the 'mainstreaming' of lifestyle sports. PR has a role to play within those lifestyle sports cultures that are on the brink of mainstream to help them come to terms with potential cultural change and implications for self-identity.

For some, there is an intrinsic tension in 'alternative' lifestyles becoming mainstream as explained by one commentator,

> ❜Skateboarding is quite an underground sport now used by the mainstream to promote cool … People who do skateboarding don't follow norms … it attracts creative independent people and there are connections to music and art … skateboarders have a will of their own, those that do other sports have to conform … skateboarding is the inspiration for other extreme sports. Because of its cool image, suddenly everyone wants to look like skateboarders so suddenly Diesel and Levi want in on the act and you don't need the specialized companies any more, which slump once the commercial brands take over. (cited in L'Etang, 2009: 58) ❜

In this example, large brands can be seen as greedy consumers of market opportunity, to the detriment of specialist insider enterprises. The ideological tensions implicit in the relation between lifestyle sports and commerce suggests that there will be associated fractures within the communities of those sports, between those who reject commercial affiliations and those who welcome the opportunities (cited in L'Etang, 2009: 58). For example, a different journalist commented,

> ❜We tend to deal with PR companies when large mainstream brands are trying to push their new ranges or their riders, for example, an American brand that's sold over here will bring a bunch of riders over to go around the country and do demos and stuff at parks and obviously we deal with the PR aspect of that – we work with them to decide which skateparks we should go to or where we should take the team for photographs and video and stuff. Also we do have some dealings with a lot of

music companies because there's a music review aspect of the magazine, so we speak to Sony etc. [skateboards reference music and art in their designs] … companies such as Quicksilver run a lot of events in Europe so we deal with their PR departments to go over to, say, France or Spain to cover their event.   **'**

In a free market there is clearly room for a very particular form of exploitation – the use of images without any reciprocal investment. For example, a kite-surfing practitioner commented that 'We struggle to get sponsorship', yet Audi, Mercedes Benz, Peugeot and Ford have all used images of kite surfing (L'Etang, 2009: 59). Therefore, it may eventually be a sense of injustice combined with pragmatism that persuades adventure sports to embrace marketing more fully in order to benefit financially by working to establish sponsorship opportunities (L'Etang, 2009: 59). Branding opportunities are important to adventure sport because they can help compensate for the lack of conventional sports coverage, the consequence of the current distortions in media reporting which focuses on a small selection of (largely) male-dominated sports (L'Etang, 2009: 59). The prime factors that discourage big brand sponsorship are the lack of media coverage (implying the absence of a readership or informed community) and relatively few spectators and small media audiences. Of course, it is also fair to point out that those brands that use those images so promiscuously risk their communications being seen as an inauthentic form of impression management (L'Etang, 2009: 59).

Applying the Circuit of Culture to PR's Role in Lifestyle Sport

PR in liaison with marketing can help to imbue lifestyle sports with meaning in terms of the identities of lifestyle networks and organizations. However, the extent of such work will not be consistent across all lifestyle sports because there is a continuum ranging between mainstream sports and newly forming sports. For example, BMX has achieved Olympic status and has necessarily acquired, and will continue to acquire, bureaucratic structures to organize financing, elite and development programmes. It is likely that the sport will acquire more sophisticated PR expertise to navigate more complex relationships with local governments, schools, local communities, as well as seeking corporate funding. As the range of publics with which BMX needs to communicate diversifies, so PR will be required to communicate that identity to ever-increasing audiences and stakeholders. The achievement of Olympic status already denotes considerable lobbying skills. The dangers and 'extremeness' of the sport (well exemplified for British audiences in the spectacular crashes of Shanaze Reade in the Beijing 2008 Olympic finals) remain, but the alternative and lifestyle elements, while important for marketing purposes, have surely been compromised. The challenges for PR include the navigation of discourses that retain the original BMX identity for marketing purposes to sell the sport for sponsorship, yet, at the same time, retention of honesty about the acquisition of a certain conventional status; maintenance of the relationship with participants who espouse the lifestyle and BMX ideology; distinction of this lifestyle sport in relation to other competing lifestyle sports; retention of authenticity and credibility. Rinehart and Grenfell (2002) contrasted two BMX venues: one of which was free, grass roots and child-centred; the other commodified, corporate and adult-driven. They aimed to explore BMX as an emergent 'extreme sport' and to understand the meanings that participants created of their activity at these two different locations. This inevitably entailed a consideration of the issue of 'mainstreaming of the alternative' and the contrasts between the 'old-timers' who clung to values of authenticity and altruism and younger, newer participants who apparently had less problem with commodification, 'Indeed, they often seek more mainstream participation'. PR evaluates and engages with such identities in order to tailor more appropriate goods and services. Within the marketing-consumer PR process there are strategic moments at which salient language and values are employed to understand and communicate with target audiences. In order for PR to be trustworthy and believable as a source, it is essential for PR to represent identities as accurately and as authentically as possible.

PR activity should involve reflection upon the co-realities of a lifestyle sports organization (such as the International Coastering Association), cause or lifestyle sport that is being promoted. Internal reflection is part of the organizational identity formation and mission. It is this process which can help an organization achieve self-understanding of its culture, and construct the symbolic images and language in which to communicate its vision (corporate or organizational identity), and to relate to its external stakeholders.

PR also creates (and to some degree objectifies) identities when it goes through the process of defining publics (Leitch and Neilson, 2001). Members of publics and networks will actively construct their own meaning of individual and group identity. However, PR and marketing are more concerned about 'shared meanings' in communities. PR and marketing use their knowledge and understanding of significant micro-cultures, active publics and target audiences to create a space for engagement at which identities can be co-created or reinforced, often through commercial products and services such as magazines, DVDs, websites, clothes, and equipment. The challenge for PR is in trying to engage in meaningful communication and feedback with collective categories, which may be relatively unstable or fluid, and whose members are only in communication with subsidiary networks, some of which may be remote. The motivation behind such activities is frequently, though not always, commercial gain (for example, social marketing and PR campaigns to increase participation in sports have different behavioural and attitudinal goals). But reaching a particular marketing demographic inevitably lies behind much promotional and marketing activity. The commercial co-option of lifestyle sports to market other goods such as cars has become endemic. Lifestyle sports connote a variety of aspirational values including freedom, bravery, expertise, challenge, and taming the wild.

Many lifestyle sports have emerged since the 1970s from within the context of promotional culture and are already conscious of image as part of their community of 'edge-sport' practice, for example snowboarders. Such an identity already plays in to media stereotypes about 'adrenalin junkies' and sensation-seekers. Representatives of those sports can involve themselves actively in the identity creation of their sport and reflect upon whether their PR, promotion and impression management is truly authentic or just somewhat conventional. By falling into a stereotype they may just become 'another one of those "adrenalin junkie" sports' and become less able to distinguish themselves from close competitors in a way that could be detrimental in relationships with local communities or government, or in trying to widen participation.

The moment of production describes the process by which creators of cultural products imbue them with meaning. (Hall, cited in Curtin and Gaither, 2007). In lifestyle sports this process is a key part of the central proposition of an ideology of alternative authenticity. The 'bottom-up' creative emergence of new sports that combined risk, danger, music and art (popular culture) while rejecting formality and rules, is a major reason why the features and emergence of lifestyle sport are so fascinating. From a PR perspective, the emergence and very strong identities of such sports suggests that PR is not solely in the hands of political and corporate worlds, and that in fact we do inhabit some form of 'PR democracy'. Production is also relevant to the creation and marketing of events, such as adventure race series for example, Rat Races or Polaris. These require a concept, positioning and in some cases accessibility. While many adventure races are serious 'expedition' challenges of several days, monitored in tracking rooms and covered on TV, such as the Southern Traverse in New Zealand (mentioned earlier), event organizers have stepped in to create a new market of more manageable dimensions for 'weekend warriors' of weekend or even one- or half-day challenges as tasters and as a way to develop the market.

Consumption in the circuit of culture describes the interpretation, decoding and re-coding of messages by consumers as they engage with media or direct experiences of lifestyle sports culture. Their engagement with lifestyle sports cultures also contributes to the development of those cultures and shifts over time, for example as a lifestyle sport becomes more professionalized, or distinguishes itself from other similar lifestyle sports. Again one can see that the public images of a lifestyle sport are constructed from many experiences and opinions at street, club, local, national, and international level. All sport is a form of communication and specific cultures are enacted at the point of consumption and in the social life and worlds that encapsulate that experience.

Regulation is an interesting concept in the context of anti-authoritarian or alternative sporting lifestyles. As Lyng pointed, out there appears to be a,

' Core paradox represented by the very existence of edgework activities. In one perspective, edgework is seen as a means of freeing oneself from social conditions that deaden or deform the human spirit through overwhelming social regulation and control. In the other perspective, edgework valorizes risk-taking propensities and skills in demand throughout the institutional structures of risk society. Thus, in one view, edgeworkers seek to escape institutional constraints that have become intolerable; in the other, edgeworkers strive to better integrate themselves into the existing institutional environment … people may, on one level, seek a risk-taking experience of personal determination and transcendence in an environment of social over-regulation, whereas on another level they employ the human capital created by this experience to navigate the challenge of the risk society. (Lyng, 2005: 9–10) >

The identity of adventure sport may depend on their lack of regulation and PR rhetorical skills may be required on behalf of such sports to argue convincingly against such restraints (Palmer, 2004). Such advocacy and knowledge of public affairs and political processes could assist these sports to retain their distinctive identity and legitimate their practice. On the other hand, PR strategies and tactics may be employed on behalf of local and national government authorities to explain why regulation is necessary. In such contexts, PR performs rhetorical public communication in the court of public opinion and the media, which is why some commentators believe that it contributes to democratic practice.

In some sports there are no specific rules of engagement, just free expression, although there may be a form of linguistic regulation through the specific terms applied to particular 'tricks' or 'moves'. There are alternative climbing conventions too between British 'adventure climbing' and the safer bolted climbs with fixed gear that are common elsewhere. Nevertheless, some lifestyle sports contain regulatory aspects, for example, the use of a Global Positioning System (GPS) may be forbidden in adventure races where part of the test is traditional navigational skills using only map and compass. Some adventure races also specify the order and length of adventure race sections and administer penalty points for those who return late. But regulation is clearly relevant in terms of the lifestyle sport environment, for example, local government may determine where skating, rollerblading, parkour or BMX may or may not take place. Many skaters have heavily criticised the provision of skating parks for their technical inadequacy and lack of consultation. Furthermore, the risk that is intrinsic to many lifestyle sports often flouts convention and defies regulation, specifically laws, for example BASE jumping. BASE jumpers perform their own PR posting their exploits on the web, such as the twentieth anniversary jump off the Trollwall, Norway. Should lifestyle sport incur misadventure, then it is at least possible that legal liability will be sought by relatives.

Edgework is gradually being industrialized and regulated by the new and expanding adventure industry. Discourse work is required to support this process to create the illusion of risk and adventure.

PR contributes to the representation and mediatization of lifestyle sports on behalf of various stakeholders. For example, the producers of lifestyle gear will be keen to have their products covered by editorial review sections or placed in pictures of well-known exponents (product placement). PR is a major, if not the dominant source of news stories and features, even in mainstream news media, and certainly in magazine media. Similar to journalism, PR both reflects common assumptions and trends and stimulates new ideas on behalf of different organizations and clients.

The representation of lifestyle sport shares similar challenges to the mainstream sport in terms of gender, race and age. Many lifestyle magazines represent those they perceive to be their audience, often middle class ABC1 males with a 'good spend', who can afford the top of the range products, buy the magazines and celebrate their identity of lifestyle sport participant and enthusiast through reading and associated online discussion. Magazines and websites offer aspirational locations and lifestyles that are sources of fantasy to the novice afficianado who desires the social cachet.

Many lifestyle sports have their own media, often online specialist communities and magazine media. The journalism in these is often 'embedded', written by those who are also enthusiasts and participants, and key to co-constructing the identities of these sports. In magazines they are operating within the free market and need to sell magazines to survive and to continue writing about the sports they love. This means that magazine editors often have close, almost collaborative relationships with producers of specialist products or 'gear'. As one journalist commented, 'It is promotional work' and another said that, 'through the magazine we promote the sport, help put on a lot of events across the country … I also make skateboard videos as well … so I guess that constitutes promotion as well'.

One commentator pointed out that,

> It's vital for people in the BMX industry to liaise with us, and us with them, and get their products in the magazine and pictures of their riders and portray the sport as positively as possible so that everyone can benefit.

This relationship undercuts the purists, who might regard their sport as being outside promotional culture.

These quotations demonstrate clearly some of the relationships between media relations and journalism within the domain of adventure sports. The producers need coverage of products in targeted magazine media and their PR and marketing personnel will aim to gain positive mentions in editorial. The magazine editors need source material for their own business survival and are to some degree dependent on the producers and their PR practitioners, who will write promotional material to support the marketing promotion. The promotional landscape in lifestyle sport may be characterized by mixed messages from different sources; minority media at least partially dependent on advertising; missed opportunities for sponsorship and some apparent corporate parasitism. It appears to be the case that lifestyle sport practitioners could usefully take into account deeper considerations of promotional culture and the role of PR to establish and enhance the unique identities of the different lifestyle sports and their associated subcultures to ensure a better understanding and appreciation among the wider public.

Some adventure sports have governing bodies that often have limited resources to spend on PR activities. Nevertheless, their aims are typically PR focused and expressed using PR discourse. For example, International Mountain Biking UK, which does not employ a PR specialist, articulates its aims as 'Developing positive relationships with government agencies and Local Authorities ... cultivating partnerships ... working with other cycles organizations to maximize benefits for mountain biking.'

Likewise the 'vision' of British Orienteering includes 'expanding numbers of people ... widening the range of places' (www.britishorienteering.org.uk) and that of the Scottish Canoe Association is, according to one canoeist, 'to promote the sport of canoeing as widely as possible ... as a family sport, not just for rufty tutfty types [repositioning] ... [and improving] relationships with other water-users' (see also www.canoescotland.org).

Although adventure sports are exciting they are sometimes difficult to access for both spectators and media. Some, such as adventure racing or mountain biking, may take place overnight (possibly several nights), which means that televisuality is variable. In adventure racing it is necessary to use devices such as tracker boards to allow media to see the team competition developing and to generate interest. In general terms adventure sports find it much easier to generate coverage in tourism and lifestyle media than in sports media.

Summary

The key PR issues that arise for adventure sports are those of mixed identity, ideological tensions and risk that impact public awareness, identity and reputation, all within the PR remit. At present it seems that there are few PR specialists in this field and that PR considerations only develop out of event management and the need for publicity and promotion. PR activity is largely limited to media relations and marketing promotion rather than strategic issues management and risk communication, slightly surprising given increasingly legalistic cultures. The promotional landscape in adventure sport may be characterized by mixed messages from different sources; minority media at least partially dependent on advertising; missed opportunities for sponsorship and some apparent corporate parasitism. This chapter suggests that while engaging in PR activity may contribute to the mainstreaming of lifestyle sports, it can offer opportunities for cultural visibility and commercial success, as well as a better understanding of the many different activities and subcultures that exist under the 'lifestyle sport' definition.

Further Reading

Kay J and Laberge S (2002) The 'new' corporate habitus in adventure racing. *International Review for the Sociology of Sport*, 37 (1): 17–36.

Kellett P and Russell R (2009) A comparison between mainstream and action sport industries in Australia: a case study of the skateboarding cluster. *Sport Management Review*, 12: 66–78.

O'Brien D and Hunting J (2013) Sustainable surf tourism: a community centred approach in Papua New Guinea. *Journal of Sport Management*, 27 (2): 158–72.

Puchan H (2005) 'Living extreme': adventure sports, media and commercialisation. *Journal of Communication Management*, 9 (2).

Rinehart R (1998) Inside of the outside: pecking orders within alternative sport at ESPN's 1995 'The Extreme Games'. *Journal of Sport & Social Issues*, 22 (4): 398–415.

Thorpe H and R Rinehart (2012) *Journal of Sport & Social Issues*, 37 (2): 115–41.

Thorpe H and B Wheaton (2011) 'Generation X Games', action sports and the Olympic Movement: understanding the cultural politics of incorporation. *Sociology*, 45 (5): 830–47.

Thorpe H (2010) Bourdieu, gender reflexivity, and physical culture: a case of masculinities in the snowboarding field. *Journal of Sport and Social Issues*.

Wheaton B and B Beal (2003) 'Keeping it real' subcultural media and the discourses of authenticity in alternative sport. *International Review for the Sociology of Sport*, 38 (2): 155–76.

9

Understanding PR and Sport in Society

Introduction

This chapter aims to draw together critically focused themes that have emerged within the book to reflect upon some theoretical and practical implications. It reflects on the practice of PR in sport in relation to adjacent and competing roles and explores societal as opposed to organizational dynamics. Finally, the chapter applies Bourdieu's field theory to develop an interpretation of occupational dynamics and roles in sport PR.

The chapter covers:

- PR work and roles in sports practice
- Theoretical framework: Bourdieu's field theory
- Field theory in sport and sports PR
- Discussion and implications

Key Concepts

- Capital
- Cultural intermediary
- Distinction
- Doxa
- Habitus
- Fields

- Field theory
- Lifestyle
- Power
- Public sphere
- Thought leadership

Media, Sport Business and Capital

Sport business is an elite operation that intersects the higher echelons in political, economic, media, and social circles and networks. Individuals may move from one elite sphere to another through celebrity. Sport business favours male elite professional sports that either are, or can be commercialized, and the intersection between sport business and sport media reinforces that inequity. Increasingly, news media cover sport business stories regarding ownership, capitalization, financial health, funding, management, purchasing, and supply in addition to sport content. Not only do certain sports dominate, but elite sports bodies, corporations and major sports sponsors are also able to dominate the **public sphere** and converged media, lending support for the 'deep pockets' argument. In contrast, there is far less coverage of women's sports or disabled sports that generally are not funded at the same level by government or sponsors (the most obvious exception to this is tennis, largely due to the campaigning and feminist advocacy of Billie Jean King in the 1970s). There is an implicit collusion between media, sport business and capital that distorts the pattern, content and value of circulating discourses. Sports PR implicitly contributes to hegemonic constructions through discursive formations that link consumerist aspirations and identities with corporate and governmental economic priorities, social projects and development.

PR Work and Roles in Sports Practice

Promotional imperatives are central to capitalized sports business and reputational challenges and issues abound. Nevertheless, the identity and boundaries of sports PR sometimes appear to be unclear and variable. PR practice in sport is less visible than one might expect in a business redolent with competition and capital. In fact, PR work is done at all levels but it is not always acknowledged as a discrete occupation, often subsumed in marketing and branding activities. Coverage of PR as a business discipline was slight in *SBI* in the period 2005–2012. There was a special section in 2005 that defined PR as media relations and publicity for sponsorship, that did not appear to acknowledge strategic functions clearly central to sports business and described earlier in this book. Not until 2012 did a **thought leadership** section focus again on PR and communications, and it signalled what might be a significant change in approach along with acknowledgement of strategic aspects and their importance to sports business. In it the Editor argued,

' Success, failure, bust-ups, make-overs … and that's just in the boardroom. The
business of sport is innovative, secretive, sensitive and hugely competitive. There's
big money and big ambitions and the big egos that go with them. And as sport

has become more mainstream and the business behind it more sophisticated, the role of PR, media relations and communications has become more important and, out of necessity, more demanding and complex … The term "sports PR" includes reputation management, sponsor communications, marketing, brand-building, press office operations, event promotion and crisis management … media training has become another high-value strand of the sports PR sector … Today sports PR demands a deep understanding of [the] complex and diverse digital media environment. (Roberts, 2012b: 81)   **)**

Nevertheless, despite this apparently more visionary approach, some contributors to the thought leadership section still emphasized responsibility for responding to crises (no mention of their involvement in simmering issues that might precede them), media handling and a dissemination model of PR. However, others articulated a clear strategic role that is encouraging for those with ambitions to pursue a career in this area.

Thought Leadership in Sports PR: a sports business perspective

'Across sport everybody has to communicate, whether they are governing bodies, teams athletes or stadiums … there are far more communications channels available and it is essential that they are able to deliver the right messages to the right audiences by using the channels to best effects.' (Giles Morgan, Group Head of Sponsorship and Events, HSBC, quoted in *SBI*, 2012j: 84)

'PR, however good, has never won a sports bid on its own. PR consultants should know they are a servant, not a master … PR and communications must first help to breathe life into a bid's brand and narrative (its motivation, its character, its difference from other bids, its legacy) … PR's second key role is at home. No sports organization will proffer its highest honour to bid in the teeth of local or national resistance.' (Dennis Landsbert-Noon, Chairman EMEA Media and Sports Practices, Burson-Marsteller, quoted in *SBI*, 2012g: 82)

'It's about identifying appropriate channels to deliver particular messages and about making complex strategic calls.' (Roberts, 2012b: 81)

Interestingly, the final contributor to the thought leadership issue was a journalist, Keir Radenage, who had given media relations advice to various sports organizations including FIFA. This dual occupational role is of interest in itself, indicating precisely the continuing ease with which journalists move into PR, demonstrating that boundaries between these occupations remain porous. Radenage explained the emergence of PR as an inevitable consequence of commercialization that required pragmatic solutions to heightened media interest. However, he also suggested that the rise of sports PR had led to reduced journalism access to players, a common complaint that has been raised about PR in a range of contexts since the 1940s (at least in the UK).

> ❝ Back in the day you simply didn't have directors of communication at football clubs or even governing bodies. It was a different era then and sport was played more or less for its own sake. Sports PR was born out of commercialization and the need of governing bodies, teams and sponsors to find people with knowledge and experience who could help ensure they were well represented in the media. In fact it may have gone too far as one of the complaints about PR people [from journalists] is that they seem to think their job is to keep the press at bay. That simply antagonizes them and if often counter-productive … Good PRs are all about the story and not themselves. (Keir Radenage quoted in *SBI*, 2012g: 85) ❞

The idea of the PR worker as behind the scenes facilitator also goes back to the 1940s and 1950s in the UK. Much PR work has been and remains centred about media publicity, the maintenance of technical websites, blogs and social media outlets, frequently focused on fan relations; and roles that concentrate on the output of information via digital media and professional print and broadcast media. As technicians their main day-to-day role is the production and dissemination of information. For example, in British football, practitioners are largely focused on the media and fans. Their work is primarily structured around matches, editorial content for programmes and websites, match day entertainment, drafting material for managers and players and monitoring social media and blogs. The role includes a customer and complaints handling aspect, responding to fan criticism and communicating with supporters clubs, in some cases holding open forums where supporters question the manager and players in an open meeting because as one practitioner stated, 'the fans are the most important group' and can, as another said, 'be fickle', depending on match results because 'the performance on field really affects the mood of your customer'. Nevertheless, relational work is also carried out with a wider range of stakeholders including commercial partners and sponsors, suppliers, shareholders, and any customers who may use or hire club facilities. Inevitably larger, more successful clubs have more potential for reach and influence and can think about responding to issues on the public and social agenda both in the immediate community and more widely. Recruitment activities to ensure another generation of supporters/consumers is also important, so schools, teachers and local junior clubs are important. Effort may be directed towards youngsters, for example in 2007

Heart of Midlothian FC developed the Magnificent Seven scheme through which every seven-year-old in Edinburgh and the Lothians was invited to a presentation on a week-day evening, taken for a tour round the stadium, introduced to players and mascots and given two free tickets. In this way youngsters are given some insight into the culture and values of the club and in some cases to begin to see the club as part of their own community, possibly to be incorporated into their own identity. Internally public relations practitioners have also to consider employee relations including footballers for whom media training is required.

The overlap between PR, media and agents is also an interesting intersection, indicating that PR's boundaries may also be opaque in this area with the boundaries between PR and journalism (above) and between PR and marketing/branding (evidenced in the lack of distinction in *SBI*). These relationships are constantly negotiated around particular tasks or resources. Agents may carry out media work behind the scenes, for example suggesting to media that a player is of interest to a club that may lead to others believing that a player is unsettled in their present club and might be open to a move. Increasingly it seems that agents take on the role of media representative. However, football agents are football experts primarily rather than marketing or PR specialists. From a journalists' perspective both agents and PR practitioners can be seen as a barrier to access with a sports star.

Theoretical Framework: Bourdieu's Field Theory

The rest of this chapter focuses on the application of **field theory** as a way of understanding the occupation of sports PR, beginning with a brief explanation of the key elements that form Bourdieu's field theory. Within PR, Bourdieu's ideas have been taken up by a number of academics most notably Edwards (2005, 2008, 2009, 2011) and Ihlen (2005, 2007; Ihlen et al., 2009). Bourdieu is chosen here partly because he had useful and interesting things to say about sport and society, and partly because his ideas can be used to interpret issues relating to public relations structures, practices, role, scope and professional status.

Bourdieu conceptualized fields as bounded spheres within which agents competed for dominance. Fields present particular sets of beliefs known as **doxa** and structure the social world as defined by practice. Within fields, systems of classification emerge; norms, values and attitudes are intertwined with practices and processes that produce systems of classification

Think Critically

Compare the marketing deals achieved by a selection of footballers compared to sports stars in a range of other sports? How do these compare? What are the implications of your findings for footballers, agents, clubs and PR practitioners?

that operate as 'a structured and structuring structure' (Bourdieu, 1986: 171). Being part of a field means internalizing, practising, enacting the values of field and its systems – a feature, process and 'generative formula' known as **habitus:**

> ❛ The **habitus** is necessarily internalised and converted into a disposition that generates meaningful practices and meaning-giving perceptions; it is a general, transposable disposition which carries out a systematic universal application. (Bourdieu, 1986: 170) ❜

Habitus emerges from accretions of experience and environment and facilitates the elaboration of **sociocultural capital** that positions its owners symbolically within power dynamics of the field. In sports business **cultural capital** played a clear role in the ability of the following graduate to get into the business,

> ❛ Kiernan landed himself a job in the sports industry straight off a non-sporting bachelors programme…' Having a history degree wasn't a problem at all when trying to get into the sports industry… In fact I think it was beneficial to do a non-sporting degree, because it means you have quite a broad range of skills to draw upon like essay-writing, presenting, reading and researching. I think I got the job … because I had a good academic degree from a decent university with quite a lot of extra-curricular sporting interests. I'd also been recommended by someone who had previously worked there. (Chauhan, 2013: 96) ❜

The quote shows how distinctive markers may be used in the competitive job market. Similarly in PR (in the UK at least) there continues to be a pattern of recruitment that rather surprisingly does not favour those with a degree in the subject, something that suggests that PR is shaped by cultural values rather than by the values and principles of professionalism that would enforce specialist qualifications as a barrier to entry to the occupation.

> ❛ Class habitus, the internalized form of class condition and the conditioning it entails … [is] practice-unifying and practice-generating. (Bourdieu, 1986: 101) ❜

Capital requires labour and investment, and while it is not an innate power inherited benefits are possible through class advantage. For example, one practitioner commented on the challenges of getting into sports PR,

> ❛ The main gripe I have with the industry is that you do get some fantastic graduates from some of the best universities in the country and they're earning nothing for six months, and the only ones who can do that are ones who have quite wealthy parents who can fund them. I think that's going to be a detriment to the industry because it stops the hungry brilliant people that haven't got funding. ❜

Capital has value and is the consequence of relationships but as it is scarce it is the focus on competition within the field (Bourdieu, 1990: 122 cited in Ihlen, 2007: 66). **Capital** comprises three key types: **economic** (money, property); **cultural** (knowledge, skills, educational qualifications); **social** (connections, networks, memberships of certain groups); and appears in various forms such as political, personal, functional, professional, linguistic, intellectual and scholastic (Ihlen, 2007: 66 citing Bourdieu, 1991). Capital demonstrates and communicate **habitus** through the possession and display of assets:

> The habitus is necessarily internalised and converted into a disposition that generates meaningful practices and meaning-giving perceptions; it is a general, transposable disposition which carries out a systematic, universal application. (Bourdieu, 1984: 170)

Status, and therefore **power** are linked to the amount of relevant capital and **symbolic value**. Fields are **homologous** so that the structure of smaller fields reflects power structures (Edwards, 2011: 62). According to Bourdieu capital is the 'energy of social physics' (Bourdieu, 1990: 122 cited in Ihlen, 2007: 66) a phrase that could be understood as **dominance**.

Lifestyles are the products and sign systems of **habitus**, the indicators that mark valued capital. **Distinction** is the process arising from that which categorizes markers between more or less valued capital and groups,

> Principles of division, inextricably logical and sociological, function within and for the purposes of struggle between social groups; in producing concepts, they produce groups, the very groups which produce the principles and the groups against which they are produced. What is at stake in the struggles about the meaning of the social world is power over classificatory schemes and systems which are the basis of representations of the groups and therefore of their mobilization and demobilization: the evocative power of an utterance which puts things in a different light (as happened for example, when a single word, such as 'paternalism', changes the whole experience of a social relationship) or which modifies the schemes of perception, shows something else, other properties, previously unnoticed or relegated to the background (such as common interests hitherto marked by ethnic or national differences); a separative power, a distinction, *diacrisis*, *discretio*, drawing discrete units out of indivisible continuity, difference out of undifferentiated. (Bourdieu, 1984: 479)

In addition to the subtle understandings that Bourdieu portrays of dynamic power and competitive relationships in a societal context, his analysis highlights processes in which field assumptions are created and maintained through practice and language. His analysis has strong relevance to both sport and sport PR and it is to this that attention is now given.

Field Theory in Sport and Sports PR

Field Theory in Sport

In his classic study *Distinction: a social critique of the judgement of taste* (1986), Bourdieu applied his scheme to French society, usefully referring on several occasions to sport practices. He highlighted the elements that lay behind the distribution of different types of sport across society, exploring those that were stigmatized and those advantaged in terms of social capital,

' To understand the class distribution of the various sports, one would have to take account of the representation which, in terms of their specific schemes of perception and appreciation, the different classes have of costs (economic, cultural and 'physical') and benefits attached to the different sports – immediate or deferred 'physical' benefits (health, beauty, strength, whether visible, through 'body-building' or invisible through 'keep-fit' exercises) economic and social benefits (upward mobility etc.) immediate or deferred symbolic benefits linked to the distributional or positional value of each of the sports considered (i.e. that all of them received from its greater or lesser rarity, and its more or less clear association with a class, with boxing, football, rugby or body-building evoking the working classes, tennis and skiing the bourgeoisie and golf the upper bourgeoisie), gains in distinction accruing from the effects on the body itself (e.g. slimness, sun-tan, muscles obviously or discreetly visible etc.) or from access to highly selective groups which some of these sports give (golf, polo etc,). (Bourdieu, 1984: 20) '

This book has provided examples of these processes in play societally, and explored how economic capital invests in branding to connote values in relation to certain sports, for example attention has been given to golf's elite connotations in some cultures. However, within some fields the capital is social, but not necessarily capitalized, for example in the case of the minority sport Eton Fives in the UK. Eton Fives is an historic sport that originated at the exclusive fee-paying school Eton College in the mid-nineteenth century. This has remained its base and recruitment is still dependent on the 30 or so public schools (the term is a misnomer since these schools are actually fee-paying private schools) that play the game and special events at Eton. Such sponsorship is limited, but interesting in its associations. For example HSBC has sponsored the Prep Schools Championship and the champagne company Paul Roche has sponsored the University Championships. Internationally, the sport has bases in Switzerland, Nigeria, and India a consequence of public school masters who travelled to these countries from the 1900s. The sport's rarity, origins and class base clearly marked out a distinctive group. However, in order to survive the sport has latterly attempted to move away from its traditional base and also to achieve social and community goals by seeking to attract boys and girls from local state schools.

This example illustrates the dynamics within this particular sports field, the doxa, habitus, power connections, assumptions, and values. The historical trajectory illustrates how the elite field of Eton Fives reflected social, political and economic power structures in

British society, but that more recently it has taken a more populist and community-based approach in order to survive, necessarily blurring its original distinction.

Field Theory in Sports PR

Sports PR is a specialist field both within PR, where strategic positioning and communication power are valued, and within sports business where economic capital is prioritized alongside a frequent mobilization of the term 'passion' that legitimizes discourse that disguises commercial gain.

> ## Think Critically
>
> Analyse a sport with which you are familiar and apply Bourdieu's schema. How does this help understand the sport and its relationship to society?

The field of PR, however, is not clearly bounded and in sports business merges opaquely with marketing and branding and sometimes with sports agents and journalists who occupy some of the same social space and participate in shared networks. This necessarily leads to intense competition at the periphery over symbolic power and language within the dialectical relationship between habitus and doxa in the context of open systems. As one PR consultant explained,

' We were attending a sporting dinner and sports agents were there as well. We see them and we talk to them quite a lot, it's just in the milieu of going about and working in sport ... sport is a small world and highly fragmented which means there are always going to be close relationships, business and personal. '

PR practitioners operate within the PR field and compete with each other and with those with similar expertise (marketing) both within and between different fields, for example within sport, politics, the law, medicine) and between different subfields (for example football or badminton) that structure status and symbolic value via the doxa. The field of PR is divided into subfields of consultancy and in-house, and within and between that into specialized areas such as consumer, employee communications within different economic sectors (sport, tourism, health, environment). Since the field of power encompasses these, public affairs has a higher status and more symbolic power than press officer; those working for large consultancies and important powerful clients have higher status than freelance self-employed consultants or those working for less influential interests. Public relations specialists navigate a context of overlapping expertises and are best recognised for their facility with the media, although the online converged and fluid media environment challenges previously established practices and processes in a way that influences self-understanding and introduces a new classification of expertise in the field, shaking up established norms in ways that are not yet fully understood.

Edwards argued that 'In PR the **doxa** relates to the role of the profession in society, the techniques they use to realize that role and the rationale given to clients and others to justify PR importance' (Edwards, 2011: 62). However, the **doxa** relates to the occupation's competitive position *in a particular field or subfield*, and it is the techniques the occupation *is actually able to use* in the context of its position in that particular field or subfield in relation to its discursive position (rationale) that is significant, not only with regard to its clients but also to *itself* (reflexive self-impressions) as well as in relation to the position of its field or subfield to other fields and subfields, and the dynamics of power and influence within and between these.

In other words, because PR does not have completely convincing distinctive status in the sports subfield, workers may be unable to exercise strategic intention or to contribute to the policy level, instead being retained in a service function rather than elite consultancy supported by acknowledged expertise. This lived reality frames the occupation's sense of itself. Within the competitive PR professional field it appears that the relatively lower status is reinforced, exemplified by the lack of sports special interest groups in professional bodies and the fact that it is relatively recently that professional bodies awarded prizes in this subfield in annual awards ceremonies – a signifier of symbolic capital.

Furthermore, within the field of sports business the gendered nature of PR practice raises interesting questions as to the likely status and progression of the PR specialism in a business environment where few women have succeeded in reaching the most senior levels as discussed in a previous chapter.

In Conclusion

While much of this book has been taken up with description and analysis of practices and language in the sports PR business context, the undercurrents of power can be readily detected within the complex, adjoining, and to some degree overlapping and homologous political, sociocultural, economic fields, sports and business subfields, and converged media. There is no doubt that sport has acquired power through capital, but interesting questions remain about the exercise of communication power by PR practitioners, the roles they play and the expertise they deploy. The invisibility and behind the scenes nature of much of the work of **cultural intermediaries** such as PR makes investigation challenging, but central to an understanding of the often taken for granted practices facilitated by habitus and doxa to which sport contributes in contemporary society. Although this book contributes some insight into PR issues relevant to sport, the sports business practices and values relating to PR and PR in sport, it also indicates the necessity for more substantial empirical research in this area that can indicate more precisely the flows of communication power in sportscape.

Summary

This chapter has reflected on the role of PR within sport and society and suggested that within sports business a relatively limited notion of the scope of PR tends to dominate so that everyday practicalities of PR are focused on techniques of communication. Bourdieu's ideas have been applied to indicate deeper sociocultural understanding of the significance of sports PR, its structures, boundaries, challenges, operations, and values. It has shown that the connection between and among a variety of fields and subfields within which contestation for power is enacted within the context of societal power and capitals affects the operation and recognition of public.

Further Reading

Cleland JA (2009) The changing organizational structure of football clubs and their relationship with the external media. *International Journal of Sport Communication*, 2 (4).

Coombs DS and Osborne A (2012) Sports journalists and England's Barclay's Premier League: a case study examining reporters' takes on modern football. *International Journal of Sport Communication*, 5 (3): 413–25.

Edwards L (2007) PR practitioners' cultural capital: an initial study and implications for research and practice. *Public Relations Review*, 24: 367–72.

Edwards L (2005) Rethinking power in public relations. *Public Relations Review*, 32: 229–31.

Ihlen O (2007) Building on Bourdieu: a sociological grasp of public relations. *Public Relations Review*, 33: 269–74.

Kitchin PJ and Howe PD (2002) How can social theory of Pierre Bourdieu assist sport management research. *Sport Management Review*, 16 (2): 123–34.

References

Adler D (2011) A stellar performance. *SBI*, 172: 14–15.

Allison L (Ed.) (2005) *The Global Politics of Sport: the Role of Global Institutions in Sport.* London: Routledge.

Allison L and Monington T (2005) Sport, prestige and international relations. In Allison, L. (Ed.) (2005) *The Global Politics of Sport: the Role of Global Institutions in Sport.* London: Routledge.

Anderson W (2006) American v. national football league: using PR to 'win' a war against a monopoly. *Public Relations Review*, 32 (1): 53–7.

Anderson W (2008) Pete Rozelle: a historical review of how the NFL commissioner used PR. *Public Relations Review*, 34 (2): 152–5.

Andreff W (2004) The taxation of player moves from developing countries. In R Fort and J Fizel (Eds) *International Sports Economics Comparisons.* Westport CT: Praeger: 87–103.

Andreff W (2008) Sport in developing societies. In W Andreff, J Boland and S Szymanski (Eds) *Handbook of the Economics of Sport.* Cheltenham: Edward Elgar Publishing.

Andrews DL and Jackson S (Eds) (2001) *Sports Stars: the Cultural Politics of Sporting Celebrity.* London: Routledge.

Anstead N and O'Loughlin B (2011) Twenty20 as media event. *Sport in Society*, 14 (10): 1340–57.

Appadurai A (1996) *Modernity At Large: Cultural Determinants of Globalization.* Minneapolis: University of Minneapolis Press.

Armstrong G and Giulianotti R (Eds) (2004) *Football in Africa: Conflict, Conciliation and Community.* London Palgrave.

Askwith R (2004) *Feet in the Clouds: a Tale of Fell-running and Obsession.* London: Aurum Press.

Bale J and Christensen MK (2004) *Post-Olympism? Questioning Sport in the Twenty-First Century.* Oxford: Berg.

BBC News (2012) Argentine Olympic advert riles Falklands, 4 May. Available at www.bbc.co.uk/news/world-latin-america-17948002 (accessed 1 October 2013).

Beech J and Chadwick S (2004) *The Business of Sports Management.* London: Pearson Education.

Bennett T (1988) The exhibitionary complex. *New Formations*, 4 Spring: 73–102.

Benoit WL (1995) *Accounts, Excuses and Apologies: a Theory of Image Restoration Strategies.* Albany NY: State University of New York.

Benoit WL (1999) Image repair discourse and crisis communication. *Public Relations Review*, 23: 177–86.

Benoit WL and Hanzicor R (1994) The Tonya Harding controversy: an analysis of image restoration strategies. *Communication Quarterly*, 42: 416–33.

Benson R and Neveu E (2005) *Bourdieu and the Journalistic Field*. Cambridge: Polity.

Beutler I (2008) Sport serving development and peace: achieving the goals of the UN. *Sport in Society*, 11 (4): 359–69.

Black D (2010) The ambiguities of development: implications for 'development through sport'. *Sport in Society*, 13(1): 121–9.

Blain N, Boyle R and O'Donnell H (1993) *Sport and National Identity in the European Media*. Leicester: Leicester University Press.

Bloxham C (2006) *SBI*, 25.

Boorstin DJ (1992) *The Image: a Guide to Pseudo-events in America*. New York: Random House.

Bourdieu P (1984) *Distinction: A Social Critique of Taste*. Translated by R. Nice. Cambridge MA: Harvard University Press.

Bourdieu P and Wacquant LJD (1992) *An Invitation to Reflexive Sociology*. Cambridge: Polity Press.

Bourgeois N (1995) Sports journalists and their source of information: a conflict of interests and its resolution. *Sociology of Sport Journal*, 12: 195–203.

Bowden G, McDonnell I, Allen J and Toole W (1999, reprinted 2003) *Event Management*. Oxford: Butterworth Heinemann.

Boyd-Barrett O (1977) Media imperialism: towards an international framework for the analysis of media systems. In J Curran, M Gurevitch and J Woollacott (Eds) *Mass Communication and Society*. London: Edward Arnold: 174–95.

Boyd-Barrett O (1998) Media imperialism reformulated. In DK Thussu (Ed.) *Electronic Empires: Global Media and Local Resistance*. London: Edward Arnold: 157–76.

Boyd J and Stahley M (2008) Communitas/corporatas tensions in organizational rhetoric: finding a balance in sports public relations. *Journal of Public Relations Research*, 20: 251–70.

Boyle R (1992) From our Gaelic fields: radio, sport and nation in post-partisan Ireland. *Media, Culture and Society*, 14: 623–36.

Boyle R (2006) *Sports Journalism*. London: Sage.

Boyle R (2013) Reflections on communication and sport: on journalism and digital culture. *Communication and Sport*, 1 (1/2): 88–99.

Boyle R and Haynes R (2000) *Power Play: Sport, the Media and Popular Culture*. London: Longman.

Boyle R and Haynes R (2006) The football industry and public relations. In J L'Etang and M Pieczka (Eds) *Public Relations: Critical Debates and Contemporary Practice*. Mahwah NJ: Lawrence Erlbaum Associates: 221–41.

Braman S (2002) A pandemonic age. In WB Gudykunst and B Mody (Eds) *Handbook of International and Intercultural Communication*. Thousand Oaks CA: Sage: 309–24.

Brazeal L (2008) The image repair strategies of Terrell Owens. *Public Relations Review*, 34 (2): 145–50.

Brit Sport 2009 *The Definitive UK Sports Industry Guide*. Sport Business Group Companies Ltd.

Britcher C (2006) The ones to watch. *SBI*, 116: 36–7.

British Horseracing Authority (2012) Statement from BHA Chief Executive regarding the John Smith's Grand National. Available at www.britishhorseracing.presscentre.com/Press-Releases/Statement-from-BHA-Chief-Executive-regarding-the-John-Smith-s-Grand-National-29e.aspx (accessed 1 October 2013).

Brookes R (2002) *Representing Sport.* Oxford: Oxford University Press.

Broom GM, Casey S and Ritchey J (1997) Toward a concept and theory of organization – public relationships. *Journal of Public Relations Research*, 9: 83–93.

Broom GM, Casey S and Ritchey J (2000) Concept and theory of organization – public relationships. In JA Ledingham and SD Bruning (Eds) *Public Relations as Relationship Management: a Relational Approach to the Study and Practice of Public Relations.* Mahwah NJ: Lawrence Erlbaum Associates: 3–22.

Bruce T and Tini T (2008) Unique crisis response strategies in sports PR: rugby league and the case for diversion. *Public Relations Review*, 34 (2): 108–15.

Bruning SD and Ledingham JA (1999) Relationships between organizations and publics. Development of a multi-dimensional organization–public scale. *Public Relations Review*, 25: 157–70.

Campbell V (2004) *Information Age Journalism: Journalism in International Context.* London: Arnold.

Cartmell M (2012) G4S under fire for comms stance. *PRW*, 20 July: 3.

Chadwick S and Beech J (Eds) (2006) *The Marketing of Sport.* London, FTPH.

Chauhan E (2013) Good karma. *SBI*, 189: 18.

Chehabi H (2001) Sport diplomacy between the United States and Iran. *Diplomacy and Statecraft*, 12 (1): 89–106.

Choi P (2000) *Femininity and the Physically Active Woman.* London & Philadelphia: Routledge Taylor and Francis Group.

Coakley J and Dunning E (Eds) (2000) *Handbook of Sports Studies.* London: Sage.

Coalter F (2006) *Sport-in-Development: A Monitoring and Evaluation Manual.* London: UK Sport.

Coalter F (2007) *A Wider Social Role for Sport: Who's Keeping the Score?* London: Routledge.

Coalter F (2009) 'Sport-in-development: accountability or development?'. In R. Levermore and A. Beacom (Eds) *Sport and International Development.* Basingstoke: Palgrave.

Coalter F (2010a) *Sport for Development Impact Study.* London: Comic Relief.

Coalter F (2010b) The politics of sport-for-development: limited focus programmes and broad gauge problems? *International Review for the Sociology of Sport*, 45: 295–314.

Cook C (2012) RSPCA want rempval of 'killer fence' Becher's Brook at Grand National. *The Guardian*, 1 May. Available at www.theguardian.com/sport/2012/may/01/grand-national-rspca-bechers-brook (accessed 1 October 2013).

Cooper J (2009) Sports show must go on. *SBI,* 144: 9.

Cornelissen J (2008) *Corporate Communication: a Guide to Theory and Practice.* London: Sage.

Cornelissen S (2008) Scripting the nation: sport, mega-events, foreign policy and state-building in post-apartheid South Africa. *Sport in Society: Cultures, Commerce, Media, Politics*, 11 (4): 481–93.

Corporate Golf World (2005a) Enter the dragon. 11–12.

Corporate Golf World (2005b) King Curt. Spring/Summer: 8–9.

Crawford G (2004) *Consuming Sport: Fans, Sport and Culture*. London: Routledge.

Culture, Media and Sport Committee (2011) *Football Governance: Seventh Report of Session 2010–12*. London: The Stationary Office. Available at www.publications.parliament.uk/pa/cm201012/cmselect/cmcumeds/792/792i.pdf (accessed 1 October 2013).

Cunningham J (2013) Going the extra mile. *SBI*, 186: 70.

Curtin P and Gaither TK (2007) *International PR: Negotiating Culture, Identity and Power*. London: Sage.

Cutler M (2011) Time to take action. *SBI*, 173: 12–13.

Cutlip, M and Center A (1950) *Effective Public Relations*. Upper Saddle River NJ: Prentice Hall.

Daily Mail (2013) Shamed cyclist Lance Armstrong drops out of swim meet after outcry over his lifetime ban from competition, 4 April. Available at www.dailymail.co.uk/news/article-2303762/Lance-Armstrong-Disgraced-cyclist-drops-swim-meet-outcry.html (accessed 1 October 2013).

Darnell S (2012) Olympism in action, Olympic hosting and the politics of 'Sport for Development and Peace': investigating the development discourses of Rio 2016. *Sport in Society*, 15 (6): 869–87.

David P (2005) *Human Rights in Youth Sport*. London: Routledge.

Dawson A (2013) Dispatches from the skate war. *Metro*. July 18th: 32.

Dayan D and Katz E (1994) *Media Events: the Live Broadcasting and History*. Cambridge MA: Harvard University Press.

de Certeau M (1988) *The Practice of Everyday Life*. Berkeley CA: University of California Press.

Debord G (1994) *The Society of the Spectacle*. New York: Zone Books.

Dimitrov R (2008) Gender violence, fan activism and PR in sport: the case of 'Footy Fans Against Sexual Assault', *Public Relations Review*, 34 (2): 90–99.

Dinan W and Miller D (2007) *Thinker, Faker, Spinner, Spy: Corporate PR and the Assault on Democracy*. London: Pluto Press.

Domingues B (2010) The inaugural Youth Olympics: bringing the game to a new generation. *SBI*, 160: 73.

Downing J, McQuail D, Schlesinger P and Wartella E (Eds) (2004) *The Sage Handbook of Media Studies*. London: Sage.

Dozier D, Grunig J and Grunig L (1995) *Manager's Guide to Excellence in Public Relations and Communication Management*. Mahwah NJ: Lawrence Erlbaum Associates.

Dutta-Bergman M (2005) Civil society and public relations: not so civil after all. *Journal of Public Relations Research*, 17(3): 267–89.

Dutta M (2008) *Communicating Health: a Culture-centred Approach*. Cambridge: Polity.

Edwardes D (2010) Parkour's leap of faith. *SBI*, 162: 9.

Edwards L (2008) PR practitioners' cultural capital: an initial study and implications for research and practice. *Public Relations Review*, 34: 367–72.

Edwards L (2009) Symbolic power and PR practice: locating individual practitioners in their social context. *Journal of Public Relations Research*, 21 (3): 251–72.

Edwards L (2011) PR in society: a Bourdieuvian perspective. In L Edwards and C Hodges (Eds) *Public Relations, Society and Culture: Theoretical and Empirical Explorations.* London: Routledge: 61–74.

Edwards L (2012) Defining the 'object' of PR research: a new starting point. *Public Relations Inquiry*, 1 (1): 7–30.

Edwards L and Hodges C (2011) *Public Relations, Society and Culture: Theoretical and Empirical Explorations.* London: Routledge.

Eisenegger M (2005) Reputation nurturing as a core function of PR. Presented at the International Communication Association. 26–30 May, New York.

Evans O (2011) Sports social network. *SBI*, 174: 19.

Evans O (2012a) An unlikely hero. *SBI*, 176: 26.

Evans O (2012b) Sport's biggest losers *SBI*, 177: 27.

Evans O (2012c) Unique style, mass appeal. *SBI*, 176: 28–9.

Farnsworth D (2006) Whose shirt is it anyway? *SBI*, 118: 58.

Featherstone M (2007) *Consumer Culture and Postmodernism.* London: Sage.

Ferguson M (Ed.) (1990) *Public Communication: the New Imperatives: Future Directions for Research.* London: Sage.

Fletcher R (2008) Living on the edge, the appeal of risk sports for the professional middle class. *Sociology of Sport Journal*, 25: 310–30.

Fombrun C and van Riel C (2003) The reputational landscape. In JY Balmer and S Greyser (Eds) *Revealing the Corporation: Perspectives in Identity, Reputation, Corporate Branding and Corporate Level Marketing.* London: Routledge: 223–33.

Fortunato J (2008) Restoring a reputation: the Duke University lacrosse scandal. *Public Relations Review*, 34 (2): 116–23.

Fry A (2006) Understanding the Eastern promise. *SBI*, 111: 44–6.

Fry A (2008a) Agencies size up the market. *SBI*, 133: 16.

Fry A (2008b) Blooming marvellous. *SBI*, 132: 30.

Fry A (2008c) Come dine with me. *SBI*, 131: 38–41.

Fry A (2011) Building bridges for brands. *SBI*, 173: 52.

Galtung J (1996) *Peace by Peaceful Means: Peace and Conflict, Development and Civilization.* International Peace Research Institute Oslo. London: Sage.

Galtung J and Ruge MH (1965) The structure of foreign news: the press coverage of the Congo, Cuba and Cyprus crises in 4 Norwegian newspapers. *Journal of Peace Research*, 2(1): 64–90.

Gandy O (1982) *Beyond agenda-setting, information subsidies and public policies.* Norwood NJ: Ablex.

Giddens A (1996) *Sociology* (2nd edn). Cambridge: Polity Press.

Giese R (2000) She got game. In P Donnelly (Ed.) *Taking Sport Seriously: Social Issues in Canadian Sport.* Toronto: Thompson education: 83–6.

Gilchrist P (2005) Local heroes or global stars. In Allison L (Ed.) *The Global Politics of Sport: the Role of Global Institutions in Sport.* London: Routledge.

Gillis R (2008) Country on a mission. *SBI*, 132: 64–5.

Glantz M (2009) The Floyd Landis doping scandal: implications for image repair discourse. *Public Relations Review*, 36: 157–63.

Glendinning M (2006a) Building a winning platform. *SBI*, 106: 49–56.

Glendinning M (2006b) Sports security reassures insurance market. *SBI*, 110: 46–7.

Glendinning M (2008a) Don't bet on us, says the CFT. *SBI*, 133: 12–13.

Glendinning M (2008b) Moscow – the heart of Russia's revival. *SBI*, 131: 65.

Glendinning M (2008c) Hospitality rides the slowdown. *SBI*, 133: 10.

Glendinning M (2009a) A tale of two cities. *SBI*, 142: 30–32.

Glendinning M (2009b) Assessing the impact. *SBI*, 143: 74–5.

Glendinning M (2012) Breaking barriers. *SBI*, 182: 15.

Grand D and Goldberg A (2011) *This is your Brain on Sports: Beating Blocks, Slumps and Performance Anxiety for Good*. Indianapolis IN: Dog Ear Publishing.

Gratton C and Henry I (Eds) (2001) *Sport in the City: the Role of Sport in Economic and Social Regeneration*. London: Routledge.

Grunig J (1992) *Excellence in Public Relations and Communication Management*. Mahwah NJ: Lawrence Erlbaum Associates.

Grunig J and Hunt T (1984) *Managing PR*. New York: Holt, Rinehart & Winston.

Gudykunst WB (2002) Cross-cultural communication: introduction. In WB Gudykunst and B Mody (Eds), *Handbook of International and Intercultural Communication*. Thousand Oaks CA: Sage: 19–24.

Gudykunst WB and Mody B (Eds) (2002) *Handbook of International and Intercultural Communication*. Thousand Oaks CA: Sage.

Habermas J (1989) *The Structural Transformation of the Public Sphere: an Inquiry into a Category of Bourgeois Society*. Cambridge: Polity Press.

Hall S (1969) The technics of persuasion. *The New Statesman*, 948–9.

Hall S et al (1978) *Policing the Crisis: Mugging, the State and Law and Order*. London: Macmillan.

Harcourt T (2009) Exporting expertise. *SBI*, 142: 51.

Hargreaves J (1994) *Sporting Females: Critical Issues in the History and Sociology of Women's Sports*. London: Routledge.

Harman L (2012) Cloozup and personal. *SBI,* 180, 7: 21.

Haunts (2005) *Sidewalk*, 103: 76.

Hay P (2009) Kindred digital hire indicates new focus. *PRW,* 24 July.

Haynes R (2005) *Media Rights and Intellectual Property*. Edinburgh: Edinburgh University Press.

Heath RL (1980) Corporate advocacy: an application of speech communication perspectives and skills – and more. *Communication Education*, 29: 370–7.

Heath RL (1991) Ethics of internal rhetoric on management response to external issues: how corporate culture failed the asbestos industry. *Journal of Applied Communication*, 18 (2): 153–67.

Hearit KM (2001) Corporate apologia: when an organization speaks in defence of itself. In R Heath (Ed.) *Sage Handbook of Public Relations*. Thousand Oaks CA: Sage: 501–3.

Helitzer M (1999) *The Dream Job: Sport$ Publicity, Promotion and Marketing* (3rd edn). University Sports Press in partnership with Team Marketing Report Inc. in co-operation with the Graduate School of Recreation and Sport Sciences and the EW Scripps School of Journalism. Athens OH: Ohio University.

Herman E and Chomsky N (1988) *Manufacturing Consent*. New York: Pantheon.

Hill A (2012) Crossing the divide. *SBI*, 175: 18–19.

Hoberman J (1995) Toward a theory of Olympic internationalism. *Journal of Sport History*, 22 (1): 1–37.

Hoberman J (2011) The myth of sport as a peace-promoting political force. *The SAIS Review of International Affairs*, 31 (1): 17–29.

Hodges C (2006) *Relaciones Humanas: the Potential for PR Practitioners as Cultural Intermediaries in Mexico City*. Unpublished doctoral thesis, University of Bournemouth.

Hodges C (2011) Public relations in the postmodern city: an ethnographic account of PR occupational culture in Mexico City. In L Edwards and C Hodges (Eds) *Public Relations, Society & Culture: Theoretical and Empirical Explorations*. London: Routledge: 33–46.

Hognestad H and Tollison A (2004) Playing against deprivation: football and development in Nairobi, Kenya. In G Armstrong and R Guilianotti (Eds) *Football in Africa: Conflict, Conciliation and Community*. London: Palgrave: 210–28.

Holladay SJ and Coombs WT (2013) Public relations literacy: developing critical consumers of public relations. *Public Relations Inquiry*, 2 (2): 125–46.

Holtzhausen D (2000) Postmodern values in PR. *Journal of Public Relations Research*, 12 (1): 93–114.

Holtzhausen D (2002) Towards a postmodern research agenda for PR. *Public Realtions Review*, 28 (3): 251–64.

Hopwood M (2005) PR practice in English county cricket. *Corporate Communications: an International Journal*, 10 (3): 201–12.

Hopwood M (2006) The sports integrated marketing communications mix; and Sports PR. In S Chadwick and J Beech (Eds) *The Marketing of Sport*. London: FTPH: 292–317.

Hopwood M, Kitchin P and Skinner J (2010) *Sport Public Relations and Communication*. Oxford: Elsevier.

Houlihan B and White A (2002) *The Politics of Sports Development: Development of Sport or Development though Sport?* London: Routledge.

Hoye R, Smith A, Nicholson M, Stewart B and Westerbeek H (2006) *Sport Management: Principles and Applications*. Oxford: Butterworth Heinemann Elsevier.

The Herald (2012):3.

Huesca R (2002) Participatory approaches to communication for development. In W Gudykunst and B Mody (Eds) *International and Intercultural Communication* (2nd edn). Thousand Oaks CA: Sage: 499–518.

Hung C-J F (2007) Toward the theory of relationship management in PR: how to cultivate quality relationships? In E Toth (Ed.) *The Future of Excellence in Public Relations and Communication Management: Challenges for the Next Generation*. Mahwah NJ: Lawrence Erlbaum Associates: 443–76.

Hunt G (2008) Press release from Southern Traverse. Available at www.southerntraverse.com/Images/PDF/Januarynewsletter.pdf (accesses 1 October 2013).

Ilhen O (2002) Rhetoric and resources: notes for a new approach to public relations and issues management. *Journal of Public Affairs*, 2 (4): 259–69.

Ihlen O (2005) The power of social capital: adapting Bourdieu to the study of PR. *Public Relations Review*, 31 (4): 492–6.

Ihlen O (2007) Building on Bourdieu: a sociological grasp of PR. *Public Relations Review*, 33 (3): 269–74.

Ihlen O, van Ruler B and Frederiksson M (2009) *Public Relations and Social Theory: Key Figures and Concepts*. New York and London: Routledge.

Irwin R, Sutton W and McCarthy L (2002) *Sport Promotion and Sales Management*. Champaign IL: Human Kinetics.

Jackson S and Haigh S (Eds) (2008) *Sport and Foreign Policy in a Globalising World*. London: Routledge.

Jaques T (2009) Issue and crisis management: quicksand in the definitional landscape. *Public Relations Review*, 35 (3): 280–86.

Jarvie G (2006) *Sport, Culture and Society: an Introduction*. London Routledge.

Jerome A (2008) 'Toward prescription: testing the rhetoric of atonement's applicability in the athletic arena', *Public Relations Review*, 34 (2): 124–34.

Jhally S (1989) *The Codes of Advertising: Fetishism and the Political Economy of Meaning in the Consumer Society*. London: Routledge.

Johnson J (1996) *Promotion for Sports Directors*. Champaign IL: Human Kinetics.

Kay T (2012) Accounting for legacy: monitoring and evaluation in sport in development relationships. *Sport in Society*, 15 (6): 888–904.

Kent M and Taylor M (2002) Toward a dialogic theory of PR. *Public Relations Review*, 28: 21–37.

Kidd B (2008) A new social movement: sport for development and peace. *Sport in Society*, 11 (4): 370–80.

Klein J (2012) In 1972 Hockey's Cold War boiled over. *New York Times*, 1 September, www.nytimes.com/2012/09/02/sports/hockey/in-hockeys-1972-summit-series-between-canada-and-soviet-union-cold-war-got-colder.html?pagewanted=all&_r=0 (accessed 7 October 2012).

Knoppers A and Elling E (2004) We do not engage in promotional journalism: discursive strategies used by sports journalists to describe the selection process. *International Review for the Sociology of Sport*, 39 (1): 57–74.

Kruckeberg D and Starck K (1988) *Public Relations and Community: A Reconstructed Theory*. London: Praegar.

Kruger A (1999) Strength through joy: the culture of consent under fascism, Nazism and Francoism. In J Riordan and A Kruger (Eds) *The International Politics of Sport in the 20th Century*. London: Routledge: 67–89.

L'Etang J (1994) Public relations and corporate social responsibility: issues arising. *Journal of Business Ethics* 13 (2): 111–23.

L'Etang J (1995) Ethical corporate social responsibility: a framework for managers. *Journal of Business Ethics*, 14 (2): 125–32.

L'Etang J (1996) Public relations and diplomacy. In J L'Etang and M Pieczka (Eds) *Critical Perspectives in Public Relations*. London: ITBP.

L'Etang J (2006) Public relations and sport in promotional culture. *Public Relations Review*, 32 (4): 386–94.

L'Etang J (2008) *Public Relations: Theory, Practice and Critique*. London: Sage

L'Etang J (2009a) Public relations and diplomacy in a globalised world. *American Behavioral Scientist*, 53(4) 607–26.

L'Etang J (2009b) PR and promotion of adventure sports. In B Wheaton and J Orm-rod (Eds) *On the Edge: Leisure, Consumption and the Representation of Adventure Sports.* Brightton: Leisure Studies Association: 43–70.

L'Etang J (2010) Cross-cultural sport public relations and communication. In M Hop-wood, P Kitchin and J Skinner (Eds) *Sports Public Relations and Communication.* London & New York: Butterworth Heinemann.

L'Etang J (2011) Public relations and marketing: ethical issues and professional practice in society. In G Cheney, S May and D Munshi (Eds) *The Handbook of Communication Ethics.* ICA Handbook Series. London: Routledge: 221–40.

L'Etang J (2013) Critical perspectives in sports public relations. In P Pedersen (Ed.) *Routledge Handbook of Sports Communication.* London & New York: Routledge Taylor and Francis Group.

L'Etang J and Pieczka M (Eds) (1996) *Critical Perspectives in Public Relations.* London: ITBP.

L'Etang J and Pieczka M (Eds) (2006) *Public Relations: Critical Debates and Contemporary Practice.* Mahwah NJ: Lawrence Erlbaum Associates.

Ledwith D (2011) Smile, you're on the Internet. *SBI*, 166 (4): 20–21.

Leitch S and Neilson D (2001) Bringing publics into public relations: new theoretical frameworks for practice. In R Heath (Ed.) *Handbook of Public Relations.* Thousand Oaks CA: Sage: 127–138.

Lewis J, Williams A and Franklin B (2008) A compromised fourth estate? UK news journalism, public relations and news sources. *Journalism Studies*, 9 (1): 1–20.

Lievrouw LA (2011) *Alternative and Activist New Media: Digital Media and Society.* Cambridge: Polity Press.

Linstead S, Fulop L and Lilley S (2009) *Management & Organization: a Critical Text.* Basingstoke: Palgrave Macmillan.

Loch Lomond Golf Club (n.d.) www.lochlomond.com/#/membership/ (accessed 1 October 2013).

Lott G (2012) Keeping it social. *SBI*, 181: 8.

Lopiano DA (2000) Modern history of women in sports. Twenty-five years of Title IX. *Clinics in Sports Medicine*, 19: 163–73.

Lowes MD (1987) Sports pages: case study in the manufacture of sports news for the daily press. *Sociology of Sport Journal*, 14: 143–59.

Lundgren R and McMakin A (2009) *Risk Communication: a Handbook for Communicating Environmental, Safety and Health Risks.* Hoboken NJ: Wiley.

Luoma-aho V (2009) On Putnam: bowling together – applying Putnam's theories of community and social capital to public relations. In O Ihlen, B van Ruler and M Frederiksson (Eds) *Public Relations and Social Theory: Key Figures and Concepts.* London: Routledge: 231–51.

Lyng S (2005) Edgework and the risk-taking experience. In S Lyng (Ed.) *Edgework: the Sociology of Risk-taking.* London, Routledge: 3–16.

Madison DS and Humera J (2006) Introduction: performance studies at the intersections. In DS Madison and J Humera (Eds) *The Sage Handbook of Performance Studies.* London: Sage: xi–xxv.

Magee K (2012a) Ready for the media scrum. *PRW*, 26 January: 26–7.

Magee K (2012b) The struggle to measure up. *PRW*, 6 July: 22–5.

Maguire J (1993) *Power and Global Sport*. Routledge: London.

Maguire J (2006) Sport and globalization: key issues, phases and trends. In A Raney and J Bryant (Eds) *Handbook of Sports and Media*, Mahwah NJ: Lawrence Erlbaum Associates: 435–47.

Manzenreiter W (2008) Football diplomacy, post-colonialism and Japan's quest for normal state status. *Sport in Society: Culture, Commerce, Media, Politics*, 11 (4): 414–28.

Marriott S (2007) *Live Television: Time, Space and the Broadcast Event*. London: Sage.

Martinkova I (2012) Pierre de Courbetin's vision of the role of sport in peaceful internationalism. *Sport in Society*, 15 (6): 788–97.

Mattinson A (2012) Coke fuels Olympic fire. *PRW*, 27 July.

Mattinson A (2013) The reputation evangelist. *PRW*, 25 January: 18–19.

McCullagh K (2009a) The language of sport. *SBI*, 142: 24–5.

McCullagh K (2009b) Looking for leadership? *SBI*, 142: 39.

McCullagh K (2009c) Just don't flaunt it. *SBI*, 144: 8.

McGrath J (2009) Jumps racing faces axe in Australia. *The Telegraph*, 10 May, available at www.telegraph.co.uk/sport/ (accessed 2 March 2013).

McGrath J (2012) John Smith's pull-out from sponsoring the Grand National brews up a storm for Aintree. *The Telegraph*, 25 November, available at www.telegraph.co.uk/sport/ (accessed 2 March 2013).

McKie D and Munshi D (2007) *Reconfiguring Public Relations: Ecology, Equity and Enterprise*. Abingdon: Routledge.

McNair B (1996) Performance in politics and the politics of performance: PR, the public sphere and democracy. In J L'Etang and M Pieczka (Eds) *Critical Perspectives in PR*. London: ITBP: 35–53.

McNair B (2000) *Journalism and Democracy: an Evaluation of the Political Public Sphere*. London: Routledge.

McPhail T (1981) *Electronic Colonialism: The Future of International Broadcasting and Communication*. Newbury Park: Sage.

McPhail T (2006) *Global Communication: Theories, Stakeholders and Trends*. Boston MA: Allyn and Bacon.

McPhail T (Ed.) (2009) *Development Communication: Reframing the Role of the Media*. Chichester: Wiley-Blackwell.

Meikle G and Young S (2012) *Media Convergence: Networked Digital Media in Everyday Life*. Basingstoke: Palgrave Macmillan.

Melkote S (2002) Theories of development communication. In W Gudykunst and B Mody (Eds) *International and Intercultural Communication* (2nd edn). Thousand Oaks CA: Sage: 419–36.

Merkel U (2008) The politics of sport diplomacy and reunification in divided Korea: one nation, two countries and three flags. *International Review for the Sociology of Sport*, 43: 289–311.

Miller A (2011) Capital gains. *SBI*, 171: 12.

Miller D (1998) PR and journalism: promotional strategies and media power. In A Briggs and P Cobley (Eds) *The Media: an Introduction*. London: Longman: 65–80.

Miller D and Dinan W (2008) *A Century of Spin: how PR became the Cutting Edge of Corporate Power*. London: Pluto Press.

Mitrook M, Parish N and Seltzer T (2008) From advocacy to accommodation: case study of the Orlando Magic's PR efforts to secure a new arena. *Public Relations Review*, 34 (2): 161–8.

Mody B (2002) Development communication: introduction. In W Gudykunst and B Mody (Eds) *International and Intercultural Communication* (2nd edn). Thousand Oaks CA: Sage: 415–19.

Mondello M, Schwester R and Humphreys B (2009) To build or not to building: examining public discourse regarding St. Petersburg's stadium plan. *International Journal of Sport Communication*, 2: 432–50.

Motion J and Leitch S (1996) A discursive perspective from New Zealand: another world view. *Public Relations Review*, 22: 297–309.

Neupauer NC (2001) Sports information directing: a plea for help in an unknown field. In R Heath (Ed.) *Handbook of Public Relations*. Thousand Oaks CA: Sage.

Nichols W, Moynahan P, Hall A and Taylor J (2002) *Media Relations in Sport*. Fitness Information Technology.

Nixon S and du Gay P (2002) Who needs cultural intermediaries? *Cultural Studies*, 16 (4): 495–500.

Owens J (2012a) McAlpine puts tweeters on alert. *PRW*, 23 November: 3.

Owens J (2012b) Sports bodies up comms game: Minority sports bid to secure government support on the back of exposure during the Olympics. *PRW*, 17 August: 3.

Pal M and Dutta M (2008). Public relations in a global context: the relevance of critical modernism as a theoretical lens. *Journal of public relations research*, 20: 159–79.

Palmer C (2000) Spin doctors and sportsbrokers: researching elites in contemporary sport – a research note of the Tour de France. *Sociology of Sports Journal*, 35 (3): 364–77.

Palmer C (2004) Death, danger and the selling of risk in adventure sports. In B Wheaton (Ed.) *Understanding Lifestyle Sports: Consumption, Identity and Difference*. London: Routledge: 55–69.

Pedersen P (Ed.) (2013) *Routledge Handbook of Sport Communication*, New York: Routledge Taylor & Francis Group

Pedersen P, Miloch K and Laucella P (2007) *Strategic Sport Communication,* Champaign IL: Human Kinetics.

Perry J (2012) The power of sport in peacemaking and peacekeeping. *Sport in Society*, 15 (6): 775–87.

Peters T and Waterman R (1982) *In Search of Excellence*. New York: Harper Collins.

Pfahl M and Bates B (2008) This is not a race, this is a farce: Formula One and the Indianapolis Speedway tire crisis. *Public Relations Review*, 34 (2): 135–44.

Pieczka M (1996a) Public opinion and PR. In J L'Etang and M Pieczka (Eds) *Critical Perspectives in Public Relations*. London: ITBP: 54–64.

Pieczka M (1996b) Paradigms, systems theory and public relations. In J L'Etang and M Pieczka (Eds) *Critical Perspectives in Public Relations*. London: ITBP.

Pieczka M (2000) Objectives and evaluation in PR: what do they tell us about expertise and professionalism. *Journal of Public Relations Research,* 12 (3): 211–33.

Pieczka M (2011) PR as dialogic expertise? *Journal of Communication Management,* 15 (2): 108–24.

Pieczka M and Escobar O (2013) Dialogue and science: innovation in policy making and the discourse of public engagement. *Science and Public Policy,* 40 (1): 113–26.

Poli R and Gillan P (2006) Nationality in sport: issues and problems. Paper presented at CIES Conference.

Powell D (2011) Project India: handle with care. *SBI,* 172: 15.

Price V (1992) *Public Opinion.* Newbury Park CA: Sage.

PRW (2012a) G4S under fire for comms stance. 20 July: 3.

PRW (2012b) Sponsors outperform 2012 rivals. 27 July: 3.

PRW (2012d) Hit or Miss? British horseracing authority responds to deaths at Grand National. April: 2.

Redeker R (2008) Sport as an opiate of international relations: the myth and illusion of sport as a tool of foreign diplomacy. *Sport in Society: Cultures, Commerce, Media, Politics,* 11 (4): 494–500.

Ridley R (2011) Beijing's road test. *SBI,* 172: 24–5.

Rinehart R and Grenfell C (2002) BMX spaces: children's grass roots courses and corporate-sponsored tracks. *Sociology of Sport Journal,* 19: 302–14.

Riordan J and Kruger A (Eds) (1999) *The International Politics of Sport in the 20th Century.* London: Routledge.

Robb M (2012) A little more conversation. *PRW advertising supplement,* 5 October: 13.

Roberts K (2005) Time for heroes. *SBI,* 62.

Roberts K (2005/06) When less is more – more or less. *SBI,* 109: 5.

Roberts K (2006a) Creative thinking, clear communications and an eye to the future *SBI,* 111: 5.

Roberts K (2006b) Delivering the goods. *SBI,* 109: 24.

Roberts K (2006c) Game on. *SBI,* 114 : 46–7.

Roberts K (2006d) Girls just wanna have phones. *SBI,* 114: 32–3.

Roberts K (2006e) HSBC banking on golf. *SBI,* 117: 19.

Roberts K (2006f) Jumping onto the event bandwagon. *SBI,* 116: 45.

Roberts K (2006g) Oh I say! *SBI,* 114: 16–17.

Roberts K (2006h) Scott takes Tour into new commercial territory. *SBI,* 114: 28–9.

Roberts K (2006i) Three pillars of wisdom. *SBI,* 114: 14.

Roberts K (2006j) Barça basking in brand play. *SBI,* 110: 22–3.

Roberts K (2006k) Football value out of Africa. *SBI,* 110: 5.

Roberts K (2008a) Playing for sporting power. *SBI,* 133: 7.

Roberts K (2008b) Seeing the wood for the trees. *SBI,* 132: 7.

Roberts K (2008c) The changing man. *SBI,* 131: 46–8.

Roberts K (2008d) Wild West comes East. *SBI,* 131: 66.

Roberts K (2008e) The value of keeping it real. *SBI,* 131: 7.

Roberts K (2008f) Youth games target sport's lost generation. *SBI,* 131: 34–5.

Roberts K (2008g) Challenge and opportunity. *SBI*, 134: 24–5.

Roberts K (2009a) Editorial. *SBI*, 142, February: 7.

Roberts K (2009b) What is the value of CSR? *SBI*, 143: 14.

Roberts K (2010a) Editorial. *SBI*, 162: 7.

Roberts K (2010b) Editorial. *SBI*, 163 (12/10): 7.

Roberts K (2011) Editorial. *SBI*, 171, September: 7.

Roberts K (2012a) Editorial. *SBI*, 178: 7.

Roberts K (2012b) Editorial. *SBI*, (183/10): 81.

Roberts K (2012c) Get the picture. *SBI*, 176 (3/12): 13.

Roberts K (2012d) *SBI*, 184: 39.

Roberts K and Brodie D (1992) *Inner City Sport: Who Plays and What are the Benefits?* Culemborg: Giordano Bruno.

Roberts M (2009) What is the value of CSR? *SBI*, 143: 14.

Roche M (2000) *Mega-events Modernity: Olympics and Expos in the Growth of Global Culture.* London: Routledge.

Rogers EM and Hart WB (2002) The histories of intercultural, international and development communication. In WB Gudykunst and B Mody (Eds) *Handbook of International and Intercultural Communication.* Thousand Oaks CA: Sage: 1–18.

Rojek C (2001) *Celebrity.* London: Reaktion Books.

Rojek C (2013) *Event Power: How Global Events Manage and Manipulate.* London: Sage.

Rowe D (1999) *Sports, Culture and the Media: the Unruly Trinity* (2nd edn). Maidenhead: Open University Press.

Rowe D (Ed.) (1995) *Popular Cultures: Rock Music, Sport and the Politics of Pleasure.* London: Sage.

Rushman N (2006) On with the show. *SBI*, 110: 3.

Salem G, Jones E and Morgan N (2004) An overview of events management. In I Yeoman, M Robertson, J Ali-Knight, S Drummond and U McMahon-Beattie (Eds) *Festival and Events Management.* Oxford: Elsevier

Salkeld A (1997) *A Portrait of Leni Riefenstahl.* London: Pimlico.

Sannie I (2008) Avoiding Africa's white elephant. *SBI*, 133: 31.

Sarver Coombs D (2012) A case study of Aston Villa Football Club. *Journal of Public Relations Research,* 24: 201–221.

Savage P (2009) Sportshot: bringing home the benefits. *SBI*, 145: 46.

SBI (2005a) Sims still in the driving seat. 109: 62.

SBI (2005b) Back to the future: the technology evolution. 99: 16.

SBI (2006a) Arrest sets off gaming sector jitters. 116: 51.

SBI (2006b) From life saving to sponsorship. 111: 54.

SBI (2006c) The art of attracting a niche crowd. 114: 25.

SBI (2006d) 'Rising stars' look forward with confidence. 110: 24.

SBI (2006e) London 2012 to hit tourism. 115: 14.

SBI (2006f) Security report set for launch. 109: 8.

SBI (2007a) Bidding for gold. 128: 114.

SBI (2007b) Formula earth. 121:17.

SBI (2007c) Reinventing the business. 127: 90.

SBI (2007d) Sporting Singapore gets great PR. 127: 44.

SBI (2008a) Best practice in action. 132: 46.

SBI (2008b) The queen of gymnastics. 139: 17.

SBI (2008c) Passion, power and profit. 131: 50–51.

SBI (2008d) 'Did your athlete score last night?'. 135: 47.

SBI (2008e) Country on a mission. 132: 65.

SBI (2008f)The sports business debate. 132: 36–7.

SBI (2009a) Empowering stakeholders. 143: 32.

SBI (2009b) The debate goes on … . 151: 17.

SBI (2009c) Football's new reality. 142: 8.

SBI (2009d) Peace and sport. 146: 68–70.

SBI (2009e) Lord of the Rings. 145: 26–8.

SBI (2011) Communiqué. 172: 11

SBI (2012a) Capital gains. 180: 78–9.

SBI (2012b) Social event campaigns. 281: 20.

SBI (2012c) Summer of two halves. 184: 14.

SBI (2012d) The first lady of sponsorship. 179: 30–32.

SBI (2012e) The new social order. 180: 22–3.

SBI (2012f) PR in sports bids: a servant, not the master. 183: 82.

SBI (2012g) Thought leadership in Sports PR. 183: 82–5.

SBI (2012h) Taking the specialist path. 183: 84.

SBI (2012i) View from the press box. 183: 85.

SBI (2012j) Sports business debate. 175: 65.

SBI (2012k) The billion dollar men. 175: 31–35.

SBI (2013a) New ball games. 186: 56.

SBI (2013b) Giving the hosts the most. 188: 69–70.

SBI (2013c) How significant is social responsibility to your operations? 189: 54.

SBI (2013d) Big debate. 189: 114.

Scannell P (1996) *Radio, Television and Modern Life*. Oxford: Blackwell.

Scherer J, Falcous M and Jackson S (2008) The media sports cultural complex: local–global disjuncture in New Zealand/Aotearoa. *Journal of Sport and Social Issues*, 32: 48.

Schlesinger P (1990) Rethinking the sociology of journalism: the source strategies and the limits of media centrism. In M Ferguson (Ed.) *Public Communication: the New Imperatives: Future Directions for Research*. London: Sage.

Schnitzer M, Stephenson M, Zanotti L and Stivachtis Y (2012) Theorizing the role of sport for development and peacekeeping. *Sport in Society*, 1–16.

Scholte JA (2000) *Globalisation: A Critical Introduction*. Basingstoke: Palgrave.

Seeger MW and Ulmer RR (2001) Virtuous responses to organizational crisis: Aaron Feuerstein and Milt Cole. *Journal of Business Ethics*, 31: 369–76.

Serrels M (2006) *WWE and Kayfabe: Retaining the Real*. Available at www.popmatters.com/sports/features/060504-wrestling.shtml

Shank MD (2002) *Sports Marketing: a Strategic Perspective*. Upper Saddle River NJ: Prentice Hall.

Shearman S (2012) Massive rise in tweets during London 2012. *PRW*, 17 August: 15.

Sherlock M (2006) Agents of change. *SBI*, 117: 42–4.

Sherlock M (2007) Running, swimming and riding high. *SBI*, 126: 52–3.

Sherlock M (2009) The toughest sport on dirt. *SBI*, 142: 58.

Shirky C (2008) *Here Comes Everybody. How Change Happens when People Come Together.* London: Penguin.

Signitzer B and Coombs B (1992) Public relations and public diplomacy: conceptual convergences. *Public Relations Review*, 18 (2): 137–47.

Singer O (2008) Playing regulatory games. *SBI*, 131: 18

Slack T (2004) *The Commercialisation of Sport.* London: Routledge.

Smart B (2005) *The Sport Star: Modern Sport and the Cultural Economy of Sporting Celebrity.* London: Sage.

Smith D (2006a) A protected package. *SBI*, 113: 35.

Smith D (2006b) Equipping yourself for a career in sport. *SBI*, 112: 10.

Smith D (2006c) What's mine is yours. *SBI*, 109: 20.

Smith D (2006d) Your country needs you. *SBI*, 106: 70.

Spaaij R (2009) The glue that holds the community together? Sport and sustainability in rural Australia. *Sport in Society: Cultures, Commerce, Media, Politics*, 12 (9): 1132–46.

Spaaij R (2012) Olympic rings of peace? The Olympic movement, peacemaking and intercultural understanding. *Sport in Society*, 15 (6): 761–74.

Spaaij R and Burleson C (2012) London 2012 and beyond: concluding reflections on peacemaking, sport and the Olympic movement. *Sport in Society*, 15 (6): 905–13.

Spain N (1953) *'Teach' Tennant: the Story of Eleanor Tennant – the Greatest Tennis Coach in the World.* London: Werner Lawrie.

Sports and Development (n.d.) Sport and Peace-building. Available at www.sportanddev.org/learnmore/sport_and_peace_building/ (accessed 1 October 2013).

Stein L (2012) Aloft invites agencies to pitch via Twitter. *PRW*, 30 November.

Stockdale L (2012) More than just games: the global politics of the Olympic Movement. *Sport in Society*, 15 (6): 839–54.

Sylt C (2006) F1's five-star service. *SBI*, 110: 43.

Tassell D and Terry D (2012) An overlooked path to peace and stability: sport, the state and the case of the Koreas. *Sport in Society*, 15 (6): 814–22.

Taylor M (2010) Public relations in the enactment of civil society. In R Heath (Ed.) *The Sage Handbook of Public Relations.* Thousand Oakes CA: Sage.

Terry V (2005) Postcard from the steppes: a snapshot of public relations and culture in Kazakstan. *Public Relations Review*, 31: 31–6.

Thayer L (1968) *Communication and Communication Systems.* Homewood Il: Irwin.

Theunissen P and Wan Norbani (2012) Revisiting the concept 'dialogue' in PR. *Public Relations Review*, 38 (1): 5–13.

The Guardian on-line, 1 May 2012 (downloaded 2 May 2012)

The Herald, 20 May, Reporting on the Etape Caledonian, punctures of, 16 May 2009.

Tilson DJ (2006) Devotional-promotional communications and Santiago: a thousand year PR campaign for St James and Spain. In J L'Etang and M Pieczka (Eds) *Public Relations: Critical Debates and Contemporary Practice.* Mahwah NJ: Lawrence Erlbaum Associates: 167–86.

Toth E (Ed.) (2006) *The Future of Excellence in PR and Communication Management: Challenges for the Next Generation*. Mahwah NJ: Lawrence Erlbaum Associates.

Trujillo N (1992) White knights, poker games and carpet baggers: interpreting the sale of a professional sports franchise. In E Toth and R Heath (Eds) *Rhetorical and Critical Approaches to Public Relations*. Hillsdale NJ: Lawrence Erlbaum Associates.

Urry J (2002) *The Tourist Gaze*. London: Sage.

Valentine J (2004) Audit society, practical deconstruction and strategic public relations. *parallax*, 10 (2): 20–37.

Vincent J and Crossman J (2007) Champions, a celebrity crossover and a capitulator: the construction of gender in broadsheet newspapers' narratives about selected competitors at Wimbledon. *International Journal of Sport Communication*, 1: 78–102.

Walmsley D (2011) Long-lasting legacy. *SBI*, 173: 34.

Walsh J and Mcallister-Spooner S (2011) Analysis of the image repair discourse in the Michael Phelps controversy, *Public Relations Review*, 37 (2): 157–62.

Wanta W (2013) Reflections on communication and sport: on reporting and journalists. *Communication & Sport*, 1 (1/2): 76–87.

Watts J (2010) All the trees in China: golf boom threatens rainforest, *The Guardian*, 23 April.

Whannel G (2000) Sport and the media. In J Coakley and E Dunning (Eds) *Handbook of Sports Studies*. London: Sage: 291–308.

Wheaton B (2004) *Understanding Lifestyle Sports: Consumption, Identity and Difference*. London: Routledge.

Wheaton B and Beal B (2003) Keeping it real: subcultural media and the discourses of authenticity in alternative sport. *International Review for the Sociology of Sport Journal*, 17: 254–74.

Wicks N (2010) Social media spend to rise. *PRW*, 8 October.

Williams R (1961) *The Long Revolution*. London: Pelican.

Williams R (1962) *Communications*. London: Penguin.

Williams R (1981) *The Sociology of Culture*. Chicago: University of Chicago Press.

Wilner B (2006) Worth its weight in gold. *SBI*, 113: 16–17.

Wilner B (2007) Cities of opportunity. *SBI*, 125: 62–3.

Wilner B (2011a) Vick-torious comeback. *SBI*, 171: 16

Wilner B (2011b) NASCAR's soap opera. *SBI*, 173: 19.

Wilner B (2011c) Show me the money. *SBI*, 174: 16–17.

Wilner B (2012) McFlurry of abuse. *SBI*, 176: 17.

Wilson B, Stavros C and Westburg K (2008) Player transgressions and the management of the sport sponsor relationship. *Public Relations Review*, 34(2): 99–107.

Woo C, An S-K and Cho S (2008) Sports PR in message boards on Major League Baseball websites. *Public Relations Review*, 34 (2): 169–75.

Xifra J (2008) Soccer, civil religion, and PR: devotional-promotional communication and Barcelona Football Club. *Public Relations Review*, 34 (2): 192–8.

Xifra J (2009) Building sport countries' overseas identity and reputation: a case study of public paradiplomacy. *American Behavioral Scientist*, 53 (4): 504–15.

Yeoman I, Robertson M, Ali-Knight J, Drummond S and McMahon-Beattie U (Eds) (2004) *Festival and Events Management: an International Arts and Culture Perspective.* Oxford: Elsevier Butterworth-Heinemann.

Zaner RM and Engelhardt HT (1973) *The Structures of the Life-World.* Evanston IL: Northwesterm University Press.

Index